CATHERINE & DIDEROT

Robert Zaretsky

Harvard University Press

Cambridge, Massachusetts
London, England
2019

Printed in the United States of America

First printing

Library of Congress Cataloging-in-Publication Data
Names: Zaretsky, Robert, 1955– author.
Title: Catherine & Diderot : the empress, the philosopher, and the fate of the Enlightenment / Robert Zaretsky.
Other titles: Catherine and Diderot : the empress, the philosopher, and the fate of the Enlightenment
Description: Cambridge, Massachusetts : Harvard University Press, 2019. | Includes bibliographical references and index.
Identifiers: LCCN 2018034816 | ISBN 9780674737907 (alk. paper)
Subjects: LCSH: Catherine II, Empress of Russia, 1729–1796. | Diderot, Denis, 1713–1784. | Enlightenment—Russia—History.
Classification: LCC B4215.E5 Z37 2019 | DDC 194—dc23
LC record available at https://lccn.loc.gov/2018034816

Frontispiece: Illustration by A. de Neuville, from François Guizot, *A Popular History of France, from the Earliest Times,* trans. Robert Black, vol. 6 (Boston: Dana Estes and Charles E. Lauriat, ca. 1883), p. 321. Photo by Culture Club/Getty Images.

To Julie, with all my love and gratitude

Contents

CATHERINE & DIDEROT

Prologue

On the morning of April 5, 1774, a carriage swayed past the elaborate dikes that, like giant staples, bound together the polders checkering the Dutch lowlands. Staring out the dust-matted windows of the cabin were two travelers, an elderly Frenchman and young Greek officer. The latter, Athanasius Bala, excitedly insisted their voyage "seemed so short that I can hardly persuade myself that we've reached our destination."[1] The wrinkled and sagging face of his older companion, Denis Diderot, reflected just how long and demanding their voyage had been, but Diderot's mind thrummed with plans and ideas. They were headed to The Hague, the port city that served as the Dutch Republic's seat of government. Though a good distance from Diderot's final destination, Paris, this prosperous port city would serve as a haven. He would find there the peace and perspective necessary to order his thoughts—which, as friends and foes knew, could be as wild and subversive as the Dutch landscape was tamed and predictable.

As Bala tried to glimpse what lay ahead of the carriage, Diderot instead focused on what lay behind. Slightly more than four weeks (and three carriages) earlier, he had departed from the capital city of imperial Russia—Saint Petersburg—where he had spent five months as the official guest of the individual who had assigned Bala, a royal court officer, to escort Diderot on his return voyage: the Empress Catherine II. After several years' worth of increasingly insistent invitations, the empress had finally succeeded the previous October in bringing Diderot to her capital city. What was an already formidable journey in the eighteenth century for someone in the prime of life was even more challenging for Diderot, whose sixty years of often-hardscrabble life had made for a frail old age. He had always been, moreover, the most reluctant of travelers, and was deeply attached to his friends, his family—in particular his daughter, Angélique, then pregnant with her first child—and his books. Nevertheless, at this late stage of life Diderot's reluctance to travel was outdone by his even greater reluctance to refuse the imperious call from Saint Petersburg.

The reasons, both practical and philosophical, for Catherine's invitation and Diderot's acceptance, and the remarkable series of events that followed, are the subject of this book. In nearly all of the many scholarly and popular biographies devoted to Catherine, readers can find a brief account of Diderot's sojourn in Saint Petersburg. And while biographers of Diderot in general devote more space to the subject, there are, remarkably, no historical narratives devoted exclusively to an event that had galvanized the attention of enlightened Europe. At the end of the nineteenth century, the French literary historian Maurice Tourneux published *Diderot et Catherine II,* which is less a narrative than a collection of historical documents and commentaries. A century later, the British novelist Malcolm Bradbury issued his superb novel *To the Hermitage,* which weaves, with side-splitting results, Diderot's experience in Tsarist Russia with the narrator's own visit as an academic attending a Diderot conference in post-Soviet Russia. As a novelist, though, Bradbury took the liberty of, in his words, "improving" on history when he thought necessary.

No doubt Diderot himself is to blame, in part, for this odd state of affairs. As Bradbury notes in his book's preface, his protagonist is "now generally remembered only as a Parisian district or a Metro stop."[2] In

2013 the commemorations for the tri-centenary of Diderot's birth led to calls, mostly from intellectuals and writers, to place his remains in the Pantheon—France's hall of fame for its national heroes and, increasingly, heroines. But the calls have remained unheeded, Diderot's bones remain buried in their original resting place (the church of Saint Roch), and his name remains tied to a subway station in an unfashionable neighborhood in southeastern Paris.

Quel dommage. For what also remains is the subversive power of Diderot's life and writing. The monumental work conceived, edited, and partly written by Diderot—the twenty-eight-volume *Encyclopédie*—presented his age's greatest challenge to the rules that governed society, politics, and religion. Among the relatively few of his works of fiction and philosophy published during his life, a couple of titles earned their author a lengthy stay in prison—an experience that, more than once, he risked repeating later in life. Since his death, just five years before the event for which many would hold him responsible—the French Revolution—several of Diderot's most radical works have been discovered and published. *Rameau's Nephew, D'Alembert's Dream, The Nun,* and *Jacques the Fatalist and His Master* continue to challenge, in lasting ways, our literary sensibilities and moral sentiments. Soon after we begin one of these novels, we find ourselves rubbing our eyes, stunned to find an eighteenth-century writer whose technique and talent seem rooted in our own century.

But Diderot is subversive for another, if somewhat paradoxical, reason. We tend to think of the great thinkers as isolated and imperious individuals who sacrifice the life of everyday duties and pleasures in the pursuit of ideas and ideals. Yet Diderot collapses this stereotype: his character combined heart-stopping originality with heart-warming congeniality. He was fully engaged in the political and social issues of his day, but at the same time remained fully engaged in the lives of his friends, family, and (yes) mistresses. Not only was Diderot one of the most provocative thinkers of his age, but as Bradbury (who was clearly smitten by the

Frenchman) observes in his preface, he was also "the most pleasing of all the philosophers."[3] In the time and attention he gave to maintaining his friendships, supporting his family, and assisting struggling writers (even though it cost him precious time and energy), Diderot acted on his profound conviction that human beings seek the good for others as well as for themselves. More so than the vast majority of his philosophical peers then and now, Diderot was a mensch.

In a certain respect, the same claim can be made for his host in Saint Petersburg. Few eighteenth-century monarchs were as consistently humane, and affectingly human, as the Empress of All Russias, Catherine II. She displayed these qualities not just in her interactions with her subordinates, but also with her subjects—at least to the degree possible for an absolute ruler of the vast and backward empire over which she reigned. It was, in part, Catherine's desire to apply her humane impulses by transforming them into law and institutions that led her to reach out to French philosophes like Diderot. As a largely isolated teenager in Saint Petersburg, Catherine had discovered and devoured the works of Enlightenment thinkers like Montesquieu and Voltaire, and sought to rule in the spirit of these writings once she came to power. (That Catherine also expected the approbation and applause of enlightened Europeans, and in particular of prominent philosophes, marks her as fully human.) Who better, Catherine believed, to discuss the lamentable state of her country's legal and civil codes than, as she repeatedly called him, this "extraordinary" man? And who better, thought Diderot, to legislate the Enlightenment than this ruler who, he repeatedly insisted, combined "the intelligence of Caesar and the beauty of Cleopatra"? This, then, was the promising background when, in October 1773, Diderot arrived in Saint Petersburg and was granted, much to the chagrin of the imperial court, the unprecedented freedom to visit Catherine in her private quarters at the Hermitage every afternoon in order to converse about philosophical and political matters.

Five months later, the promise had mostly bled into the boggy land on which Saint Petersburg had been built. During his return trip to Holland, Diderot struggled to make sense of the several dozen encounters he had with the Russian ruler. At the same time, he continued to tweak and revise the manuscript of *Jacques the Fatalist and His Master.* Whether by design, accident, or some combination of the two, the relationship in Diderot's novel between Jacques and his master resembles the bond between Diderot and Catherine. Jacques, who is a valet, rightly believes himself better qualified to give orders than his master, while the master recognizes the justice of Jacques's claims but insists upon the traditional social and political order. In the novel, the arbitrary and unjust nature of life in the Ancien Régime becomes the stuff of much laughter, but also raises discomforting questions that thinkers like Diderot insist on asking. The master himself sighs, "I know all too well that philosophers are a breed of men who are loathed by the mighty because they refuse to bend the knee to them."[4]

The relationship between Catherine and Diderot raises these same questions and reflects this same dynamic. Their series of conversations, which began in mutual admiration and ended in mutual incomprehension, mixes moments of lèse-majesté and bristling majesty, combines great intellectual intimacy and even greater distance imposed by social and political conventions, and underscores the uneasy and perhaps impossible coexistence between the Empire of Reason and the Empire of All Russias. During his return voyage to Holland, Diderot finally grasped just how impossible this coexistence was. As soon as he set foot in The Hague, he began drafting a series of scathing observations on Catherine's reforms. Diderot concluded that the Empress of Russia—the individual who had feted him in Saint Petersburg, funded him in desperate times, and portrayed herself to the world as an enlightened ruler—was, quite simply, a "despot." Challenging Her Imperial Majesty to say whether she planned to maintain or abdicate her despotic hold on power, Diderot warned: "If in reading what I have written and in listening to her conscience, her heart beats with joy, then she no longer wants slaves. If she trembles, feels weak and goes pale, then she has taken herself for a better person than she really is."[5] Upon reading these words, Catherine did indeed tremble, but from anger, not fear. "This is a piece of genuine babble," she exclaimed, insisting that her so-called philosophe had lost his mind.[6]

When Diderot has Jacques quip that life is little more than a series of misunderstandings, he offers, perhaps unwittingly, a summary of his liaison with Catherine. Yet their unlikely friendship, if that is the word, poses fascinating questions about the Age of Enlightenment, particularly the knotty ties between idealists and realists, thinkers and rulers. It was an age that placed great (though not unlimited) stock in reason and progress, but at the same time placed in the person of an enlightened ruler the power to apply the one and accomplish the other. In the case of Catherine and Diderot, this merging of roles was mostly unsuccessful. While this failure was perhaps inevitable, it is also wonderfully instructive. Historians know that the past must not be reduced to a lesson plan for the present, but they also know that the past, when distilled into a story, can do more than simply entertain. In this respect, the story of the friendship between Catherine and Diderot can at least prod us to greater modesty as we explore the ideals and limits, the successes and defeats, of those who have preceded us.

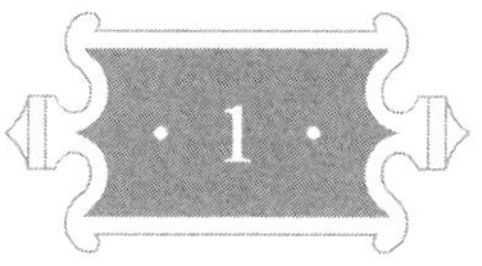

The Sea at Scheveningen

YOU HAD PROMISED TO STAY HOME, BUT IT SEEMS EVERYONE OWNS YOU EXCEPT YOUR OWN FAMILY. AH, WHAT A MAN!

—NANETTE TO DIDEROT

In the early summer of 1773, a Frenchman walked with a slight stoop along the promenade that stretched between the Dutch city of The Hague and the beach town of Scheveningen. He often slowed to a stop, turning his head toward the sea, then back to his fellow strollers; men garbed in sober coats, their heads filled with mostly commercial affairs; small groups of women, long scarves tied around their necks and large straw hats pinned to their hair, looking as if they were on their way to confession.[1] A discordant but not distressing sight for the traveler, unaccustomed to seeing women walking unaccompanied, and largely unadorned, back home in the streets of Paris.[2]

The passers-by, no doubt, had in turn taken the measure of this strange man. Gazing at the sea, wearing an old black frock coat, his thinning hair tossed by the briny wind, he was an older man, perhaps pushing sixty, who seemed startled to be where he was—like a sleeping child bundled by his parents into a carriage at night and awakening the next day to find himself in a place he has dreamed about but never visited.

For Denis Diderot, the dreamer in question, the barrier between the imagination and the world was not as staunch as the great dikes that separated land from sea. It was the sea's "vast sameness, neither still nor stormy," he later wrote to his mistress, Sophie Volland, "along with its constant murmur, that makes me dream." Here on the beach, he confessed, he dreamed best.[3] What better reason did he need to walk along the coast when he broke away from his reading and writing?

Diderot often lingered at Scheveningen, a spot where the sight of the sea was freed of the docks, ship masts, and port buildings that crowded one's view at The Hague. It was, as he later wrote in an account of his visit, his "favorite promenade."[4] He was not alone in that preference: by the second half of the century, Scheveningen had become a favorite site—a stage of sorts—for tourists who wished to encounter, in all of its slate gray fullness, the North Sea. Holland itself had become something of a stage for the dramatic framing of sea and coastline, transforming water and sand into a spectacle worthy of the tourist's time.[5] The mighty effort by the Dutch to claw their land from the sea was scorned by the envious English—the poet Andrew Marvell brushed off the Netherlands as "this undigested vomit of the sea"—and dismissed by the imperial French: Napoleon considered the Lowlands as nothing more than the "alluvium deposited by some of the principal rivers of my empire."[6]

For Diderot, however, the land was a wonder, in part because it was the work of men. He marveled over the system of dikes and canals serving as ramparts against the sea, just as he marveled at the systems of banks and commerce that had enriched the country's coffers and nurtured its spirit of toleration. There was no more powerful sign of Holland's wealth, he observed, than the "forest of masts" afloat at the port of Amsterdam. Even Carthage paled in comparison.[7] Unlike his erstwhile friend Jean-Jacques Rousseau, Diderot was not a romantic *avant la lettre:* the land defended by dikes and canals, the ports thickened by masts and warehouses, the merchant and war ships that commanded the seas also commanded Diderot's imagination, as did the dikes that held back the sea. How surprising, he thought, that in this "land of floods one nevertheless managed to sleep."[8]

But he was especially taken by the details, not the grand designs; the men and women, not the ideas and numbers. Perhaps more so than other visitors, he spent long periods watching fishermen as they struggled with their herring nets in heavy seas. Standing with him on the beach were the fishermen's wives; when not gazing at the men, Diderot turned his eyes to the women, noting how their lined faces expressed both their anxiety and resignation. His own face, registering the impressions sparking inside his head, reflected the barely suppressed terror and suspense felt by those wives. "A hundred times," he wrote, "I was overwhelmed by fear over the fate of these men, who in the midst of storms fought with the seagulls over their catches." When the trawlers, heavy with their harvest, reached shore, the women would run and embrace their husbands and sons—a sight of "timeless conjugal and familial love" that never tired Diderot.[9]

So avid was Diderot for such scenes that, when they were found wanting, he would create them. This seems to have been the case with his own family the night before he left Paris for Holland. Ever since their daughter, Angélique, married to an ambitious business entrepreneur, had left their home, Diderot and his wife, Nanette, spent their days "circling one another" in the now-empty nest. "How can I be expected," he complained to his sister, "to talk with an ill-tempered woman ready to explode at the drop of a needle?"[10] One can well imagine Nanette replying: "How can I be expected to talk to a jabbering man ready to change his plans at a moment's notice?" Still, given his advanced age and frail health, Diderot's indecision over his trip to Russia—repeatedly taking one step toward Saint Petersburg, then one step back—was certainly understandable.

The prospect of quitting his family overwhelmed the sedentary man. "Try to understand," he implored a friend: "I am leaving my wife, my sister, my daughter and my relations. . . . Now that I think about it again, the pain is too great. Let's not talk about it anymore."[11] Alas, the problem for Nanette was that her husband enjoyed nothing more than talking about it. She was as tired of her husband's dithering as she was of his self-dramatization.

By the eve of Diderot's departure, the atmosphere at home had become pure vaudeville. A friend who passed by the Diderot ménage that night, Jean Devaines, left an eye-popping account that swings from Corneille to Molière. Greeted at the door by an overwrought Diderot, Devaines followed him to his study. Bursting into tears, the old philosophe blurted out: "Behold a man in despair! I have just witnessed the cruelest of scenes for a father and husband." Seemingly unable to continue his story, Diderot moaned: "Ah! How could I ever part from them, now that I've seen the pain they are in?" As Devaines groped for words, Diderot interrupted him, having nevertheless found the strength to finish his account. There we were, he explained, seated at the dinner table, my wife and daughter on either side of me. There were no guests, of course: Diderot wanted to give these final moments to them alone. "Such a desolate spectacle," he declaimed, "the likes of which will never again be seen! Unable to speak or eat, our despair suffocated us." Grabbing his friend by the arms, Diderot paused before bursting out: "Ah, my friend: What can be sweeter than to be loved by one's family? No, the thought of leaving them is too horrible! I'll never find the inhuman courage to do so. How can the expectations of the Empress Catherine outweigh the outpourings of the heart?" Seemingly persuaded by his own words, Diderot then announced to his audience of one: "I've made my decision: I'm staying! Never will I leave my wife and daughter! My departure will cause their deaths, and I refuse to be their executioner!"

Having ended his peroration, Diderot threw himself into Devaines's arms, wetting his coat in tears. A tableau made all the more remarkable by the sudden entrance, stage left, of Madame Diderot. A small bonnet perched on her head, and hands clenched against her hips, the good woman demanded: "And here we are, eh? What are you doing, Monsieur Diderot?" Knowing the answer, Nanette did not bother to wait for a reply: "You are losing your time, and neglecting your packing, in order to recount such baloney. You're leaving first thing in the morning, but here are you are, busy spouting fine phrases." After a pause, Nanette then reveals why Diderot had little appetite: "This is what happens when you dine outside with your friends rather than at home. You had promised to stay home, but it seems everyone owns you except your own family. Ah, what a man!"[12]

Standing at Scheveningen, Diderot's absorption with the breaking of waves helped drown out the memory of the breaking of china in Paris. But, crucially, both moments were *mises en scène,* less spontaneous than scripted. Several years before, in 1765, he described various encounters he had already had with the sea. There was a terrifying shipwreck, where the "sea roars, the wind whistles, the thunder cracks, and the pale, somber glow of lightning pierces through the clouds and reveals the scene." Or a view of the same sea, but now calm, which deepens "imperceptibly as the eye moves out from the shore to the point at which the horizon meets the eye."[13]

These encounters, though, had taken place not on the French or Dutch coasts, but instead in the close and heated rooms of the Paris Salon. These were Diderot's descriptions of paintings by Claude-Joseph Vernet, an artist he had recently befriended. Shortly before he left for Holland, he had hung in his study one of his favorite Vernet paintings, *A Storm on the Mediterranean Coast.* The work's sheer realism, depicting a small group of men and women gathered on a beach following a shipwreck, overwhelmed Diderot. "O Lord!" Diderot exclaimed, "Acknowledge the waters Thou hast created: concede that they are as Thou madest them, both when agitated by Thy breath and when calmed by Thy hand."[14]

Recalling yet another of Vernet's seascapes, Diderot simply sighed: "If you've seen the sea at five o'clock you know this painting."

Oddly, until his trip to Holland, Diderot had never seen the North Sea at five o'clock—or for that matter, at any time of day or night. He had never before seen *any* body of water—or, at least, one wider than the Seine River running through his beloved Paris. After moving as a young man to Paris from his native Langres—a town southeast of the capital—Diderot never wandered far from the great city. Excursions to the country estates of aristocratic friends, the infrequent visit to Langres, and a three-month stay in the prison in Vincennes were, until 1773, the outer limits of his travels. Diderot would not have considered that a handicap, though. "I had always thought that a person was never so well off as when at home," confides a character in a work, *Supplement to the Voyage of Bougainville,* that he most probably worked on while in Holland. Pointing to a copy of Bougainville's published account of his circumnavigation of the globe, the character, who has more than a passing resemblance to Diderot, tells his companion that just as the French explorer "can go around the globe on a plank, you and I can make a tour of the universe on this floor."[15]

Yet here he was in Holland, pried from the floor of his home, just as the Dutch had pried dry land from the sea. For now, standing on the promenade, Diderot's thoughts went no further than the sea. Or, rather, the sea was driving his thoughts in many directions, one of which was perhaps his recollections of the Paris Art Salon of 1765. It was there that he first encountered Vernet's work. What struck him was the verisimilitude of his seascapes; how they managed to create something so real—though, admittedly, he was hardly qualified to attest to the reality of seas—through a means so false. As he observed, the canvas frames a "tissue of falsities, one disguising another," that nevertheless merge, from the brush of a great painter, as a seemingly true and artless vision of the world.[16]

For this reason, Diderot could, with utter sincerity, claim he knew what the sea looked like at five o'clock. The line between creation and its re-creation, nature and its depiction, blurs and disappears in the hands of great artists. In fact, truly great painters place themselves in the canvas, unaware or uncaring that it is an object to be seen by others. "If, when one is painting a picture, one supposes the presence of spectators, all is lost."[17] It is like an actor who, launching into a declamation, turns to the audience: the fourth wall collapses and the fiction or artifice is revealed. For this reason, Diderot could stop in front of a favorite painting by J.-B. Chardin in the same way as "a weary traveller goes and sits down, half unaware of doing so, in the spot which offers him a seat among the verdure, silence, waters, shade and coolness."[18] These paintings were extensions of the real world, intimate and textured, so unlike the rococo cartoons produced by Chardin's great competitor, François Boucher: "That man only takes up the brush to show me tits and buttocks. Now, I am more than happy to see such things, but I cannot have somebody pointing them out to me."[19]

Holland, in effect, allowed Diderot to measure not just how closely Vernet depicted nature, but how well nature conformed to Vernet. Nature could, Diderot warned, fall short of art. "Excellence in art, in its moral as well as its physical aspects, consists in surpassing nature, in applying more intelligence to the composition of its scenes. . . . Notice how the most terrible accidents of nature, tempests, volcanoes, thunderbolts, are more terrifying still in the fictions of the poets."[20]

Dutch academics and writers had given Diderot, celebrated as the editor of the *Encylopédie,* a hero's welcome. He toured the museums and universities, met with local notables and prominent faculty; he was, reported one friend, "mad about Dutch doctors."[21] Inevitably, as the planned two-week layover turned into a two-months-long series of victory laps, Diderot became a fixture at social gatherings. Madame de Hogendorp, the wife of a wealthy merchant, encountered the seductive Frenchman several times at these events. "He is kind, good and humane," she wrote to her husband. "I love to listen to him talk." In fact, she continues,

Diderot would sometimes drop in at the good woman's residence to "pass a couple of hours and listen to my woes."[22] One hopes that Monsieur de Hogendorp, across the globe in India on business, shared his wife's happiness on this score.

In those few lines, Madame de Hogendorp captured Diderot's personality. He had seduced men and women alike by his gift of conversation—at least when he had not shocked them. Madame Geoffrin, who hosted one of Paris's great salons, tactfully made Diderot to understand that he was no longer welcome at her weekly Wednesday gatherings. The man, she confessed, was beyond even her polite, yet steely control.[23] While Diderot was electrifying his Dutch hosts, Geoffrin wrote to a friend about the philosophe: "He is an upright man, but he is wrongheaded. And he is so wrongly constituted that he neither sees nor hears anything as it really is. He is always like a man in a dream, and who believes everything that he has dreamed."[24]

Diderot would not have disagreed. In a letter to Sophie Volland, he wonders at the "circuits we have made" during one of their conversations. "The dreams of a delirious patient," he adds, "are no more heteroclite." But that impression, he continues, is dispelled if we study what was uttered, apparently at random, during the conversation: "Since there is nothing incoherent either in the head of a man dreaming or in that of a madman, everything holds together in conversation as well. But it would at times be quite difficult to rediscover the imperceptible links that have attracted so many diverse ideas. A man throws out a word he detaches from what preceded and followed in his head; a second does the same, and then it's a free-for-all."[25]

Not surprisingly, the eighteenth century is nearly as frequently called the "Age of Conversation" as the "Age of Reason." The two activities, for Diderot and his contemporaries, could hardly be separated. In her early-nineteenth-century work *Of Germany (De l'Allemagne)* Madame de Staël offered what was as much a eulogy as a defense for this unique institution: "All classes in France feel the need to converse: the spoken word is not only, as it is elsewhere, a means of communicating ideas, sentiments, and concerns, but it is an instrument that is enjoyable to play and that, like music with some peoples and strong liquor with others, raises the spirits."[26] The ends of conversation were found in their means: the display of *esprit,* or quickness and wit; *honnêteté,* or affability, yet controlled; and *politesse,* or polish and restraint.

These hallmarks were emphasized in the entry on "Conversation" in the *Encyclopédie.* "It should be remembered that conversation is a relaxation and that it is neither a contest of arms nor a chess game; it must know how to be disregarded, more than disregarded if necessary: it must, in a word, give free rein to its wit."[27] But the philosophes increasingly found their "relaxation" in contestation. In the intellectual salons of mid-eighteenth-century Paris, conversation had become more than a web of words woven by aristocrats to distract one another and dilate on court rumors. Instead, the philosophes, as well as women like Julie de Lespinasse and Madame d'Épinay who reigned over their literary salons, slowly shaped conversation into a collective effort to discover truth and question authority, an effort that necessarily threatened to undermine aristocratic ideals and traditional assumptions. During the twilight years of the Ancien Régime, these men and women, dismissing the dusty rules of conversation that had governed the world of their predecessors, pushed the boundaries of what one was allowed to say and think.

Diderot applauded what he thought to be the beneficent influence of this new forum of conversation. "What we write influences only a certain class of citizen," he explained to his fellow philosophe (and France's finance minister) Jacques Necker, "while our conversation influences everyone." Public opinion, Diderot reminded him, "originates only from the effect of a small number of men who speak after having thought and who endlessly create, at different points in society, centers of instruction from whence their reasoned truths and errors spread from person to person until they reach the confines of the city where they become established as articles of faith."[28]

Diderot's conversation, if not always persuasive, was almost always enthralling. For his friend and frequent collaborator on the *Encyclopédie* the Abbé Morellet, Diderot's genius lay in his "vivid, supremely honest, subtle without being obscure" conversation: it was "varied in its forms, speaking with imagination, fecund in ideas and stimulating ideas in others." When Diderot spoke, he often grew so excited that he would grab hold of his interlocutor, shaking him or her by the arm or thigh. At times, marveling at the ideas he unearthed in his conversational forays, he seemed to forget the presence of others, a habit that the playwright Jean-François de La Harpe insisted was a "tic." La Harpe recounts (with some irritation) that, with "head raised and arms dangling," Diderot would "shut his eyes as if seeking inspiration" and words would begin to "tumble from his mouth."[29]

No less irritating, perhaps, for La Harpe, was Diderot's delight in both hearing and seeing himself speak. Few admired Diderot's eloquence and originality as much as he himself did—a trait he was not at all abashed to admit. He asked Étienne-Maurice Falconet, a sculptor who will play an important role in our story: "What is the difference between a modest man and a vain man?" The answer, continued Diderot, was that the former thinks but remains silent, while the latter thinks and speaks.[30] Of course, for Madame Geoffrin, the problem with Diderot was that he tended to speak before he thought. As for La Harpe, the problem was elsewhere: all the while that Diderot spoke, he was his own most ardent and attentive listener.

Given his impatience with Diderot's admiration of his own eloquence, it seems La Harpe had not read the Earl of Shaftesbury's *Inquiry Concerning Merit, or Virtue.* In itself, this would not have been surprising: Shaftesbury's work had been published more than a half-century before, in 1699. But a French translation had nevertheless appeared in 1745. Although Diderot's name does not appear on the cover, it was a secret known to many that he was the work's translator. Known to far fewer—namely, those who had read Shaftesbury in the original English—Diderot had not merely translated the work, but made it his own by inserting, grafting, or simply forcing his own thoughts onto the text: a writing and translating quirk that he would keep his entire professional life, threading across the range of his works from the *Encyclopédie* through the *Supplement to the Voyage of Bougainville* to the *History of the Two Indies.*

Though a student of John Locke—in fact, Locke, as his parents' attending physician, brought him into the world in 1671—Shaftesbury rejected his mentor's description of the human mind as a tabula rasa—a blank slate to be filled by the scribbling of sensory stimuli. Inspired by the Cambridge Platonists, Shaftesbury instead insisted that human beings are endowed with a sixth sense, that of sympathy. A faculty for grasping moral truths, Shaftesbury argued, is no less embedded in us than our faculties of sight and smell. We naturally sympathize with our fellow creatures, just as we naturally collaborate with them. "If any Appetite or Sense be natural, the Sense of Fellowship is the same." No less natural and basic principle of our constitution, he claimed, is our "Sense of Right and Wrong." When we seek to do what is right, Shaftesbury argued, we do what is good; and when we do what is good, we add to the "Existence of well-being" of society.[31]

Though Shaftesbury, with admirable but misplaced confidence, extrapolated from his aristocratic pedigree and refined sentiments to those shared by all of humankind, and confused what ought to be with what is, the young Diderot nevertheless embraced his claims. He was especially taken by Shaftesbury's argument that virtuous behavior is selfish behavior: we strive to be good because it makes us feel good. That sense, in turn, is reinforced by the recognition and applause our fellow men and women bestow upon us for our striving. Key for Diderot was Shaftesbury's conviction that "Virtue and Interest may be found at last to agree."

As improbable as it appears, the scion of English aristocracy and the offspring of French artisans seem to have agreed on the foundations of morality. But this was, in part, because Diderot lost elements of

Shaftesbury in translation, all the while finding elements of his own thought. In effect, Diderot agreed less with Shaftesbury, than with a Shaftesbury remade in his own image. With his endearing combination of naivety and subtlety, Diderot recalled his approach to translating Shaftesbury's book: "I read and reread him, I filled myself with his thoughts, and then, so to speak, I closed his book when I took up the pen. Never has someone else's work been used with such liberty."[32]

Not only did Diderot use Shaftesbury with liberty, but Shaftesbury also liberated Diderot from the need for a religious basis for morality. Thanks to our inner moral sense, we no more needed God to be capable of virtue than we did to be capable of seeing or hearing. While Shaftesbury's latitudinarianism remained within the precincts of Christianity, Diderot used him as a trampoline to launch himself well beyond the borders of religious belief. This, in turn, helps explain Diderot's intense desire for applause—and his willingness to applaud himself. It was not, or not only, childish vanity or mere egotism. To the contrary, there was a moral purpose to such public performances, and the admiration that ensued. For Diderot, virtue was first and foremost a public activity—an activity that could not be performed often enough. To the faithful who insisted that virtue was its own reward, Diderot replied that the reward still had to be recognized—if not, as Diderot now began to suspect, by God, then certainly by one's peers.

During those early years in Paris, especially the 1750s, Diderot rarely missed an occasion—in conversation or in print—to insist on man's goodness. Indeed, he insisted so often and loudly that he seemed to be trying to convince not just others, but also himself. When done well, literature ignites the tinder of goodness already within our hearts. After reading Samuel Richardson's novel *Clarissa,* Diderot could hardly restrain himself. "If we sought to persuade men that, apart from all ulterior considerations, all we need to be happy is to be virtuous, what service would Richardson not render humanity?"[33] While La Rochefoucauld conveyed a harsher view of life through maxims, Diderot marveled, Richardson reveals a more uplifting view through realistic narrative. Thanks to this Englishman, Diderot declared, "I love my fellow men and my duties better, feel greater pity for those who do evil . . . and greater respect for those who do good."[34]

In a word, Diderot felt "greater love for virtue, the only good the heavens can grant us."[35] Don't bother turning to history for such truths, for it has none to offer. Instead, fiction alone can provide this kind of moral epiphany. "I dare say," Diderot assures (the all-too-dead) Richardson, "that the truest history is empty while your novel is filled with truths."[36] For the reader, the result was not only an aesthetic experience, but a moral one as well. Echoing less Richardson than Jean-Jacques Rousseau, Diderot faulted society, not nature, for the ascendancy of evil over goodness. In his *Discourse on Dramatic Poetry,* he asks: "Is human nature good?" His answer was swift: "Yes, my friend, and very good. It is not human nature which should be blamed but miserable convention, which perverts man." He appealed to what he assumed was a universal attraction for good works and character, whether in life or literature. "What moves us like the story of a generous action?" he demanded. "Where is the wretch who can listen coldly to the woes of a good man?"[37]

And, for that matter, where is the wretch who could remain cold while attending a play of Diderot's on this very theme? In many places, it turns out. In 1756 Diderot dashed off a play inspired by the Italian playwright Carlo Goldoni's popular comedy *The True Friend.* Diderot's reworking of Goldoni transforms what was a witty and forgettable farce into a sententious and forgettable drama. It follows the predictable arc of the hero, Dorval, who masters his great passion for a woman who loves him but is betrothed to his best friend. Over the course of five acts, Dorval finds the words to persuade his love interest to marry his friend, finds the courage to defend the friend from thugs, finds the compassion to sacrifice his personal fortune for the less fortunate, and finds the self-abnegation to marry someone he does not love. By play's end, we are exhausted, not enthralled, by Dorval's serial self-sacrifices. This character, described by Diderot as melancholy in bearing except when he is speaking about virtue—he is then "transfigured"—is less a paragon than a caricature of moral integrity.

For this reason, instead of laughs, as in Goldoni's farce, there are speeches—*many* speeches—in Diderot's morality play. In essence, Diderot drapes the appearance of a drama over a paean to probity. He goes as far as having one of the play's characters explain the moral function of plays in this age of reason and its benefits: "These are the lessons our theaters announce—lessons they cannot announce too often." Clearly, such heavy-handed didacticism worried its author. In a letter to Voltaire, Diderot sensed the play failed as a play: "I do not know what the public will think of my dramatic talent, but I don't care. I wanted to give them a man whose heart was marked by the ideal of virtue and love of humanity. Now, they will have seen it."[38] Diderot's fears were well founded. In 1771, when the Comédie-Française finally staged the play, it had the life span of a mayfly: it closed after one night.

But readers of his revised text, published the following year, saw something different and far more fascinating. Having first hijacked Goldoni's theatrical fluff on behalf of virtue, Diderot meta-wrapped it with what he called the "True History of the Play." This consisted of a conversation between a philosophe named "Diderot" and Dorval, the play's protagonist, who, it transpires, not only lived through the play's events but also turned them into the play we have just read. In their discussion, each time "Diderot" takes issue with the play, criticizing a scene that is too unlikely or dialogue that is too overwrought, Dorval replies that these were precisely how the words were spoken and the scenes unfolded. When "Diderot" presses him on a particularly distasteful scene, dismissing it as a cheap "coup de théâtre," Dorval quickly agrees, but confesses he couldn't do otherwise—"This was not fiction, but a fact"—all the while allowing, for the sake of verisimilitude, that it "would have been better if things had happened differently."[39]

La Rochefoucauld famously insisted that hypocrisy is the debt vice pays to virtue, but Diderot wished for something better: namely, that fiction be the debt that truth pays to virtue. If necessary, the moralist could and should sacrifice mundane facts on the altar of enduring moral truths. By the same token, while it was important for the philosophes to be good, it was even more urgent for them to display their virtues. For this reason, Diderot explained to Voltaire, the philosophes had to go public with their campaign on behalf of virtue. "It is not enough to know more than they [the ranks of bishops and cardinals, priests and monks] do; it is necessary to *show* them that we are better and that philosophy makes more good men than sufficient or efficacious faith." Diderot conceived this campaign in both individual and collective terms. A philosophe's public display of benevolence and tolerance, reason and reasonableness, was less a self-advertisement—though it certainly was that—than a model for the society they hoped to bring into being. It is, he declared, "at least as important to make men better as to make them less ignorant."[40]

Shortly after he arrived in The Hague, Diderot met Frans Hemsterhuis, a prominent Dutch thinker who sorely tested Diderot's views on man's ability to be virtuous though godless. Hemsterhuis was as famous in his own day as he is forgotten in ours. Honored with the unlikely moniker "the Batavian Socrates," he had studied philosophy at university but was unable to find a teaching position. So, unlike Socrates, he became a government official, devoting his free time to his philosophical investigations.

Given the amount he wrote, he seems to have had much free time. Shortly before Diderot's arrival, Hemsterhuis had published a short work titled *Letter on Man (Lettre sur l'homme).* Hardly had Diderot's bags been unpacked than Hemsterhuis delivered a copy of his book to Diderot, who was staying at the stately residence of a friend, Prince Golitsyn. For Diderot, it was something of a backhanded welcome to The Hague. Written in French, *Letter on Man* takes aim at the philosophy of Benedict Spinoza, the native son Holland didn't quite know what to do with. Though Spinoza had died almost a century earlier, his name remained very much alive. "No one else, not even Hobbes," the historian Jonathan Israel remarks, "was denounced as often as Spinoza." In fact, Hobbes himself was left breathless by Spinoza's frontal assault on traditional religion. According to one of Hobbes's early biographers, Spinoza's writings "cut through him a bar's length, for he [Hobbes] durst not write so boldly."[41]

Elaborating a thoroughly materialist and determinist approach to the world and our place in it, Spinoza held that mind and matter, as well as God and nature, were one and the same. Spinoza's God is an immanent being—his own cause, in other words—and provides the substance for everything else in the world. In effect, God is the world, the world is God, and always the twain shall meet. One consequence of Spinoza's reasoning is that nothing in the world, or within humankind, was beyond the reach of our intellect. More disturbingly, Spinoza's metaphysics led inescapably to a world, or a God, in which everything was already determined. Everything that happens, happens necessarily.

Historians of European thought still argue over the impact of Spinozism. The case can be made that never before had a system of metaphysics so strongly influenced politics and society, shattering the pillars of traditional truth claims and bringing down the aging roof of political authority on both throne and altar. Not surprisingly, in the early 1670s, soon after Spinoza settled in The Hague, the city's Calvinist elders denounced his "idolatrous and superstitious" writings.[42] They worried that his "utterly godless doctrines" had begun to "creep in more and more both here and elsewhere."[43]

At Scheveningen, however, Diderot was quite at home not just with republicanism, but with godlessness as well. In the published account of his voyage to Holland, he (unfairly) proclaimed the Dutch to be a "superstitious people, hostile to philosophy and free thought concerning religion." Yet, importantly, he also praised them for not persecuting those who took such liberties.[44] Indeed, Diderot savored the political atmosphere that allowed so much freedom to think and say what one wished. To Sophie Volland, he extolled the "republican spirit" of the Dutch, regardless of their social station; to Madame d'Épinay, he asserted that the Dutch seemed "possessed by a republican demon."[45] To both women, he delightedly quoted a saddle maker who declared he was removing his daughter from a convent. " 'I worry,' said the good man, 'that those underhanded monarchical ways are contagious.' "[46] "Here merchants speak with the majestic tone of kings." While this has become all too common in our own age, this perspective was rare and valuable in Diderot's day. As he understood, a class of citizens with a literal stake in society was essential for a healthy nation: "There is no country for those who own nothing, or those who can take everything."[47]

As for Spinoza's godlessness, Diderot was more circumspect. There is no indication that he visited the house at Paviljoensgracht, near the city's outskirts, where Spinoza spent his final years. He may have avoided it for reasons of prudence, seeing no need to strengthen the parallels others had drawn between Spinoza's philosophy and his own work. This seemed to be the case with the good Hemsterhuis, who had come out as an anti-Spinozist. While praising the freedom of the press in Holland, Hemsterhuis also deplored the amoralists and atheists that had abused this freedom. Offering his book as a cure for the "prodigious quantity of writings which ridicule belief in God's existence, the soul's immortality and religion's necessity," the Dutch Platonist declared that "reason, when freed from imagination and prejudice, can never lead us to systems of materialism and free thinking."[48]

When he lashed out at atheists, Hemsterhuis did not name names. But Diderot understood that he was squarely in the Dutchman's crosshairs. In the margins of the copy Hemsterhuis had given him, Diderot scoffed at the claim that only a transcendental foundation guarantees virtuous behavior. By privileging a Christian and "chimerical level of duties above our real duties," Diderot argued that Hemsterhuis separated humankind from the duties of sociability and humanity.[49] Rather than locating the basis of moral behavior in a realm infinitely distant, Diderot insisted we should instead look around us. Still attached after all these years to Shaftesbury, Diderot affirmed we find the source in natural law: "An order of knowledge and ideas peculiar to the human species, which emanate from its dignity and constitute it."[50]

A far greater challenge, both philosophically and politically, than Hemsterhuis was Claude-Arien Helvétius, a wealthy aristocrat who associated with many of the *Encyclopédie*'s contributors. Between bouts of socializing in The Hague, Diderot read and reread his colleague's *De l'homme (On Man),* darkening the margins with his thoughts. Having finished the book in 1769, the author had waited several years to publish it, afraid of official reaction. "The Inquisition is more severe in France than Spain," Helvétius told a friend.[51] It was only in 1772, a year after his death, that the book reached the shelves of Parisian booksellers.

Helvétius was right to wait. More than a decade earlier, in 1758, he had published his treatise *De l'esprit (On Mind).* Even though the state censor had given the work his official imprimatur, the storm it stirred made clear that the poor official had either failed to read the book or failed to grasp its explosive contents. A methodical and mostly humorless materialist, Helvétius declared that ethics was nothing more than physics applied to the realm of human actions. The noble virtues—from self-sacrifice to selflessness—are the rouge we slap on the pocked face of our self-aggrandizing and selfish ways. Ultimately, all human behavior ripples from our base passions and appetites. What reasonable man could not perceive, Helvétius wonders, "that his virtues and vices are wholly owing to the different modifications of personal interest and that all equally tend to happiness?"[52]

If Helvétius's book shocked his readers, one contemporary wit declared, it was because it stated what readers already believed. In fact, the aristocratic novelist Madame de Graffigny complained that Helvétius had lifted his arguments, and even turns of phrase, from conversations at her literary salon.[53] Whether or not Helvétius had borrowed the words of others, Diderot in turn found them reductionist and artless. "A paradoxical author ought never to state his conclusion but always his proofs. He should enter into the mind of his reader slyly, and not by force. . . . If all that the author wrote had been heaped up pell-mell, so that there had been only in the mind of the author an unacknowledged principle of arrangement, his book would have been infinitely more agreeable and, without appearing so, infinitely more dangerous."[54]

In the end, Helvétius sinned less by his materialism than by his reductionism, collapsing any and all distinction between, say, moral sentiments and physical appetites. For Helvétius, as the historian of ideas Ernst Cassirer drily remarked, "all such sensations boil down to the same undifferentiated mass of sensation."[55] And yet the danger posed by Helvétius's clumsy work was all too real for Diderot. Both the man and his work had acquired many enemies, both at court and the church, who willfully associated Helvétius's subversive work with Diderot's *Encyclopédie.* In a dispatch from the salons where he whiled away his time, Diderot's close friend and collaborator Melchior Grimm reported his grim forebodings: "Philosophy will feel the effects for a long time of the upheaval of opinion that this author caused almost universally by his book." More particularly, Grimm continued, it would be Diderot, not Helvétius, who would pay for the malicious rumors swirling around the book: "In order to ruin Monsieur Diderot, it has been spread about everywhere that he was the author of all the passages in the book of Monsieur Helvétius that revolted people."[56]

Underscoring the resemblances between *De l'esprit* and *"le système horrible"* of Spinozism, the church banned the book while royal authorities debated imprisoning its author. Helvétius ultimately dodged the dungeon, but nevertheless paid a steep price in terms of public humiliation. By the order of the Paris Parlement, an executioner displayed a copy of *De l'esprit* outside the entrance of the Palais de Justice, then shredded and burned it.[57] Helvétius was stripped of his honorific titles and, in order to avoid imprisonment, signed a crushing retraction of his work that had been dictated by the royal censors. "I wish in all sincerity," Helvétius declared, "that all of those unfortunate enough to have read my book excuse me for not having considered the disastrous impression it would leave."[58] While Helvétius groveled, Diderot and his colleagues ran around with their hair on fire, frantic that *De l'esprit* not only threatened the gains they had so far made but also risked the future of the *Encyclopédie.*

The fires were for the moment contained, if not stamped out. Having escaped punishment by issuing an abject apology, Helvétius had learned at least one lesson: not to publish another such book—at least during his lifetime, if he wished to spend that life at home and not in the Bastille. And so it was a little more than a year after his death—witnessed by his wife and friends but not a confessor—that Helvétius's magnum opus was printed in Holland and promptly outdid his earlier work in its scandalous claims. Helvétius claimed that pleasure and pain are the only causes, the "unknown principles," behind all human activity. As all of our ideas derive from physical stimuli, it is pointless "to admit a faculty of judging and comparing distinct from the faculty of sensation." In a word, the physical world—which includes our own sensations—is the sole basis for morality and justice. "I can form an idea of my five senses," Helvétius declares, "but I confess I have no more idea of a moral sense than of a moral castle and elephant."

From this axiom, it is but a short step to the belief that everything that leads to pleasure is good, while everything that leads to pain is evil. The ideals praised by moralists and poets—loyalty and courage, love and friendship—are, in fact, names of convenience we slap on animal instinct and individual interest. Impatient with those who "continue to use words void of meaning," Helvétius insists that the truth will set us free. Or, rather, that it would set us free were we not chained to our quest for pleasure and flight from pain.

The political and social consequences of Helvétius's analysis of human nature were momentous. Because all of us seek just one thing, our own pleasure, we are all of us tyrants in the making, ready to run roughshod over others—to inflict pain on them—in order to reach that goal. As a result, we require a fair and balanced government devoted to the reconciliation of individual desires with the general good—a task best assumed by a democratic republic or an enlightened ruler. Not surprisingly, this line of reasoning terrified many of Helvétius's colleagues and friends. In a letter to Diderot's co-editor, the mathematician Jean le Rond d'Alembert, Voltaire exclaimed that if any powerful men were to read the treatise, "they would never pardon us."[59]

In Parisian court circles, it hardly helped matters that Helvétius had dedicated the book to the Empress Catherine, explaining that the Enlightenment now shone most brightly in "northern lands," while in the south—i.e., France—"superstition and eastern despotism" now reigned.[60] Nor did it improve relations between Paris and Saint Petersburg that Prince Golitsyn, who was playing host to Diderot at that very moment in The Hague, had become a one-man public relations firm for Helvétius's book, passing out copies at every opportunity, including one to the French ambassador, the Marquis de Noailles. Not amused, Noailles suspected that Diderot might have penned the dedication. Even if he had not, the Frenchman nevertheless had "shown the same sentiments enclosed within the book."[61]

Yet Diderot would never have written such a preface. Not only would he have never sung the praises of Frederick the Great, as did the preface's author, but he was never able to accept the narrow and reductionist theses of the book. Whereas Voltaire worried over what those in power would make of Helvétius, Diderot instead worried over what Helvétius himself made of the moral consequences of materialism. The book presented

Diderot with another opportunity to wrestle with the knotty issues raised by determinism.

The notes he scribbled in the margins soon spilled onto paper, pooling into a small work called *A Refutation of Helvétius.* "Is it really true," he asked, "that physical pain and pleasure, which are perhaps the sole principle of animal behavior, are also the sole principle of human conduct?" Not at all, Diderot replied. Helvétius had failed to distinguish between man and men: "So different is each individual that if he could create a language specific to himself, there would be as many languages as there are men. No man would say 'hello' or 'goodbye' like any other man." Helvétius, Diderot insisted, had also confounded causes and preconditions. Of course, the faculty of sensation, which allows us to act and react in the world, is embedded in human beings. But this particular faculty, along with the physical sensations it registers, is nothing more than the necessary condition for such activity. He declared that it is "a mere *sine qua non,* and that the direct and immediate motives of our aversions and desires are something quite other."[62]

Diderot was also shocked by Helvétius's scientific hubris, the conviction that his axioms concerning man's nature were as irrefutable as Newton's principles concerning physical nature. "Admit that you are uselessly hitting your head," Diderot warns, "as I have also done on matters I will never plumb. If I mention myself, it is because I am conscious of my own attempts and aware of my own obstinacy. And yet, though I've more than the stuff you require, I have not found the truth. In fact, questions that seemed complex have turned out to be simple, while those that seemed simple were beyond my comprehension."[63]

In the end, the novelist no less than the humanist in Diderot rebelled at Helvétius's impoverished and oppressive portrait of humankind. Although we are made of matter, influenced by our drives, and shaped by our world, we are not mere marionettes. Drawing from Locke's philosophy that innate ideas do not exist and that all knowledge is derived from experience, Helvétius caricatured rather than continued the English empiricist's work. In fact, Diderot added mischievously, Helvétius was himself a living argument against his own thesis that pleasure and pain are the sole motivating forces in our lives. After all, Helvétius was independently wealthy and married to a beautiful woman, but rather than spend his time in bed, wrapped in sensual pleasures, he committed himself to the exhausting and thankless task of writing his book. Diderot agreed that the sources of moral law must be universal, but he rejected Helvétius's claim that physical sensibility alone is the unique cause to all of our actions. Hunched over the book, rubbing his brow over his colleague's reductionist claims, Diderot impatiently dashed off in the margin: "I am a man and I need causes proper to man."

Taking in the view from Scheveningen—an ideal vantage point from which to reflect on the ways the Dutch had reshaped the natural world—perhaps reminded Diderot that he had a similar ambition, but one aimed at the human world. In the *Encyclopédie,* Diderot announces the moral ends of this unprecedented work: he and his contributors, he vowed, must "inspire a taste of science, a horror of falsehood and vice, and a love of virtue, because everything which does not ultimately aim at happiness and virtue is nothing."[64] As he told Helvétius, "I am convinced, I say, that all in all, the best thing to do for one's happiness is to be a good man: in my opinion that is the most important and interesting work to be done, that is the one I shall remember with the greatest satisfaction in my last moments."[65]

In the end, for Diderot, anything that does not place man at the center of the world isn't worth a moment's reflection or physical exertion. What would become of the universe, he asks, if man were "banished from the surface of the earth." The answer makes Diderot shudder: "This pathetic and sublime spectacle of nature becomes nothing but a mute and melancholy scene. . . . Setting aside my own existence and the happiness of my fellow beings, what does the rest of nature matter to me?" With or without him, Diderot believed, nature would abide. But whether his fellow beings would prosper without him was less clear. He was, after all, a philosophe, one who had dedicated his life to bettering the lives of his fellow beings. While the goal never varied, the means to attain it did. One path was paved by writing for others, another by conversing with others. The first path led to his becoming editor of the *Encyclopédie*—a work, accomplished with the help of dozens of collaborators, whose aim was to gather the sum of human knowledge and bequeath it to future generations. Diderot's justification can either still stir, or simply sting, our hearts: We have undertaken this project, he wrote, "so that our descendants, in becoming better informed, may at the same time become more virtuous and content, and so that we do not leave this earth without having earned the respect of the human race."[66]

The second path, however, led through Scheveningen to Saint Petersburg, where Catherine the Second, Empress of Russia, had invited him—more than once—to converse. As Diderot rightly sensed, the invitations were as imperious as they were imperial. "The desires of a sovereign like the empress, the wishes of a benefactress are commands which even the least sensible of men must honor. Such a woman must be seen at least once in a lifetime, and I will see her."[67] As his own lifetime grew shorter, Diderot could no longer find excuses, telling friends that if he "did not make that voyage, I will stand badly with myself, badly with her."[68] Were he to feel badly with himself, it was only in part due to his sense of gratitude. No less important, though, was his sense of philosophical duty. If change cannot come from below, it needs to be imposed from above. Who better to undertake this task than this remarkable woman, mentored by an equally remarkable philosopher? "To her," Diderot insisted, "one can really speak the truth." That Diderot wrote this *after* his sojourn in Russia, where he discovered that talking truth to power was not so simple, suggests that Diderot was not entirely truthful with himself.

Reading Voltaire in Saint Petersburg

I WANT THE LAWS TO BE OBEYED, BUT NOT BY SLAVES.

—CATHERINE II

"I HAD BEEN EXPECTING DIDEROT AT ANY MOMENT." Having penned this line, its author paused; she realized that her wait, which had in effect already lasted several years, would not end as soon as she had expected: "To my great regret, however, I have just learned that he has fallen ill in Duisburg."

Still, the letter writer perhaps found some solace in the knowledge that Diderot had actually crossed the Rhine and made it as far as Duisburg. In any case, the news would not disturb her routine. It remained what it had always been and always would be—as fixed, she once observed, as "the lines of a sheet of music." Having risen at six o'clock, she remained in her bedchamber for two hours, alone with official reports and personal letters. Annotating the former with briskness, she replied to the latter at greater length, at times in Russian but much more often in her native German. Or, as with this letter, in her beloved French, which she wrote well enough to gently mock herself. Warning its recipient that her letter promised to make him yawn, she invited him to "toss it on the fire, if you want, but do remember that boredom is my métier: it is a right that belongs to kings."[1]

Catherine II smiled as she finished this line, knowing full well that Voltaire, her correspondent, would sooner throw his wig in the fire.

As was her habit, Catherine shared with Voltaire news about events private and public, personal and political. Not only did these realms merge in the life of a monarch, but over the course of their correspondence—begun shortly after Catherine became empress in 1762—Voltaire had become one of Catherine's treasured confidants. In an early letter to him, she in fact confessed that ever since the day in 1746 when his works had fallen into her fifteen-year-old hands, she "could not put them down, and the only other books I wanted were such as were as well written and instructive. . . . In the end, I invariably returned to the author who first directed my taste and afforded me my greatest enjoyment. If I have any knowledge, it is to him alone that I owe it."[2]

Catherine owed Voltaire more than her knowledge; she also owed the renowned thinker and writer for his uncritical support of her person and policies, which were priceless possessions—what today we might call "social capital"—in the Age of Reason. Every ruler wishing to burnish his credentials as an "enlightened despot" sought Voltaire's attention—this was, most famously, the case with Frederick the Great of Prussia—but Catherine's case was particular. How could it be otherwise for a German-born woman believed by many Europeans—including Voltaire, at first—to have taken power illegitimately? Did she not, after all, depose her husband Peter III? More scandalously, did not the overthrown tsar die shortly after from what was announced to be a case of "hemorrhoids"?

In July 17, 1745, Sophia Augusta Fredericka, the fifteen-year-old Princess of Anhalt-Zerbst—a Prussian region now part of Poland—spent her wedding night alone in Saint Petersburg. Looking out the window of her bedchamber in the Winter Palace, the monumental Baroque structure that sprawled along the bank of the Neva River, she could hear her husband, Grand Duke Peter, drilling his valets as if they were imperial soldiers. Listening to the clatter of footfalls unable to sound in unison despite the barked commands of the sickly teenager chosen to be Russia's next tsar, his bride strove to order her thoughts. Sophia's pride had been wounded by Peter's obvious disinterest in her; but that same pride prevented her from complaining. Her heart, she later wrote, "did not foresee great happiness." But what her soul did foresee was something far greater: "I had something, I know not what, that never for a single moment let me doubt that sooner or later I would succeed in becoming the sovereign Empress of Russia in my own right."[3]

That "something" was manifest from the moment the young German princess crossed the frigid Russian frontier in February 1744. Scarcely had Sophia arrived at the imperial court than a fever struck her, leaving her delirious when not unconscious. Bed-ridden and bled repeatedly by doctors, Sophia remained under the personal care of Elizabeth, Empress of Russia, for nearly a month. Elizabeth's watchfulness did not stop when the princess was finally well enough to appear in public: the empress sent her young charge a jar of rouge to enliven the ghostly pallor of her thinned face. What hardly needed rouge, though, was the teenager's preternatural sense of self. While still teetering between life and death, Sophia, raised in the Lutheran church, had the will and wit to refuse the visit of a Protestant minister. Instead, she insisted on seeing an Eastern Orthodox priest, Simoen Theodorsky, who was clearly impressed by this young foreigner's request.[4]

He was not alone: at this moment, Elizabeth perhaps realized her great gamble had paid off. It was the childless empress who had orchestrated the marriage. Determined to ensure a smooth succession—her father, Peter the Great, had ended the traditional law of dynastic succession through the male line, allowing the tsar to choose whomever he or she wished—Elizabeth sought an appropriate wife for her chosen heir. For cultural and dynastic reasons, Elizabeth believed that the House of Anhalt-Zerbst would answer her needs. Not only was Peter, who was a grandson of Peter the Great, also German-speaking—his mother Anna had married a Holstein prince—but Sophia was, due to the thick and related branches of the European aristocracy, Peter's second cousin. In fact, Sophia had met her future husband in Eutin, in Peter's native Holstein, when she was barely ten. The boy struck her as "sickly and delicate;" more worrisome, relatives whispered that he was "inclined to drink."[5]

Elizabeth's decision that Sophia suited her own dynastic plans offered prospects that the young girl's parents, relatively obscure aristocrats, could not refuse. But once settled in Russia, Sophia had few illusions about those same prospects. Her husband Peter, though seduced by the example set by Frederick the Great, had neither the Prussian king's capabilities nor culture. Instead, all he seemed to have acquired from Frederick was his infatuation with the pomp and circumstance of the military. When not busy changing into his many brightly laced uniforms, Peter spent hours playing with toy soldiers that, in order to keep them hidden from Elizabeth's officials, he stowed under Catherine's bed. Made of wood, lead, papier-mâché, and wax, these toy soldiers were periodically reviewed by Peter, who would strut past them wearing boots, spurs, and a scarf.[6] Peter was similarly dressed when, one day, his dog caught a rat that was scampering across his toy battlefield. As he was executing it from a miniature gallows and in full military ceremony, Catherine walked in on the macabre scene. Looking back on the scene years later, she reflected: "It could at least be said in the rat's defense that it had been hanged without anyone having asked or heard its defense."[7]

Catherine must have empathized with Peter's victim: she felt as defenseless as the rat. While Peter played with his toys, his wife assumed the duties that he shirked. Converting to the Russian Orthodox religion and taking the name Catherine, she dedicated herself to studying not just the Russian language, but also, under the guidance of Theodorsky, the Russian Orthodox faith. It was on her own, though, and by fits and starts, that she undertook a broader course of study. When she had first arrived in Russia, Catherine's hunger for books surprised a court where sycophancy was more common than literacy. Typical of her adolescent taste was the French version of the Spanish tale *Tiran the Fair,* an account of a wayward knight now mostly remembered as the butt of Cervantes's mockery.

The novels, however, quickly gave way to weightier fare. In 1751 she began reading Pierre Bayle's *Historical and Critical Dictionary.* The work's heft, packed into four thick volumes, was more than physical. One of the most subversive and subtle works of the early Enlightenment, Bayle's masterpiece was not a dictionary in the sense we now understand the term. Rather than a neutral compendium of definitions, it is a riot of articles on a multitude of subjects. Each of these relatively straightforward accounts, in turn, hatches voluminous footnotes that colonize most of the text and often diverge from the article's contents. Historians still debate today, as did Bayle's own contemporaries, what his true position was on the religious controversies of his day: for some, he was an atheist, for others an agnostic; there are those who insist he was a Christian, there are others who claim he was a clandestine Jew. Readers will never know who the real Pierre Bayle was, but they do know that he demands their full and active intellectual engagement. By refusing to stake a position, the Huguenot émigré forces his readers to do so; by throwing together conflicting accounts of, say, miracles, he obliges his readers to use reason to sort them out; by planting a forest of words—some six million—he tasks his readers with blazing their own path. For those readers who doggedly make it to path's end, they will have discovered that questions will always have a step on answers—a state of affairs that leads to skepticism, not dogmatism, and to toleration, not discrimination. Bayle observed, "I do not know whether one could not say that the obstacles to a good examination do not come so much from the fact that the mind is void of knowledge as that it is full of prejudice."[8]

In her later years Catherine stated she had read the first three volumes and most of the fourth (which was lost in a fire before she could finish it) in the short span of two years—a claim meant to emphasize either her enlightenment credentials or her emotional isolation, or indeed both. "Every six months I finished a volume," Catherine observed, "and from this one can imagine in what solitude I spent my life."[9] One can also imagine the ways in which Bayle's insistence upon reason as the sole means to distinguish between truth and falsehood—or, more accurately, the probable and improbable—helped to shape the young woman's worldview. The critical skills employed by Bayle in his approach to the world sharpened Catherine's ability to navigate the perilous landscape of the imperial court.

By the time volume four went up in smoke, Voltaire was ready to pick up the torch of enlightenment. In 1754 Catherine, who had decided "not to leave my room as long as I did not feel myself strong enough to overcome my melancholy," came across the French philosophe's two-volume *Summary of Universal History,* which had just been published. The *Summary* represented Voltaire's effort to secularize earlier "universal" histories written by Catholic theologians and told through the prism of Christian teleology. Reacting against this interpretation, however, Voltaire committed a different kind of teleological fallacy. In a word, he had "Voltairized" the past. As the philosopher Lucien Lévy-Bruhl noted more than a century ago, Voltaire did not derive his knowledge of humankind from history; instead, "he transferred to history the humanity he already knew, from the observation of his contemporaries."[10] Crucially, Voltaire's notion of humanity—and despite the work's universal claims, it remained largely Eurocentric—insisted on the desirability, if not inevitability, of progress, and on reason's power to parry and perhaps prevail against religious superstition and intolerance.

Voltaire's prudent optimism about humankind's future, and his impassioned attacks against those who threatened it, enthralled Catherine. In the months leading to her taking power, she noted that laws are "sacred because they live on after rulers pass on." As a result, "the state's interest resides in judging its citizens in accordance with the laws."[11] In a paean to liberty that would have warmed Voltaire's heart, the grand duchess exclaimed in her private notebook: "Liberty, the soul of all things, without you all things are dead. I want the laws to be obeyed, but not by slaves. Our goal is to work towards mankind's happiness, guarding against capricious or tyrannical behavior."[12]

But we need to also guard against Catherine's studied effusions in her correspondence with Voltaire. As she later told the delighted old man, "Whatever knowledge I might have, I owe it to your writings."[13] But the grand duchess's intellectual debts were, in fact, more diverse. Indeed, in 1755 she came to an emotional and intellectual turning point, one she called a "revolution in my thinking"—a revolution sparked by her discovery of two writers: the Baron de Montesquieu, who died that same year, along with the historian Tacitus, who had died more than a millennium earlier. But their works offered insights and counsel that none of Catherine's confidants could. Montesquieu, the author of the monumental (and, at times, monumentally flawed) *Spirit of the Laws,* offered Catherine a theoretical means not just for understanding the Russian identity—in particular, whether Russia was, as the contemporary debate framed the issue, a European or an Asian nation—but also for tailoring her own role as the country's ruler. While we will take up her debt, deep and acknowledged, to Montesquieu in Chapter 4, it is important to note here that, as a German transplant in Russia, Catherine embraced Montesquieu's fundamental insight that a vital core of natural laws applies to all human beings, but they are expressed differently according to place and time. As an observer of the contradictions and confusions of a multiethnic and multilingual empire overseen by an absolute ruler, Catherine reflected on whether Montesquieu was right to dismiss Russia, due to its immense size and lack of fundamental laws, as having a despotic form of government. Her eventual answer was no, though she would rule as if it was yes.

As for Tacitus, his *Annals* begin with the death of Augustus, casting a severe eye on his successors, judging them as ruthless, feckless, or both. No doubt Catherine was as impressed by Tacitus's recognition that the institutions of the Roman Republic were woefully inadequate for maintaining its empire as she was by his portrait of Augustus as maintaining the fiction of republican rule while governing as an autocrat. Equally clear, Tacitus's account of the brutal, bloody struggles for power within the imperial court branded the young mind of a woman who was a witness, and increasingly an actor, in such struggles. A few years later, in 1762, Catherine must have had occasion to recall Tacitus's opening line about Tiberius's rule: "The new reign's first crime was the assassination of Agrippa Posthumus, Augustus's sole surviving grandchild."[14]

By 1752 seven years had passed between Catherine and Peter without a pregnancy, much less a birth. Perhaps, as Catherine declared, Peter had never consummated their relationship. Whether the young man suffered from a physical handicap, as some rumors suggested, or was sterile, has never been ascertained. What is clear, though, is that Catherine, who not only needed to satisfy Elizabeth's expectations but also needed to satisfy her own emotional and physical needs, looked elsewhere. In 1753, at the urging of one of her confidants, Catherine turned to Sergei Saltykov, an imperial chamberlain who had been paying her court. While the affair was ephemeral, its probable consequence was not: in 1754 Catherine gave birth to a son, Paul. Relieved that an heir to the throne had been born, Elizabeth did not fret over the infant's true paternity. Instead, she had the baby immediately taken away from Catherine and installed in her own apartment. Six days passed before Catherine, a guest at Paul's baptism, finally saw her child. Nearly a month then passed—marking the end of her confinement—before she held him for the first time. When the infant was again whisked away, a devastated Catherine retreated to her bed: "I pretended to have new pains in my leg that prevented me from getting up, but the truth is that I neither could nor wanted to see anyone, because I was despondent."[15]

Her despondency did not, however, lead to passivity—to the contrary. She later recalled, "Aided perhaps by my depressed state of mind at the time . . . I searched to find deeper causes for the various events which presented themselves to my sight."[16] Catherine's sight was not limited to events unfolding during her waking life, but also included the "dreams" she began to have. In a breathtakingly candid letter to Sir Charles Hanbury-Williams, the British ambassador who had become both her mentor and her confessor, Catherine recounted one such fantasy. Once she learns of Elizabeth's death, Catherine confided, she would place her son in safekeeping, then call upon her followers to come to her antechamber. Clearly sketching the beginnings of a coup, Catherine adds that she would turn to the guards should she see "any commotion, or even the slightest signs of it."[17] A few years later, actual events would oddly resemble Catherine's imagined intrigues.

In fact, despondency, which had become Catherine's default position, turned to drama by the end of the decade. In 1756 she launched an affair with Stanislas Poniatowski, a young Polish nobleman assigned to the imperial court. Elegant and eloquent, worldly and witty, Poniatowski differed in another important respect from Saltykov: he was genuinely in love with Catherine. He was especially taken by the young woman's mixture of nobility and lightheartedness: "One moment she would be reveling in the wildest and most childish of games; a little later, she would be seated at her desk, coping with the most complicated affairs of finance and politics."[18] Finding herself trapped in a loveless marriage and adrift in court intrigue, Catherine was in turn taken by someone who offered her affection and advice. With Poniatowski, Catherine had a second child in 1758, a daughter named Anna, who encountered the same fate as her half-brother Paul: Elizabeth had the infant brought to her. As for Catherine, she was once again "left abandoned like a poor wretch."[19] Weak at birth, Anna died little more than a year later. As at the infant's baptism, so too at her funeral: Catherine was allowed to attend the ceremony, yet she makes no reference to the event in her memoirs.

During this period Elizabeth's physical health had begun to falter, as did her emotional well-being. She suffered not only two physical collapses—whether epilepsy or apoplexy was the cause remains unclear—but also fears that her court festered with conspiracies. In particular, Elizabeth suspected Catherine of intriguing behind her back. Was it not possible, she thought, that Catherine was planning to replace her husband with her son in the coming succession, with the intention of serving as regent until the boy came of age? But at the same time she was not heartened by the prospect of Peter's ascension to the throne. The empress, who was keenly aware of Peter's penchant for things Prussian and his childish activities at court, had no illusions over the young man's political ability or emotional maturity. Though a descendant of Peter the Great, the grand duke had inherited neither the physical nor the intellectual qualities of his grandfather. Increasingly, the empress made clear her disappointment, muttering in the presence of court officials: "My nephew is an idiot."[20]

The idiot was the growing bane not only of Elizabeth's life, but Catherine's as well. From scoffing disinterest, Peter's attitude toward his wife had changed into scornful resentment. Not only had he alienated Catherine, but his unabashed admiration for Frederick the Great, who had just launched a war against Russia, had also alienated much of the court. As a result, Catherine was in the most difficult of positions: neither in love with nor loved by a husband she thought unworthy of rule over either Russia or herself, her fate nevertheless seemed bound to his. By 1759 her predicament had fully crystallized: "Things took such a turn that it was necessary to perish with [Peter], by him, or else try to save oneself from the wreckage and to save my children, and the state."[21]

In April, armed with this clear-eyed understanding of her situation, Catherine was commanded to appear before Elizabeth. The empress, harried by the fear that Catherine was part of a Prussian conspiracy at the court, demanded a full accounting. During nearly three hours, and in the presence of her agitated and flustered husband, Catherine coolly defended herself against the baseless charges. Effortlessly, she also placed Elizabeth on the back foot, requesting that she be sent back to Anhalt-Zerbst in order to relieve the empress of any fears or suspicions concerning her loyalty. Impressed by the young woman's mixture of sangfroid and sincerity, Elizabeth made it known that she no longer had any doubts and promised a second and private meeting. When she returned to her private apartment and waited for the empress's call, Catherine spent her time in a fashion that befitted someone undergoing the apprenticeship for enlightened rule: "I leafed through the first volumes of the *Encyclopédie* for my amusement."[22]

R is for Riga

I HAVE PASSED MY FORTIETH YEAR, AND I AM WEARY OF HARASSMENT. MY CRY, FROM MORNING TO NIGHT, IS PEACE, PEACE!

—DIDEROT

"OUR PHILOSOPHER IS SO LIKE A CHILD!" wrote Madame d'Épinay to a friend of Diderot's. "He was so surprised on the day of his departure to find that he was actually departing, so frightened to have to go farther than Grandval [the country estate of his colleague and friend, Baron d'Holbach], and so miserable to have to pack his suitcases!"[1] But among the many excuses Diderot had offered Catherine for delaying his trip to Saint Petersburg, the largest had just evaporated. The previous year, the last volume of the *Encyclopédie*—the eleventh and final volume of illustrations—had rolled off the press. As for the seventeen volumes of texts—containing more than 73,000 entries, thousands of which were written by Diderot himself—the last volume, covering entries from Venerien (relating to Venus and fleshly pleasures) to Zzuéné (a town on the Egyptian Nile), had reached the booksellers in 1765. Finally, he told Sophie Volland, he was free of the thankless task to which he had been yoked for more than twenty years. Not only had it failed to make his fortune, but it also, he said, "nearly forced me to either flee France or lose my liberty, and which consumed a life which could have otherwise been devoted to more useful and glorious ends." With an audible sigh, he wrote: "My grand and cursed work is finished."[2]

It is easy, in the age of social media and Internet, to overlook the true greatness of Diderot's work—or, for that matter, its originality. Efforts to encompass and arrange all of human knowledge in writing stretch from Pliny the Elder's massive *Natural History,* compiled in the first century CE, to the early seventeenth century and Francis Bacon's *Great Instauration,* his encyclopedic project to arrange the fruit of empirical investigation on what he called "the branches of the tree of knowledge." (Having contracted pneumonia after stuffing snow into a dead chicken to see how long he could preserve its flesh, Bacon died before he could finish his work.) Bacon's tree cast a long shadow into the next century, when the Scottish journalist Ephraim Chambers published his *Cyclopedia: Or, Universal Dictionary of Arts and Sciences.*

Not only had Chambers written the work alone—a performance, he modestly noted, "to which a Man's whole Life seems scarce equal"—but he also launched a complex series of events that led to the *Encyclopédie.*[3] Convinced there was a market in France for Chambers's work, a group of Parisian book publishers joined forces for its translation. Rather like today's Silicon Valley venture capitalists, they invested money with a succession of editors, each of whom proved either incompetent, untrustworthy, or both. Doubling down on their initial investment, the publishers took a remarkable gamble: they hired, along with the mathematician Jean d'Alembert, Diderot, a young and obscure provincial recently arrived in Paris, to co-edit the book.

Indeed, obscurity was the least of his dubious qualities. More worrisome, certainly, was Diderot's intellectual radicalism. By the mid-1750s, when he leaped at the publishers' offer, Diderot had already published a number of works that outraged throne and altar. An ancestor to Eve Ensler's *Vagina Monologues,* Diderot's novel *Indiscreet Jewels* tells of the contrasting experiences and worldviews of more than two dozen women as told by, well, their vaginas. Even more disturbing, at least for the Catholic Church, was his *Letter on the Blind,* a short story in which Diderot invites the reader to see the world with the eyes, as it were, of a blind man. Given his lack of sight, he conceives of not just the world but also of God in a way terribly different from the rest of us. As he tells his interlocutor, "If you wish me to believe in your God, you must make me feel him."[4]

As it turned out, it was Diderot who was blind: How could he not see the trouble he was courting? The surges of skepticism and materialism in his books, like those of some of his fellow philosophes, threatened the country's political and religious authorities. In July 1749, shortly after Diderot became co-editor of the *Encyclopédie,* two royal officials presented themselves at his Paris apartment, rifled through his papers, and, as his wife and daughter looked on, bustled Diderot off to the massive prison of Vincennes just south of Paris. While his wife and friends panicked, Diderot fell into depression, confessing to—or warning—the prison warden "that despair will soon finish what my bodily infirmities have greatly advanced."[5] Fortunately, his frantic publishers explained to court officials that they had sunk 250,000 livres in the affair and insisted Diderot was essential to an enterprise that would bring France not just glory but also revenue. Their pleas prevailed: Diderot, vowing never again to publish such unorthodox writings, was released three months later.

Once back at his desk, Diderot did not translate Chambers's work; he transformed it. The *Encyclopédie* is no more a compendium of facts and figures than, say, Paris is a collection of boulevards and buildings. In fact, take city streets: they will, if we let them, lead us to destinations entirely new and unexpected. So, too, with Diderot's conception of his encyclopedia: rather than take us from points A to B, it takes us to points where our rulers do not want us to go, but reason and curiosity insist we go. In his entry "Encyclopédie," Diderot revealed his aim: by assembling knowledge scattered across the world, the work will guarantee that "the compendium of centuries past is not useless to centuries to come."

But such happiness could be harvested only after the razing of ancient woods and breaking of familiar ground. It is by the blade of reason that "precedent comes to be shaken and scarcely one work of dogma survives." Diderot is pitiless: "Everything must be examined, everything investigated, without hesitation or exception."[6] Diderot also expected much of his readers, making the *Encyclopédie* a deeply subversive but deliberately elusive and indirect work. Living under a regime where censorship was a given and imprisonment a near certainty for those who contested its legitimacy, he had no choice.

Even indirection risked the wrath of throne and, more importantly, altar. The first couple of volumes that Catherine leafed through in Saint Petersburg could well have been the last. In early 1752, after volume 2 appeared, Louis XV banned the publication of further volumes. How could he do otherwise, when the Jesuits greeted the second volume's appearance as a "system of impiety which tends toward nothing less than the submerging of Faith, Religion, Virtues, the Church, Subordination, the Laws and Reason."[7] Rumors quickly swept Paris that the authorities were preparing to hunt down the dictionary's editors and put them to death. It was, remarkably, thanks to the enlightened support of the official censor, Chrétien-Guillaume Lamoignon de Malesherbes, and the king's mistress, Madame de Pompadour, that Diderot was not again tossed into a prison keep and that he and his colleagues were able to continue their work. Characteristically, Diderot could not help but flaunt his victory, though he did so behind the shield of a pseudonym: "I will give myself to that grand work which I have undertaken to carry out, and in a way that will one day make all my persecutors blush."[8]

Despite these obstacles and dangers, Diderot managed to shape the *Encyclopédie* according to his deeply democratic values. On subjects too sensitive to critique, such as religion and politics, Diderot used an approach we might call *à l'Onion.* Orthodox experts were called upon to write on subjects like "soul" and "angel," producing articles of such stupefying scholasticism that they seem like self-parodies. But Diderot did not stop there. At times he tacks on his own commentary, marked by an asterisk, which sends up the incongruities and lunacies lacing the original articles. At other times Diderot appends his era's own version of hyperlinks, cross-listings, which take the reader to other "sites" in the encyclopedia that contradict the original entry—so that, as he wrote, the "entire mud edifice" of baseless claims will collapse into a "vain heap of dust." Diderot was not above tossing around a bit of dust himself. Scratching his head over the entry "Aguaxima," Diderot throws up his hands. He knows it's a Brazilian plant, but nothing else. Why then, he asks, should he bother to include it? Not for native Brazilians, who already know more about the plant than he does; not for his fellow French, who couldn't possibly care. But there it is, in volume 1, for one simple reason: "To oblige those readers who prefer finding nothing in an article, or even finding nonsense, than not finding an article at all." Years later, in his novel *Jacques the Fatalist and His Master,* Diderot will delve, with dazzling results, into this dialectic between the writer and reader.

Even the most dedicated and diligent of editors, however, can do little to control events that unfold outside their ateliers. In 1758 this banal truth was underscored with the publication of Helvétius's *De l'esprit.* Though the *Encyclopédie* did not end up in the same pile of ash outside the Palais de Justice, its future nevertheless seemed combustible. The royal authorities had explicitly tied the nature, and thus the fate, of the *Encyclopédie* to *De l'esprit.* "In the shadows of a dictionary which assembles an infinity of useful and curious facts," the public prosecutor intoned in a speech before Parlement in January 1759, "one has admitted all sorts of absurdities, of impieties spread by all authors." As a result, he had no choice but to conclude that there was a conspiracy afoot "to propagate materialism, to destroy religion, to inspire a spirit of independence and to nourish the corruption of morals."[9] The other shoe dropped that same month, when the king declared that the *Encyclopédie,* which had reached volume 7 and the word "Gythium," was suspended from going any further down the alphabet.

Many of Diderot's contributors, unwilling to court the throne's wrath, did not bother to wait for the official pronouncement. Announcing their shock—shock!—that the *Encyclopédie* attracted such disreputable types and despicable ideas, they walked away as quickly as their pride would allow. Several prominent figures, including the influential economists François Quesnay and Anne-Robert Turgot, ended their collaboration, while the celebrated naturalist Georges-Louis Buffon—who had contributed several articles—decided to tend the royal gardens full-time.

Struck by the hailstorm of invective from critics, the lightning bolt delivered from Versailles, and the flight of trusted collaborators, Diderot's thoughts turned black. "What relentless and evil enemies we have!" he confided to Sophie: "Honestly, when I compare our friendships to our hatreds, I find the former to be frail and inconsequential. We know how to hate, but do not know how to love."[10] Yet while others were buckling or bolting, Diderot rallied himself and his closest collaborators. Shortly after the work's suspension, he met with a small core of contributors: D'Alembert, the Baron d'Holbach, and Chevalier Louis de Jaucourt. When they convened at the home of André Le Breton, their publisher, though, d'Alembert revealed, as Diderot later wrote, "his well-known and childish hot-headedness." Declaring that any attempt to continue the work was pure "folie," he announced that he was washing his hands of the entire affair. As the others looked on or away in stunned silence, d'Alembert continued to "babble and pirouette" across the room. With an awkward flourish, he then walked out on his former colleagues, marking the end of his relationship to the *Encyclopédie.*[11]

D'Alembert's theatrical exit, rather than serving as yet another obstacle, instead galvanized the energies of Diderot and his colleagues. Once d'Alembert had left and the conspirators had recovered their wits, they "vowed to see the project to its end . . . with the same freedom as it had begun." With the active complicity of Le Breton, Diderot moved his workplace to d'Holbach's private library, which contained more than 3,000 works. There he and his small crew committed themselves to writing the remaining ten volumes, intending to have them published all at once in Amsterdam. The financial interests of Le Breton and his partners—the publishers owed nearly 250,000 livres to their several thousand subscribers and their writers and printers—along with the tacit support of sympathetic officials, in particular Malesherbes, helped keep the *Encyclopédie* alive during these testing times. But the moral conviction and courage displayed by Diderot—who was keenly aware of the risks he was running—were even more vital and, at least when compared to Le Breton's motivations, much less venal.

During the crisis Voltaire flung frequently conflicting and consistently frantic advice. Dictating dozens of letters from distant Ferney, his estate—conveniently located a short distance from the safety of Geneva—Voltaire was understandably worried. Though he had little patience with Helvétius's brutal materialism and expressed serious qualms about the quality and content of many of the *Encyclopédie*'s articles, Voltaire, the individual most closely identified with the Enlightenment, never lost sight of the importance of Diderot's enterprise. For this reason he urged Diderot to maintain a unified front against his critics; when that failed, he next urged Diderot to consider the offer made by Frederick the Great to move the entire operation to Prussia.

In his reply, Diderot was gracious enough not to remind Voltaire that Frederick, just a few years earlier, had made him his prisoner for several months in the gilded cage of Sans Souci, his summer palace. Instead Diderot asked Voltaire to consider the moral matter at hand. Moving the *Encyclopédie* to another country, he wrote, was a splendid idea; as with most splendid ideas, though, it was fantasy. First of all, he could not—or, more accurately, would not—break his contract with his publishers and abandon his contributors. Second, by fleeing to another country, Diderot and his team would do precisely what their enemies most ardently wished. The only answer, Diderot declared, was that which courageous men would make: "To despise our enemies [and] to combat them." No less important, he added, he and his colleagues would continue to "take advantage of the imbecility of our censors." Rather than finish his letter on a note of defiance, however, Diderot instead turned melancholic. If Voltaire thought Diderot was attached to the *Encyclopédie,* he could not have been more mistaken: "I am weary of harassment. My cry, from morning to night, is peace, peace!"[12]

True to his word, Diderot and his band of encyclopedists continued their semi-clandestine activity. This was especially the case for the Chevalier de Jaucourt, the unsung hero of the enterprise. A wealthy Protestant aristocrat, Jaucourt channeled his money and mastery of arcane information into the *Encyclopédie;* remarkably, he and his tireless team of researchers were responsible for over 10,000 articles in the remaining six volumes of the *Encyclopédie.* For Diderot, Jaucourt's relentlessness proved indispensable. External battles against the censors and church, and internal battles against doubters like d'Alembert, continued to drain the editor's energy or distract him from full engagement. Tellingly, while only sixty-four articles in the final six volumes are credited to him, Diderot felt like little more than a "galley slave," seemingly chained forever to his writing bench.[13]

Before long, however, the galley slave received a surprising offer of freedom. In September 1762 the Russian nobleman Ivan Shuvalov, founder of the Russian Academy of the Arts, wrote to Voltaire. The two men had first corresponded in 1756, when Shuvalov gathered, at Voltaire's request, otherwise inaccessible government documents and private papers for the latter's writing of the *History of Russia under Peter the Great.*

Shuvalov's assistance in this undertaking was to be expected: his lover, the Tsarina Elizabeth, had commissioned Voltaire to write this account of her father, Peter.

As Elizabeth discovered, Voltaire needed to be asked only once: What could be more compelling than the retelling of Peter's life? Here was a ruler who had undertaken, more or less single-handedly, to heave his backward and slumbering empire into the eighteenth century. Yes, of course, he built an army that had imposed itself on Europe and Asia. More importantly, though, Peter had built a new capital, the aptly named Saint Petersburg, and a modern system of laws, institutions, and practices. "All princes have besieged cities and fought battles," Voltaire explained, but "only Peter the Great has been the reformer of manners, the creator of arts, of a navy and commerce."[14] The lesson France should draw from Peter's example was thus obvious. "Princes, who reign over states long since civilized, may say to themselves, 'If a man, assisted only by his own genius, has been capable of doing such great things in the frozen climes of ancient Scythia, what may not be expected from us, in kingdoms where the accumulated labors of many ages have rendered the way so easy?'"[15]

It was now Shuvalov who was asking for Voltaire's assistance. Would he, the Russian diplomat wondered, relay an offer to his friend Diderot? The empress, conscious of the *Encylopédie*'s great importance and the challenges Diderot faced, wished to offer "all the support you find necessary to expedite its publication." It was a gesture worthy of Peter the Great, but one that came with two catches. First, the empress proposed that the work be continued in Riga. The Baltic port, as the yet-to-be published fourteenth volume of the *Encyclopédie* explained, was only 84 lieues (approximately 300 miles) south of Saint Petersburg. (While Diderot did not know the precise distance from Paris—more than 300 lieues—he had no need of a map to know it was too far.) The second item that gave Diderot equal pause was that Shuvalov's sovereign was no longer Elizabeth. Instead it was Catherine—who, a few months earlier, had stunned European capitals, first by organizing the overthrow of her husband, Peter III, then by announcing a few days later that she had unexpectedly become a widow. Her husband, it appeared, had died of "hemorrhoidal colic."[16]

This news dispatch from Saint Petersburg was perhaps fresh in Diderot's thoughts when he read the message that Voltaire had relayed from Shuvalov. (It certainly had been in the thoughts of his erstwhile co-editor, d'Alembert, who had earlier been asked by Catherine to serve as Paul's tutor. In his reply to Catherine, d'Alembert politely declined the proposition; in a subsequent letter to Voltaire, d'Alembert was instead inclined to wittiness: "I am also suffering from hemorrhoids, and they seem to be too serious in that country."[17] While the Parisian salons admired the *bon mot,* Catherine did not: Ten years later, when d'Alembert sought Catherine's help in releasing several French officers captured while fighting alongside the Poles, an icy *nyet* was his answer.[18])

Bursting with excitement, Voltaire enthused over Catherine's proposal in his cover letter to Diderot. "And so, my illustrious philosophe, what have you to say about our Russian empress? What times we live in! While France persecutes philosophy, the Scythians cultivate it."[19] Voltaire recognized that his friend had contractual obligations, but he ardently hoped that Diderot would nevertheless accept Catherine's princely offer. One could hardly expect the illustrious philosophe to feel otherwise. The great question then troubling the Republic of Letters was "How best to achieve the goals of the Enlightenment?" On this crucial matter, Voltaire never wavered. Ever since his youth, when he cut a figure as a quick wit and stylish versifier, Voltaire had played to the courts. Though he grew disillusioned with this world over the years, and had no illusions about the abilities or intelligence of the Bourbons who followed Louis XIV, he maintained that stability and monarchy went hand in hand. Moreover, Voltaire insisted—as did Grimm and d'Alembert—that only a *despote éclairé,* an enlightenment despot, could pull society toward the light. In his correspondence with his fellow philosophes, he never tired of pushing a "courtly" politics. But crucially, Voltaire did not confuse loyalty with servility. To the contrary, he argued that loyal collaboration with monarchs and their institutions would allow philosophes, by dint of their wisdom and wit, to "govern those who govern us."[20]

Diderot, however, was less willing to embrace the "Scythians." As he treated Frederick's offer, so too did he Catherine's. "No, my dear and illustrious brother: We are going to neither Berlin nor St. Petersburg." To accept the offer would betray the very men who had invested their financial and political capital in the project. The *Encyclopédie,* he reminded his illustrious but at times flighty friend, "does not belong to us," but instead belonged to Le Breton and his associates. Besides, Diderot declared, he had no intention of giving up the game. Their motto, he told Voltaire, was this: "No quarter given to the superstitious, to the fanatics, to the ignoramuses, to the fools, to the evildoers and to the tyrants."

When it came to tyrants, Diderot had already proclaimed his convictions a decade earlier, with the publication of the very first volume of the *Encyclopédie.* In the article "Autorité politique" (Political Authority), he located the power to command others not in heaven but instead in nature and reason. "No man has by nature been granted the right to command others. Liberty is a gift from heaven, and every member of the same species has the right to enjoy it as soon as he is in possession of reason." The aftereffects of this axiomatic claim are seismic. If nature and reason frame the freedom of the individual, it follows that rulers rule at the pleasure of an enlightened people. The power that issues from popular consent, Diderot states, set the conditions of a ruler's powers. With astonishing frankness, the philosophe thus demolishes the traditional claims of divine or dynastic to rule as one sees fit. Instead, it is "from his subjects themselves that the prince derives the *authority* he exercises over them, and this *authority* is limited by the laws of nature and of the state." The state, far from belonging to the ruler, instead belongs to the ruled, who permit the prince to rule according to the light of reason and laws of the land. In effect, Diderot takes Louis XIV's famous claim "L'État, c'est moi" and turns it upside down: A king must now declare to his people, "L'État, c'est vous."

Standing at the threshold of full-blown republicanism, one that sanctions the people's right to remove a ruler who violates human reason and natural law, Diderot goes no further. Should a people fall under "an unjust, ambitious and violent king," their sole redress is to "calm him by their submission and assuaging God by their prayers." Diderot did not imagine, at least not yet, that Catherine would require such a response from her people. Naturally, he found excessive, if not obscene, Voltaire's praise of the newly installed empress. On the other hand, he hesitated to place Catherine in the same company of those who, like Frederick II, collected philosophes like baubles, all the while ruling as tyrants. Though deeply allergic to absolutism, Diderot believed that Catherine would prove a different kind of ruler—one who would be deferential to the enlightenment ideals, disposed to humanitarian sentiments, and dedicated to ensuring the happiness of her subjects. In fact, during the mid-1760s Diderot would frequently meet with Melchior Grimm and Prince Dmitry Golitsyn, Catherine's ambassador to Versailles, to "reorganize" the Russian state from top to bottom.[21]

These hopes were given what seemed striking confirmation in 1765. For several months Diderot had been scrambling to gather a dowry for his daughter, Angélique. To that end he began to send out feelers, seeking a buyer for his beloved library of more than three thousand books. When Diderot's initial efforts failed, his friend Grimm decided to work his far-flung network of aristocratic acquaintances. Without informing Diderot, Grimm contacted Ivan Betsky, Catherine's chamberlain, to see if the empress would intervene on Diderot's behalf. In his reply to Grimm's query, Betsky's prose matched his employer's largesse. Beyond the "particular esteem our august sovereign has for men of learning," Betsky declares, Catherine was stricken by Diderot's specific circumstances: "Her compassionate heart could not but be moved upon learning that this philosophe, so celebrated in the Republic of Letters, finds himself forced as a loving father to sacrifice the object of his pleasures, the source of his research and companions for his leisure." Having melodramatically driven up the library's value, Betsky informs Grimm that Catherine wished to match its newfound worth. Not only would Catherine give Diderot not a sou less than fifteen thousand livres for the library, but she imposed two equally striking conditions: Diderot would not only keep his library during his lifetime—only after his death would the books be sent to Saint Petersburg—but for an additional one thousand livres a year, Diderot would also serve as his library's librarian. No need for the philosophe to reply, Betsky concluded: the money had already been sent to Diderot via Prince Golitsyn.[22]

Diderot did, indeed, reply, but the letter has not survived. Clearly, though, he was flabbergasted by the offer. The Russian empress had just showered the philosophe with the recognition denied him by Versailles. In an excited letter to Diderot, Voltaire posed the question asked by many others in the Republic of Letters: "Who in Paris would have suspected, fifty years ago, that the Scythians would so generously reward the virtue and knowledge treated like beggars amongst ourselves?"[23] Inevitably, Voltaire shared his gratitude with the empress herself, thanking her on Diderot's behalf: the Republic of Letters, he declared, "is at your feet." No less inevitably, but more disingenuously, Catherine wondered why such a fuss was being made: "I would never have thought the purchase of a library would bring me so many compliments."[24]

Diderot eventually echoed Voltaire's sentiments in a second letter he wrote the following year to Betsky. It was spurred by Catherine's discovery that Diderot had never received his first year's salary as librarian. To make amends, she instructed Betski to send Diderot a five-year advance. Though his reply is addressed to Betsky, Diderot pauses to address the "Great Princess" directly: "I prostrate myself in front of you. I reach out and wish to speak to you, but my soul is paralyzed." Nevertheless, with a "noble enthusiasm" warming his heart, Diderot reaches for the "ancient lyre whose strings had been severed by Philosophy." Diderot followed his genuflections with an ode thanking so "great a soul" for aiding a poor stranger who "scorned by his own master, accepts in silence his grim fate." Turning back to Betsky, Diderot then recalls the destiny that the "universe" has reserved for his benefactress: "Imagine the formidable challenges Catherine has accepted! The world's eyes are riveted on her. She now must show that she is equal to the great obstacles nature creates in order to separate the gold from the dross." Oddly, though, Diderot does not assume that the outcome has already been decided: "We shall see" if this will be the case, he concludes.[25]

With his eyes fixed on this good and glorious goal, Diderot stumbled into an affair that was neither one nor the other. Three years after Catherine had purchased Diderot's library and his gratitude, she learned that a Frenchman, Claude-Carloman de Rulhière, was preparing to publish an account of the 1762 coup d'état. Rulhière's credentials were solid; as an attaché to the French embassy in Saint Petersburg in 1762, he had a front row seat to events. Much to the dismay of the court in Saint Petersburg, Rulhière proved to be a sober and serious historian. His portrait of Peter III, based on interviews with participants, was detailed and devastating. But this hardly helped Catherine's case, as Rulhière's obvious command of his material also made his description of her role in the coup all the more credible. The very fact that he refused to offer a verdict on Catherine's part in the regicide—"It is not known with certainty what part the Empress played in this event"—made his book all the more embarrassing for the empress.[26]

Diderot happened to attend the salon of Mme Geoffrin where Rulhière read aloud from his manuscript. Alarmed by its explosive contents, Catherine's librarian immediately took the author aside. He praised the account's verisimilitude, but what of it? "Not all truths," Diderot warned, "are good to speak." Besides, we cannot be too respectful or discrete when it comes to treating a ruler "who has earned Europe's admiration." For this reason, whatever glory Rulhière might win with the book's publication, "it would be better, safer and more honest to suppress it."[27]

But Diderot's plea fell flat. No doubt as flattered as he was flustered by the request, Rulhière replied that he had no intention to publish the book, and thus had no reason to burn it. Worried that the diplomat would fail to keep his word, Diderot contacted one of Catherine's advisors, announcing that the "affair was delicate, very delicate."[28] Assuring the empress of his loyalty, he wrote to say he awaited her instructions. Already aware of the manuscript's existence, Catherine had her chargé d'affaires in Paris, Nicolas Khotinsky, and Diderot meet with Rulhière in order to buy the manuscript. While Khotinsky listened, Diderot again reviewed all the reasons why Rulhière should accept the deal. But once again, even though Diderot "did everything he possibly could to persuade him," Rulhière refused to be bought.[29]

In the end, Rulhière proved to be as good as his word: the book was only published in 1797, five years after his death and one year after Catherine's. Indeed, the episode casts Rulhière in a more becoming light than it does Diderot. While the diplomat—a man in a profession in which the truth often gets short shrift—proved to be a teller of truths, as both historian and *honnête homme,* the philosophe who devoted his life to the truth sought to have it repressed. Looking back on his failed mission, Diderot lamented it was a "botched" affair.[30] Only after many years would he recognize that the bungling had to do with the plan's conception and not the execution; its purpose, and not the performance.

Why Diderot felt such urgency is unclear; Angélique was only nine years old when he first began to fret about her dowry. These worries were all the more sudden and surprising given that he had been a only furtive presence during Angélique's early years. Preoccupied by work on the *Encyclopédie* and seemingly resigned to his wife's ascendancy over their child, Diderot had largely neglected his daughter's early upbringing. By the early

1760s, though, it was as if Diderot had made a sudden discovery—namely, that he had brought into the world a fellow human being who required a teacher no less than, say, a Russian empress did a mentor. With an air of astonishment, he told Sophie that Angélique is "growing taller, gentler and stronger." But, he sighs, "she is obstinacy itself."[31] He now spent more time with her, watching and correcting her piano playing and turning father-and-child strolls into philosophical lectures. In a later letter to Sophie, Diderot blurts out: "I am mad about my daughter." How could he not be? "She tells me that her mother prays to God while her father does good deeds."[32] Indeed, Diderot becomes ever more fearful of his wife's crippling influence over their daughter. If Nanette has her way, he agonized, Angélique "will be like a hundred thousand other women, and if she gets a stupid husband—and it is a hundred thousand to one she will—it will only mean she is less unhappy."[33] The prospect of Nanette's religious piety rubbing off on Angélique was so upsetting that Diderot exclaimed: "If my child was taken by a fatal disease, I don't know if I'd be sorry. Such a death would be preferable to being left at the mercy of her mother."[34]

It was a paradoxical moment for the doting father no less than it was for the doer of good deeds. As an enlightened thinker, Diderot was determined to cultivate his daughter's intellectual and moral independence. But he also despaired over the social consequences of such an education. He saw Angélique surrounded by seducers, whether they were priests multiplying the marvels of the sacred or Don Juans whispering the wonders of the profane. While both prospects were equally terrifying, Diderot seemed especially worried about this-worldly seductions. In a particularly severe reflection, he asked Sophie what "I love you" means, remarking that when uttered by a man, it means "Mademoiselle, that if you would be kind enough to dishonor yourself, abandon your standing in the world and be exiled from society, wall yourself up forever in a convent and be the cause of your parent's deaths, all for my sake, I'd be grateful."[35]

Besieged by fears over his daughter's future, but also buoyed by her intelligence, Diderot arranged for Angélique to take anatomy lessons—taught by the remarkable (and unmarried) Mademoiselle de Biheron—and set about finding a suitable husband. At first, and quite astonishingly, he hinted to his friend Grimm that he ought to marry her, praising in a letter his daughter's intellectual and musical prowess. When Grimm, more than twice Angélique's age and the lover of their mutual friend Mme d'Épinay, gently ignored the suggestion, Diderot finally chose Abel-François Caroillon de Vandeul, a savvy business investor who, crucially, was the son of old friends from his native Langres. While Vandeul was neither a philosopher nor a scientist, he was at least a sturdy bourgeois (whose hard bargaining over the dowry irritated Diderot on several occasions) who was largely indifferent to, if not openly skeptical of, religion. Indeed, Nanette was so disturbed by her son-in-law's reputation as a free thinker that she refused to visit them for several weeks after their marriage in late 1772—a situation that, though it drove Diderot to despair, also comforted him that he had chosen, if not well, at least well enough.

Yet while Diderot was reassured that his daughter had landed as well as one could expect, he remained heartbroken by the vacuum her marriage left in his life. In a letter to Angélique, Diderot unburdened his sense of both relief and desolation. "I love you with all my heart . . . and am letting you go with a pain you could hardly conceive. At least now when I can converse with myself since I no longer have you to converse with, I can tell myself as I wipe my tears that I no longer have my daughter, but she is happy."[36]

One day in the early 1760s, two men bump into one another at La Régence, a Parisian café that, along with La Procope, had become a hive for prominent writers and artists, abuzz with literary and, more guardedly—police spies were also habitués—political conversation.[37] One is a well-off and well-regarded philosopher—let's call him "Moi"—while the other—who we'll call "Lui"—is a ne'er-do-well music tutor best known for being the nephew of the celebrated composer Rameau. Moi enjoys spending his days chasing ideas, whether they are sound or silly: ideas, he happily confesses, "are my whores." As for Lui, he spends his days chasing patrons, bourgeois or aristocratic: they are, he happily admits, his meal tickets.

While watching fellow café denizens play chess, the two men, who are acquaintances, begin to converse. In the midst of a dizzying series of conversational twists and turns, they barrel into the subject of education, particularly in regard to their children. When Lui asks Moi if he has hired tutors for his eight-year-old daughter, the latter becomes edgy: the subject, we learn, is a minefield. In order to keep peace at home, Moi confesses that he allows his wife to oversee their daughter's education. Nevertheless, despite his wife's baleful interference, Moi is determined to teach his daughter one crucial skill: "To think straight—a rare thing among men, and still rarer among women."

Rather than applauding such high-minded goals, Lui waves them away: "Oh, let her think as wildly as she likes if she is only pretty, lively and well-dressed." In the face of Moi's stubborn defense of an enlightened education, Lui holds his ground—or, rather, hacks away at the ground under Moi's feet. Rather than teaching his daughter how to dance or sing, Moi will introduce her to grammar and history, mythology and geography and, most important, "a great deal of ethics." Taking pity on his friend, Lui cries: "How easy it would be for me to prove to you the futility of all those things in the world as we know it! Did I say futility? I should have said danger."

This exchange unfolds in one of Diderot's most dizzying works, *Rameau's Nephew.* Fittingly, the book's history is as serendipitous and serpentine as its narrative. A dialogue between a narrator—cast as "Moi"—and Rameau's nephew—starring as "Lui"—the work remained in Diderot's possession until his death, unpublished and unknown even to friends. In 1805 a manuscript surfaced in Germany long enough for Goethe, who was shown it by Schiller, to translate it into German, before it again sank out of sight. Potted French translations of the German text, which had been based on a dubious manuscript, circulated for several decades until 1891, when a manuscript, written in Diderot's hand, was discovered in a Parisian attic. Shortly after, another copy was unearthed in the Hermitage, buried in a box unopened ever since Diderot's library was shipped and delivered to Catherine in 1784.

Equally mysterious is the timing of the book's composition. While scholars continue to argue over dates, much in the text suggests that Diderot began writing it in the spring of 1761. This makes sense, because it was at this very same moment that he began to sort out his conflicting duties as a father and a philosopher, wrestling with Nanette, as well as with himself, over Angélique's education. And like the struggle, the writing continued nearly to the end of Diderot's life. He continued to work on the text—tweaking and revising, scratching out and adding on—until 1779, just five years before his death and five years after his return to France from Saint Petersburg.

The struggle's inner dimension must not be overlooked; in fact, given the character of Moi and Lui, it *cannot* be overlooked. Rather than two discrete and distinct individuals dueling one another over questions of morality and politics, society and family, *Rameau's Nephew* creates two discrete characters from a single and distinctive individual: Denis Diderot. The psychological depth of his struggle can be plumbed by the sheer length of time Diderot devoted to the book. There was good reason Diderot had even greater difficulty ending this particular conversation than he did most others: at stake were the justifications for teaching virtue, not only to one's daughter but also to one's ruler.

As the conversation between Moi and Lui tumbles from one topic to another—punctuated repeatedly by Lui's astonishing pantomimes of contemporaries great or obscure—nearly every rule and value we take for granted is dented or demolished. Lui's whiplash-inducing turns of reasoning leave morality itself—a subject dear to Moi, who prides himself as a moralist—battered and bared for what Lui insists it is: a mug's game.

Morality, he argues, has nothing to do with ideals and everything to do with meals. A man willing to debase himself in countless ways in order to stave off hunger, Lui runs roughshod over Moi's traditional appeals to virtue. "The voice of conscience and honor is pretty feeble when the guts cry out," he exclaims. "Ah, Master Philosopher, poverty is a dreadful thing."[38] When Moi protests that the individual can, regardless of his state, strive for decency and humanity, Lui will have none of it: "You think everybody aims at the same happiness. What an idea! Your conception presupposes a sentimental turn of mind which is not ours. . . . You call your quirks virtue, or philosophy. But virtue and philosophy are not made for everybody. The few who can, have it; the few who can, keep it." While Moi listens with a mixture of growing horror and fascination, Lui then proceeds to stand Moi's ethics on its head: "I say hurrah for wisdom and philosophy—the wisdom of Solomon: to drink good wines, gorge on choice food, tumble pretty women, sleep in downy beds—outside of that, all is vanity."[39]

Another time, another place and Moi would have echoed Lui's hurrah. He reminds Lui that he is not a prudish pedant or shriveled cynic. Not only does he have "eyes and a heart to look at a pretty woman," but he also has hands to "feel the curve of her breast . . . and die of ecstasy in her arms." Yet while these carnal desires overwhelm us, Moi insists, they must not define us. This, at least, is his case. "I find it infinitely sweeter," he tells Rameau, "to succor the unfortunate, to disentangle a bad business, to give helpful advice, to read some pleasant book . . . to spend a few instructive hours with my children and carry out my duties." The problem, Moi grasps, is that what he finds sweeter, Lui finds sillier; situations he wishes to ease, Lui wishes to exploit; moral instructions he wants to impart to his children, Lui wants to impair with immoral instructions to his own children. Moi's righteous outrage gradually cedes to intellectual confusion, just as his moral certitude gives way to inner doubts. There is, he confesses, "some sense in almost everything you've said."[40] Yet that confession terrifies Moi. When Lui asks, "What is a good education if it is not one that leads to all the enjoyments without the trouble or danger?" Moi fumbles for a reply: "I am almost with you there, but let's not go into it." When Lui nevertheless tries to take Moi there, the latter recoils: "Let it go, I say."[41]

But the doubts will not let go of Moi. From his earlier conviction that nature is the source of virtue, he now seems less convinced. Nature no longer appears as a nurturing and pacifying force; instead, it now seems perfectly Hobbesian: a social world where self-interest runs wild and selflessness has been run out of town. Over Moi's increasingly feeble protests, Lui revels in his amorality. At times through the outpouring of language, at times through the acting out of pantomimes, Lui details how his position as a music tutor allows him to empty his patrons' pockets while keeping empty his students' heads. And why shouldn't he boast about his swindles and shady dealings? "My pupil's parents were fat with ill-gotten gains. They were courtiers, tax collectors, wholesalers, bankers, and stockbrokers. I merely helped them to make restitution. In Nature all species live off one another; in society all classes do the same." The struggle among men is as pitiless as among other animals; the sole difference is that we avert our gazes from it. "Everything that lives, man included, seeks its wellbeing at the expense of whoever withholds it."[42] Disorder, not order, rules this world: "Nothing is stable. Today at the top of the heap, tomorrow at the bottom. Accursed circumstance guides us and does it very badly."[43] In the great torrent of Lui's words, the barrier that once divided Nature from society has been breached. Whereas the latter was once thought to disfigure the former, it now faithfully reflects it.

As Lui peels back the layers of hypocrisy and self-deceit, Moi fears what, if anything, he will find underneath. Sitting in La Régence, the air thick with smoke and chatter, Moi teeters at the edge of utter moral confusion. The irony is understated, but unnerving: like an unsuspecting interlocutor in a Socratic dialogue, Moi quits the dialogue stripped of the truths with which he had entered it. The difference is that while Socrates lived a moral life and pursued the good, Lui lives an immoral life and pursues the bad. But Moi finds himself in a state of *aporia,* unable to refute Lui's lessons. Toward the dialogue's end, Moi is left to muse on the chief difference between Lui and others. "He admitted his vices, which are also ours: he was no hypocrite. Neither more nor less detestable than other men, he was franker than they, more logical, and thus often profound in his depravity."[44] Too profound, it appears, for Diderot to allow others to glimpse.

After reading the manuscript of *Rameau's Nephew,* Goethe marveled to Schiller that it "bursts like a bomb right in the midst of French literature, and we need to take extreme care to determine what—and at what angle—its fragments have struck."[45] Goethe was a tad too careful, perhaps: the shrapnel riddled not just the body of French literature, but the body of French politics as well. *Rameau's Nephew* offers the bleakest of diagnoses of life under an absolutist ruler, of what happens to the contents of our characters when subjected to the power of tyrants. Less than two years before Diderot left for Russia, Louis XV's chief minister, Maupeou, disemboweled the Paris Parlement of its centuries-old powers. Voltaire hailed the move as a blow on behalf of enlightened rule; the reactionary Parlement, he held, was an obstacle to progressive measures. For Diderot, though, while the aristocratic body was reactionary, it was no less so to a restless throne than it was to restless thought. Though the Parlement was a judicial and not a legislative institution—overseen, moreover, by aristocrats—Diderot believed it was the last bulwark, hidebound and sclerotic though it might be, against royal tyranny. (The following New Year he wrote a ballad on behalf of political freedom that ends with the celebrated lines: "And for want of a rope his hands will knot / The guts of the priest to strangle kings." The text of the poem, which Diderot read aloud to friends in 1772, surfaced twenty years later in the bloody wake of the revolutionary Terror.[46])

These political concerns acquire an existential weight by the end of the dialogue. After watching the last of Lui's pantomimes, this one of a man whose entire being seems consecrated to receiving and carrying out a superior's orders, Moi accuses him of depicting a world populated only by beggars, regardless of their social rank: "I hardly know anyone who doesn't use at least a few of your dance steps." Without missing a beat, Lui agrees: "In the whole country, only one man walks—the King. Everybody else poses."[47] Rather than drawing back from the consequences of this comparison, as he had done with earlier ones proposed by Lui, Moi now runs toward them: even the king plays the phony, he tells Lui, if only in front of God and his mistress. As if struck by an epiphany, Moi announces: "What you call the beggar's pantomime is what makes the world go round."[48] But one person will not go round with it, he declares, and will refuse to join this universal farce. It is "the philosopher who has and asks for nothing." As distasteful as he might otherwise find the position of Diogenes, Moi nevertheless prefers it to the world of shadows and masks praised by Lui. Such a life, he affirms, "is better than to crawl, eat dirt and prostitute yourself."[49]

But unlike ancient Cynics, these modern philosophers *were* asking for something: a ruler, enlightened and engaged, to effect the change that the ruled were incapable of jump-starting. For many of Diderot's contemporaries, creating the conditions that would allow for the flourishing of human happiness was as daunting a task as creating the canals and levies required for the flourishing of Dutch commerce. Even more problematic, the latter was accomplished from below: an entire society, devoted to republican and egalitarian values, shaped Holland. Could the same be expected of an entire people—especially a people steeped since time immemorial in superstition and ignorance—when it came to building the legal and moral dikes and levies necessary for a flourishing society? Or, instead, did it take the unfettered hands of an energetic ruler to sculpt the rough and resistant clay of a less than enlightened people?

As Diderot grasped, Helvétius wanted to eat this brioche and keep it, too. While he praised Catherine in the dedication in *De l'homme,* he had excoriated her predecessor, Peter the Great, in the preface to his earlier

De l'esprit. Despite the great spasms of reform Peter had unleashed on Russia, Helvétius concluded, the results were disappointing. Unable to create incremental and lasting institutional and constitutional changes—in a criticism that Diderot would echo, Helvétius noted that rulers, no matter how great, could not transmit their greatness to their successors—Peter had simply replaced older hardships with "new afflictions."[50]

Yet it was largely due to Peter's reign that Russia dominated the thoughts and discussions held in the Republic of Letters. The vast country's backwardness was not just its bane, but also its promise. Where better, in effect, to test the effectiveness of enlightened despotism than in a country whose intermediary institutions were, at least to outside observers, either faint or simply nonexistent? By midcentury, other leading candidates for enlightened despotism had fallen by the wayside. From time to time, France's Louis XV raised Voltaire's hopes for the so-called *thèse royale*—the notion that the king is the fount of all authority and, thus, all effective change. In 1766, when Louis confronted a recalcitrant and reactionary Paris Parlement, informing its aristocratic members that sovereign and legislative power resided in his person alone, Voltaire was overjoyed. "It's been a long time since I have read anything so wise, so noble and so well-written."[51] However, with the passing of Louis XV and the ascension of his son, the ineffectual Louis XVI, Versailles's attachment to the *thèse royale* passed as well.

Among the other rulers who aspired to the title of enlightened despot, Frederick of Prussia topped the list. As a youthful prince in the 1730s, he wrote a mash note to Voltaire, heaping unabashed praise on his poetic genius. Predictably, Voltaire was won over, as was his companion, Madame du Châtelet. Speaking for many in the Republic of Letters, she observed: "Since it seems that we have to have princes, although no one quite knows why, then at least it would help if they were all like Frederick."[52] It turned out, however, that even Frederick was not like Frederick. Once the prince became king, he remained as hostile to religion as any freethinker, but proved indifferent to serious social and educational reform, and all too intent on war abroad and repression at home. His interest in the Enlightenment was mostly transactional: he pursued celebrated thinkers like Voltaire and Diderot, not as sources of insight and wisdom, but instead as sources of cultural capital. As Frederick purportedly said of Voltaire, at the very moment he was welcoming the Frenchman to his court in Potsdam, "I shall have need of him for another year at most, no longer. One squeezes the orange and throws away the peel."[53]

Unlike Voltaire, Diderot wavered on the desirability of the *thèse royale.* He had no illusions over the excesses such a thesis all too often justified, setting them out in a scorching pamphlet he wrote against Frederick shortly before leaving for Holland. The immediate prod was a pamphlet Frederick had written under a poorly disguised pseudonym, mocking an essay by Diderot's close friend, Baron d'Holbach, which excoriated aristocratic privileges. Pretending to be unaware that Frederick had penned it, Diderot mercilessly shredded the pamphlet's reasoning and the writer's character. "Given the author's aversion for those who dare question rulers, he has clearly never suffered from the abuse of authority." As for Frederick's scorn for d'Holbach's insistence on humankind's capacity to find and know the truth, Diderot explodes: "When this writer says that man is not made for the truth and that error is his lot, he goes further than even he knows: it is the babbling of an infant. He exhausts the commonplaces on how error governs the world and fails to see the tableau of truths that oppose him." After a half-dozen pages ablaze with insolence and insight, Diderot concludes: "What have I learned from this pamphlet? That man is not made for the truth . . . that superstition serves a purpose, that war is beautiful, etc., etc., and that God preserve us from a ruler who resembles a philosopher like this."[54]

While he admired the short leash that intermediate bodies kept on royal power in Holland and Britain, he lambasted the efforts by the *parlements* to do the same in France. How could he not, he exclaimed, given the institution's unrepresentative and reactionary character? In a letter he wrote to Grimm in 1769, Diderot explained that when one digs deeply enough into the history of *parlement,* one discovers how "intolerant, bigoted and stupid" it has been, "preserving its Gothic and Vandal privileges and proscribing good sense" all the while "mixing up everything with its ignorance, its self-interest and its prejudices." In a word, never has there been "so violent an enemy of all liberty, be it civil or religious," than the Paris Parlement.[55]

Except, it seems, when an even more violent enemy of liberty threatened the Parlement's very existence. Scarcely two years after presenting to Grimm his brief against the Parlement, Diderot did a dramatic about-face. When, in 1771, Louis XV acted on his absolutist claims and dismissed the aristocratic institution, Diderot was appalled. What Diderot earlier execrated as a reactionary body of unenlightened nobles, he now extolled as the noble rampart against royal overreach. It alone, Diderot claimed, stood between true freedom and servitude. Though deeply flawed and often foolish, the Parlement was the one institutional brake that could prevent a monarch from morphing into a monster. Hence Diderot's panicked conclusion: "We confront a crisis which will end in slavery or liberty; if it is the latter, it will resemble what now exists in Morocco or Constantinople."[56] Or, indeed, Russia.

Glasnost

WE ARE THE SECULAR MISSIONARIES WHO PREACH THE CULT OF SAINT CATHERINE, AND WE PRIDE OURSELVES THAT OUR CHURCH IS FAIRLY UNIVERSAL.

—VOLTAIRE TO CATHERINE

On December 25, 1761, the Empress Elizabeth died. Her faltering health had been the great preoccupation of not just Catherine but also the imperial court. The child-man Elizabeth had tried to ready as her successor, but failed, became Tsar Peter III. He was neither intellectually nor emotionally prepared to assume the immense responsibilities of rule; thirty-three years old, he had not outgrown his passion for his toy soldiers, or more disastrously, for Frederick's real soldiers. His affection for his native Holstein and adoration of Frederick promised to reverse Russia's long-standing foreign policy goals, while his scornful attitude toward his adopted country and scandalous behavior at court boded ill for domestic peace.

Upon Peter's accession, Russia's ruling elite, from the old aristocracy and court parties to the imperial guard and the army, found to their dismay that the throne no more makes the man than does the office. Ignoring the practices and protocols of the court, importing German soldiers to replace the imperial guard, and insulating himself within a small group of mostly German favorites, the newly anointed tsar was oblivious to the determined opposition he had ignited. Most dramatically, Peter announced that he held historic claim—as a German prince, and not a Russian tsar—to the province of Schleswig, then under Danish rule. Refusing negotiations, he declared war on Denmark—an act of staggering stupidity that dissolved the remaining ties of loyalty that Russia's military leaders held for him. As the opposition's leader, Nikita Panin, who would go on to serve as Catherine's foreign minister, declared: "All minds were alienated from the Tsar; no one was satisfied with him; they wanted another sovereign no matter what trouble it could bring."[1]

Though she had no dynastic claim to the throne, Catherine was the alternate sovereign to whom the conspirators turned—a turn of events encouraged, if not orchestrated, by Catherine herself. After their climactic meeting in 1759, Elizabeth had shared with Catherine her growing irritation, even disgust, over Peter's character. Catherine recalled frequent conversations she had with the empress: "She spoke either through bitter tears about the misfortune of having such an heir [or] showing her contempt for him." Indeed, in letters written by Elizabeth that had come into Catherine's possession, when his aunt was not damning Peter as a fool, she was describing him as a monster.[2] But Elizabeth's clear-sightedness came too late; when she died two years later, neither she nor the court had settled upon an alternative plan of succession.

Aware of the dangers presented by her estranged husband, who acted in increasingly strange ways, Catherine cultivated the same groups that Peter had alienated. Equally important, her calm and dignified behavior with foreign as well as Russian dignitaries contrasted sharply with her husband's often drunken tirades delivered in his native German or the Russian he had never bothered to master. Finally, she had found a thoroughly dependable and utterly fearless accomplice in her new lover, Grigory Orlov. An army officer who had distinguished himself in battle, Orlov came to Catherine's attention in 1760 when he appeared at court. The mutual attraction was immediate, as was one of the consequences: when Elizabeth died in 1761, Catherine was pregnant with Orlov's child.

Led by Panin, Catherine, and Orlov, the conspirators succeeded in bringing along key constituencies in the government and military. On June 28, 1762, while Peter was at nearby Oranienbaum, training his troops for a war with Denmark that would never take place, the residents of Saint Petersburg learned dramatic news: Catherine, whom Peter had ordered to stay at the royal estate of Peterhof, had just reentered the city. With Orlov, his four brothers, and the Russian Guards behind her, she walked down the Nevsky Prospect toward the Winter Palace, where great crowds had formed to cheer her passage. The regiments defending the palace, carried by events, swore allegiance to *matushka,* or Little Mother, the sobriquet for their newly proclaimed ruler. Upon entering the palace, Catherine found Panin waiting with her son, Paul; picking him up in her arms, she strode onto a balcony to the delight of the crowd massed below. Acknowledged by the Russian Senate, blessed by the Russian Holy Synod, and hailed by the Russian crowds, the German-born Catherine began her reign that tumultuous day as Russia's *gosudarina,* or sovereign autocrat.

The following day, Peter, blind to events in Saint Petersburg, learned that his estranged wife, garbed in full military uniform and on horseback, was leading several regiments to Oranienbaum to demand his abdication. A study in irresolution and indecision, Peter realized that the only support he could count on was from the universally despised Holstein and Hessian troops under his command. Collapsing under the weight of this sudden turn of events, Peter abdicated the throne in favor of Catherine and Paul and allowed himself to be bundled by the Orlovs to the royal estate at Ropsha. Three days later, there arrived news as inevitable as it was awkward. A messenger hastened to the Winter Palace carrying a letter written by Alexei Orlov. A stunned Catherine learned that Orlov and his fellow guards had, the previous night, killed Peter during a scuffle. "Most merciful *gosudarina,* we ourselves know not what we did," Orlov swore: "We are all equally guilty and deserve to die."[3]

Given Orlov's confession and Catherine's character, the guilt almost certainly did not extend to her. But she certainly benefited tremendously from Peter's sudden disappearance. Like her fellow conspirators, Catherine understood that to keep the deposed tsar as a prisoner or send him into exile were equally dim options. With her own tenuous claim to the throne, having a dead ex-tsar on her hands was, in the end, less problematic than a living ex-tsar. Conferring with Panin, Catherine released a manifesto that announced Peter's death, attributing it—as d'Alembert's *bon mot* recalled—to an "acute attack of hemorrhoids." For good measure, the manifesto added that Peter's unfortunate death, having led Catherine to the throne, was a mark of God's intentions.[4] Was Peter's death also the newly anointed *gosudarina*'s intention? The question was debated in courts and salons across the continent, but it was also a question that Catherine was determined to render moot with rapid and rapier-like attention to both the administration of her country and its image abroad.

Though the thirty-three-year-old empress had not been formally groomed to rule, she was more than prepared, both intellectually and emotionally, to do so. Catherine grasped that she needed to include as many influential figures as possible, rather than exclude them, and to seek collaborators to work with her rather than encourage conspirators who would work against her. Instead of punishing those involved in Peter's death, or exiling those who had served under him, she rewarded the former and called upon the latter to continue to serve under her. Aware of the pomp and circumstance necessary to cement popular feeling for her person, Catherine had orchestrated for her first visit to Moscow a dizzying series of festivities and ceremonies lasting a month. The young ruler, who took a gamble by scheduling them so soon after her ascension, had an existential stake in the success of her coronation in Moscow: in the late seventeenth century, the Tsarevna Sophia damaged her own authority by her efforts to claim the throne rather than guard it on behalf of her son Peter. As a result, one of the season's highlights was a fireworks display that framed a staged representation of Catherine as Minerva, the Roman goddess of wisdom.[5] (The more perceptive members of the audience no doubt remarked that Minerva was helmeted—a preview of Catherine's future territorial expansions.)

In the end the gamble paid off, allowing Catherine to set the stage for effective rule—no small task, given the weakness of the institutional and bureaucratic bodies already in place. Surveying the institutions she had acquired, Catherine was struck by their lamentable state: "The fleet was derelict, the army in disarray, the fortresses collapsing."[6] Catherine's list covered only the physical manifestations of the state; its economic, bureaucratic, and legal structures were in even worse shape. Since the start, in 1756, of what turned out to be the Seven Years' War—a complex dynastic struggle pitting Russia, France, and Austria against Prussia and Great Britain—the state's coffers were bare. The government struggled to pay its bills and cover salaries, encouraging dissension among soldiers and corruption among bureaucrats. (In fact, by effectively outsourcing most bureaucratic duties to the Russian nobility—a small minority of bureaucrats were salaried—the tsarist state invited corruption as a way of life.) No matter how majestic the royal pageants and firework displays in Moscow, they could only for so long divert attention from Russia's financial and institutional woes, all the while adding to them.

As determined to master the mechanics of government as to assert her presence as ruler, Catherine formed a cabinet to convey her desires and demands, and attended several sessions of the Senate (which, despite its grand name, was in reality a largely toothless secular court). Shocked by its glacial pace, she prodded its members, with barely suppressed irritation, to move more quickly. She was no less imperious with her administrators. Perplexed by the confusion among her financial officials, she complained that she had been unable to learn anything about state revenues and demanded a full accounting. (That she did not receive a comprehensive state financial statement until nearly twenty years later, in 1781, underscores that even an empress had limited powers over a chaotic administration.)

From the start, Catherine set a relentless work rhythm, determined to inspire the tsarist bureaucracy by leading an exemplary life. At eight in the morning, when her secretaries arrived to discuss state affairs, Catherine had already been up for two hours, reading documents and writing letters in her study. (Indeed, before sitting down at her desk, she would light the fire in her chamber and make her own coffee so as not to be interrupted by her servants.) The conferences would end at eleven, followed by a spare, business-like lunch, usually in the company of a small number of courtiers. By one o'clock Catherine was back in her private chambers, where she would spend much of the afternoon with Orlov, whose own quarters were directly above hers. At five-thirty she would then, as she explained in a letter, "either go to the theater, or I play, or I gossip to the first people to arrive before dinner, which is over before eleven when I retire to bed in order to do the same again on the following day. And all this is ruled out as regularly as musical manuscript paper."[7]

Catherine's letter, addressed to Madame Geoffrin, painted a careful self-portrait. With artful strokes, Catherine presented herself to her French audience, if not as Minerva, then at least as an enlightened ruler. Intent on presenting her reign as the continuation of Peter's, Catherine needed all the French and philosophic friends she could find. The pomp and circumstance of her crowning in Moscow, along with the rapidity and resolve of her initial decisions, allowed Catherine to legitimate her reign to the satisfaction of most Russians. But this was not the case for an audience nearly as crucial: the literary salons of Paris. By the mid-eighteenth century, the salons had become a crossroads for the Republic of Letters, bringing together artists and aristocrats, thinkers and freethinking clerics. As Dena Goodman argues, the salons were not places of frivolity, but instead "working spaces." While wit was admired, it was not encouraged; while wit might serve as a means, it must never be the end to the work of enlightenment. The *salonnières*—the women, some aristocratic and others bourgeois, who oversaw these salons—embraced this ethic. "Like the philosophes who gathered in their homes, the salonnières were practical people who worked at tasks they considered productive and useful."[8]

It was a world that mirrored not only Catherine's values but also her aspirations. Early in her reign, Catherine began a correspondence with Madame Geoffrin. Despite lacking an aristocratic pedigree, Geoffrin nevertheless hosted one of the most influential salons in Paris. Over a span of three decades, writers and scientists on certain nights, aristocrats and foreign dignitaries on others—the groups rarely mixed—regularly congregated at her home. Geoffrin would set the tone, as well as the limits, of conversation. Whenever an excitable guest would veer too far from the conversation and approach the minefields of religion and politics, Geoffrin would gently lead him back with her celebrated phrase *"Voilà qui est bien"*—"That's enough for now."[9] Yet those with any claim to citizenship in the Republic of Letters could not have enough of Geoffrin's patronage. As the ubiquitous Melchior Grimm observed, "One would not seem distinguished presenting himself in the world without having seen her."[10]

In the give-and-take of conversation, Geoffrin and her guests would read aloud and discuss letters received from abroad. As a result, aware of the power of Mme Geoffrin's salon to broadcast her good works and reputation, Catherine took particular care in writing long and deliberately disarming letters recounting her aims and achievements for Russia.[11] Unable to bring Saint Petersburg closer to Paris, Catherine also strove, during her first years in power, to bring Paris to her imperial capital. In 1767 she personally undertook, with the help of her court, the translation of the novel *Bélisaire,* published—and promptly banned—in France that very same year. Written by the playwright Jean-Francois Marmontel, the novel includes a paean to religious toleration, which spurred the ire of the Church and led to its condemnation. (Tellingly, Catherine translated the chapter in which the Byzantine general Belisarius tells the Roman emperor Justinian that any government based not on law, but arbitrary rule, was bound to become a tyranny.) The following year Catherine went beyond this effort at collective translation with the establishment of the Society for the Translation of Foreign Books into Russian. While the society did not limit itself to translating French works, it did privilege them. The society eventually published all of Jean-Jacques Rousseau's writings, with the predictable exception of *The Social Contract.* In 1773 the society also published, with Catherine's assent, a translation of the Abbé Mably's *Observations sur l'histoire de la Grèce.* Mably's republican sympathies were not difficult to see, encouraging the translator to affirm in a footnote: "Absolutism is the condition most repugnant to human nature."[12]

Needless to say, the Enlightenment's most influential and indefatigable defender quickly became Catherine's greatest advocate. As Voltaire told Catherine, in a letter written in 1765, "Dare I tell you, Madame, that I'm a bit annoyed that you took the name 'Catherine'?" Far better, he wrote, to be called Juno, Venus, Ceres, or Minerva.[13] Catherine politely refused all of these names. While she seemed particularly bothered by Juno—"I would never exchange my name for that envious and jealous goddess"—she turned down Minerva, more simply, because "I am not presumptuous enough."[14]

The presumption, at least at the beginning, was mostly Voltaire's. In their first exchange of letters, in 1765, he announced that Catherine would "fully realize the work" begun by Peter the Great—namely, transforming Russia from a shadowy and snowbound backwater into an enlightened European nation.[15] In this respect Voltaire played a crucial role in creating what one historian called the "Russian mirage in France," a mirage that married the "myth of Peter" to the "legend of Catherine."[16] In his 1759 work *The History of the Russian Empire under Peter the Great,* he attributed superhuman powers to the tsar. From the book's very opening ("Of all the lawgivers since Mohammed, Peter is the one whose people have distinguished themselves the most after his death") to its closing lines ("He coerced nature in every respect, in his subjects, in himself, on land and sea, but he coerced it in order to embellish it"), Voltaire's history is scarcely disguised hagiography.[17] Viewing the tsar's accomplishments from Ferney, his distant estate, Voltaire announced: "Peter was born and Russia was created."[18] And yet this sentiment, with its faint echo of Alexander Pope's celebrated line about Isaac Newton—"God said: 'Let Newton be' / And all was light"—was a sharp revision of Voltaire's assessment of Peter made twenty years earlier: "He civilized his peoples, but he was a savage." The man who executed his subjects by his own hands gave way to a man who, by his own hands, hauled an entire empire onto the European map. Voltaire's softening of the more brutal lines he had drawn two decades earlier was, in part, due to the origins of the biography. Elizabeth had commissioned the work, providing Voltaire along the way with invaluable documents and valuable presents, like exotic furs. Once the work was published, Voltaire found he had failed both his Russian audience, who did not find his portrait of Peter flattering enough, and his Parisian audience, who found it grotesquely flattering. Confiding to a friend, d'Alembert said the book "makes one vomit by the baseness and platitude of its eulogies."[19]

But this meant little to Voltaire as long as he held on to his imperial audience of one, who read his missives in distant Saint Petersburg. He succeeded in this goal, maintaining a rich and varied correspondence with Catherine until his death in 1778. The letters must be handled with care, though. Just as both knew they were writing less to influence one another than to influence posterity's view of them, both also knew that their letters were less the stuff of enlightened conversation than mutual flattery. But the praise Voltaire poured on Catherine was also enlightened politics by other means. For Voltaire's "party of humanity," few conquests weighed greater than Russia on the scales of reason and progress. By its sheer size and social conditions, Catherine's empire dwarfed Frederick's Prussia or Joseph's Austria in both political and philosophical significance. For those same reasons, never did the *thèse royal* seem more relevant.[20] That Voltaire had never been to Russia, that his knowledge was based on limited sources and unlimited imagination, encouraged his conceit that change could be more effectively imposed by a ruler there than elsewhere in Europe. The wilderness that Peter had conquered could now, with Catherine, be hewn and hammered into a true civilization.

Hence the fawning but frank declaration he made to Catherine in 1773, soon after Diderot had departed for Saint Petersburg: "We are the secular [*laïques*] missionaries who preach the cult of Saint Catherine, and we pride ourselves that our church is fairly universal."[21] A number of these "missionaries" did, indeed, accept the *thèse royale*. Two of Diderot's closest friends, Grimm and d'Alembert, agreed that, especially in the barren reaches of Eastern Europe, a government led by a "just, strong and enlightened despot" was essential. Grimm, for one, could hardly contain his enthusiasm for autocratic but progressive rulers: "I love," he declared, "such despots with a passion."[22]

Undoubtedly Grimm's effusive declarations were partly fueled by his intimate ties to Catherine. Like Voltaire, Grimm was a constant correspondent with the empress; unlike Voltaire, the German-born jack of literary and diplomatic trades visited Saint Petersburg—at the very same time as did Diderot—and became Catherine's official representative for various state affairs and her most intimate confidant. As she was fond of telling Grimm—and he no less fond of hearing—he was her *souffre douleur,* or punching bag, with whom she could share fears and hopes to which no one else in her circle was privy. In 1791 the dying empress told Grimm: "I think that it is decreed on high that you and I have been created expressly so that we may each have a pen continually in hand to write to one another without stopping." As for her correspondence with

Voltaire, the empress was frank. Commanding Grimm to burn her letters, she confessed: "They are so much more sprightly than the ones I wrote to Voltaire, and could do the most awful damage."[23] Had Voltaire been alive—he died in 1778, years before this exchange—the most awful damage would have been to his *amour-propre.*

But the philosophes' commitment to Catherine was not merely selfish, nor was it terribly delusive. During her long apprenticeship to the throne, Catherine read not merely to fill her time but in order to make sense of her situation and, by extension, Russia's situation. The works of Voltaire and Montesquieu, d'Alembert and Diderot, gave her the tools to rate, and try to remedy, the social and political difficulties faced by her adopted country. Crucially, this was not just a matter of playing to the Parisian crowd. Catherine harbored a sincere moral repugnancy for cruel and inhumane practices—not surprising, perhaps, for someone who had been deeply marked by a marriage to an increasingly volatile and demeaning husband. Her refusal, following the coup in 1762, to prosecute or punish any of Peter's followers was not just practical—several of them went on to become trusted officials in her government—but personal. Her conviction that one should "do good and avoid doing evil as much as one reasonably can, out of love of humanity," was authentic.[24]

No matter of state offered a greater challenge to this belief than serfdom. It was less peculiar an institution in eighteenth-century Russia than in eighteenth-century America, if only because all Russians were, to one degree or another, subject to bondage.[25] The country's skeletal administration, along with its primitive economy, created the need for an immense pool of involuntary labor. As a result, over time all individuals were bound to other individuals, to the state, or both. This was the case for the nobility, who were obliged to serve the state in administrative or military capacities, as well as for town dwellers, who, unlike nobles, required permission to move from one town to another. As Isabel de Madariaga drily notes, in eighteenth-century Russia "all that was not specifically authorized was forbidden, and only that could be done which was specifically authorized."[26]

In a world where an individual's liberty ended at the threshold of his door and the horizon of possibilities stretched no further than his village, the lot of peasant serfs, who numbered nearly ten million, out of a total population of twenty million, in the 1762–1764 census, was nevertheless incalculably worse. They fell into various categories, as the property of the state, the church, landowners, or mine and industrial enterprises. Regardless of their official categorization, serfs were united in their abject status. They were chattel that, as with other forms of property, could be bought and sold by their owners. The lot of landowners' serfs was perhaps the most abysmal. The state set out few rules to govern the treatment of serfs, so the landowner's sway over his serfs was essentially lawless. The large estates that did create codes for their serfs, specifying transgressions and their punishment, were the exception. In general, short of killing their serfs, landowners could do as they pleased.

As grand duchess, Catherine had realized that the institution of serfdom was the decaying elephantine carcass in the room no one dared to discuss. In her notebooks, at least, Catherine did not mince her words. Upon reading one author laud the glories of serfdom, she exploded in rage: "Such praise of slavery! Why, then, doesn't the writer sell himself into slavery?"[27] The young Catherine was no more tender in regard to the "mule-headed prejudices" of Russia's landed aristocracy: "It is against the Christian religion and principles of justice to make slaves of men who are born in freedom." Remarkably, she went on to imagine a scheme in which, whenever an estate was sold, its serfs would be freed. In a century, she thought, serfdom would no longer exist.[28]

Immediately upon assuming the throne in 1762, Catherine was forced to revise her youthful idealism. A series of serf rebellions was rippling across the Urals, ignited by abysmal working conditions in the region's mines and factories. Catherine was aware of the legitimate reasons for the unrest, but alert to the reality that she could not side openly against the owners. Reflecting the depths of her dilemma was her decision to reward military and court officials with tens of thousands of serfs for their support in 1762. She simply had no choice but to use the common currency, no matter how abased, of the nation she now ruled. Nevertheless, Catherine instructed a trusted general, A. A. Vyazmensky, to break the rebellion. But he was also tasked to gather evidence concerning the treatment of the serfs, rectifying what he could and punishing those guilty of excess cruelty. Trying to balance on the razor's edge between her stubborn humanity and Russia's equally stubborn reality, she told Vyazmensky to "do everything you think proper for the satisfaction of the peasants, but take suitable precautions so that the peasants should not imagine that their managers will be afraid of them in the future."[29]

Though Catherine's balancing effort failed—her moderation emboldened the resistance of both the serfs and mine owners—she had taken the full measure of the moral and social quandary. Reflecting on a case in which the Senate, reacting to the murder of a prominent landowner by his serfs, ordered the destruction of an entire hamlet as exemplary punishment, Catherine warned against quickening the spiral of violence. Not only would it spark a "riot of all bondaged hamlets," but it would also delay, if not destroy, the hope of a "general emancipation from the unbearable and cruel yoke" of serfdom. Catherine once again tasked Vyazmensky with cutting this Gordian knot: "If we do not agree to the diminution of cruelty and the amelioration of the intolerable position for the human species, even against our will they [the serfs] will seize it sooner or later."[30]

It was not just the world of serfdom that was overcome by administrative and juridical confusion. Russian law, in general, was a chaotic sprawl of conflicting and confusing decrees, a man-made mire more daunting than the miasmal swamps drained by Peter the Great and on which Saint Petersburg now stood. Though he had planned a new code, Peter did not live to see its completion; finished after his death, it was never promulgated. It was thus with great anticipation, reported Louis XV's envoy to Russia in 1766, that Russian officials expected Catherine to announce "a code which she wishes to substitute for the multitude of contradictory edicts which are the only laws of this empire and which serve merely as a resource for the dishonesty of litigants, and even more often for that of judges."[31]

On December 14 Catherine confirmed the envoy's report: representatives of the various orders of Russian society, she announced, were to convene in Moscow in order to form a Legislative Commission. Their task would be to impose order on disorganized Russian law; their guide would be the *Velikiy Nakaz,* or *Great Instruction,* the manual that Catherine had herself written during the previous two years. While the French envoy rightly anticipated the announcement, he missed the meaning of its import: the *Nakaz* was less a legal code than a lengthy list of principles, destined to undergird effective government and ensure social stability. The great majority of those principles, in turn, were culled—or, more bluntly, copied—from one of the philosophes Catherine had read while biding her time as grand duchess: the Baron de Montesquieu. While *The Spirit of the Laws* was her mainstay, Catherine was also marked by Montesquieu's *The Considerations on the Causes of the Greatness of the Romans and Their Decline.* Ordering the book on the advice of the Swedish ambassador when she first arrived in Saint Petersburg as a fifteen-year-old, Catherine attempted to read it, but with mixed success. "When I began to read," Catherine recalled, "it led me to reflect, but I could not read it straight through because it made me yawn." Declaring it was a "fine book," the teenager then "tossed it aside to continue getting dressed."[32]

But Montesquieu's portrayal of the Romans remained with Catherine longer than the clothing she wore that day. In his reflections, Montesquieu dwells not just on the material and political nature of Rome's greatness—the ability to project power and to expand its empire—but also on the moral nature of its greatness. He considers the small but vital bundle of traits that ensured Rome's ascension: the Roman's embrace of law, his willingness to engage in self-sacrifice, and his love of country. As for Rome's leaders, they were dedicated to principles of the *res publica*—so much so that when it morphed, under Augustus, into an empire, they were wise enough to maintain the appearance of republican rule. Crucially, Montesquieu also emphasizes the place of war: the greatness of a nation, he argued, was measured in part by its military conquests. It was only when conquests became the means for various individuals and factions to achieve personal power that Rome began its long decline and fall.

Eighteen years after having picked up and tossed aside this "fine book," Catherine may have forgotten its particular claims, but she recalled its general tenor. The flame of patriotism and foundations of law, she understood, were essential to a nation's greatness. Catherine's subsequent wars of imperial expansion no doubt also found justification in Montesquieu's book. But at this early stage of her rule, Catherine grasped, thanks to the Frenchman, that love of one's country required a knowledge of that country's history and institutions, and that love of the law required that a body of laws first exist.

It is here that she turned to *The Spirit of the Laws*—with scissors and paste. Of the 526 articles forming the first part of the *Nakaz,* more than half—294, to be exact—are taken, mostly word for word, from Montesquieu's work. Slightly more than a hundred other articles are culled from Cesare Beccaria's landmark work, *Of Crimes and Punishments,* published in French translation and read by Catherine at the very moment she began her writing. Unlike the current raft of plagiarism cases against Russian officials, accused of lifting the work of others for their dissertations, Catherine made no pretense that her work was original. As she happily confessed to d'Alembert, "For the sake of my empire, I have robbed Montesquieu without mentioning him by name. If he sees my work from the next world, I hope he will pardon me this plagiarism for the good of twenty million people. He loved humanity too well to take offense."[33]

While d'Alembert accepted Catherine's explanation, he also arched his eyebrows upon learning that Voltaire gladly attributed the entirety of the work to Catherine's genius. Upon rereading the French translation of the *Nakaz,* he gushed to Catherine that it was "the century's most beautiful monument." It bestowed greater glory on the empress, he continued, than ten military victories against the Ottoman Empire. While the Minerva of the North had not slaughtered the "Turks with her own hand," he explained, it was "her genius that conceived" the *Nakaz* and her "beautiful hand which had written it."[34] Nevertheless, while "the old invalid of Ferney" (as Voltaire signed his letter) had gone overboard in his praise, the unprecedented nature of the *Nakaz* can hardly be exaggerated. A ruling monarch, recently come to power in unorthodox circumstances, and confronted by an array of economic, social, and geopolitical challenges, nevertheless had the discipline and dedication to research and write a document, containing 22 chapters and 655 clauses, meant to found the nation's law code. The heavy burden she imposed on herself took its toll; during the two years she compiled the work, she suffered from migraine headaches. Yet the result, as one specialist rightly claims, is "one of the most remarkable political treatises ever compiled and published by a reigning sovereign in modern times."[35]

With the *Nakaz,* Catherine unabashedly took the word, or words, of Enlightenment thinkers. Indeed, she took these *thinkers* as they wished to be taken: as shapers of public opinion and public policy. The trick, however, was that the Russian public was utterly unlike the publics in Western countries. An empire whose illiterate and indentured peasantry dwarfed an embryonic civil society, skeletal professional class (mostly educated in German universities), and rustic and reactionary aristocracy was an unlikely test case for enlightened principles of governance. An obstacle no less daunting was the sheer size of Catherine's empire. Neither a monarchy (as in Prussia) nor limited monarchy (as with Great Britain)—two less extreme points on Montesquieu's spectrum of governments—could hope to rule so extensive a nation. While the Petrine reforms revealed that the Russian people were not impervious to change, they also reminded the world that it took a despot, and not a monarch, to impose them. For Montesquieu, the dizzying dimensions of the Russian empire entailed the necessity of a despotic ruler.

While Catherine recoiled from the title "despot," she also understood the imperative need to establish the rule of law. Could it be otherwise for someone who had insisted, in the years leading up to 1762, that rulers should be bound by law? Someone who had exclaimed, while grand duchess: "Liberty, the soul of all things, without you everything is dead. I want the laws to be obeyed, but I don't want slaves."[36] Or, indeed, for someone who placed such great store in the good opinion of the Republic of Letters? Her first order of business, as a result, was to assert, as she did in the opening line of the *Nakaz,* what many still questioned in the mid-eighteenth century: that Russia was a European state. Having thus distanced her country from the shame attached to "Asiatic despotism," Catherine then divorces herself from the disgrace implicit in the title *despot.* To Montesquieu's axiom that "a great empire entails a despotic authority," Catherine makes a subtle and telling change: not only is the Russian monarch sovereign, but "a great empire entails a sovereign authority." While despotism conforms to the Ottomans or Persians, Catherine insists, it ill-suits a European nation like her own.

But does citing Montesquieu's principles make one principled, and does echoing his love of liberty make one a sower of liberty? Catherine would have replied: yes, but with conditions. For Montesquieu, law codes and intermediary bodies (institutions with legal powers) constrain, as they should, a ruler's ability to do as he wishes. Yet such bodies were rare and slight in a Russian empire held together by bound subjects and slave labor, and maintained by fear of the knout and submission to tradition. While Catherine scrambled to distance her rule from the bad odor of despotism, and harbored a philosophical antipathy to the exercise of arbitrary power, she was nevertheless unwilling to surrender the powers of a despot. Her resistance is partly explained by her justifiable fears regarding those who might contest her legitimacy. No less important, though, Catherine quickly grasped that to rule Russia, to continue the work of Peter and introduce reforms that would benefit its people, required despotic powers.

Ultimately Catherine was unable to square this particular circle; the *Nakaz* reflects Catherine's inner conflict. The document's constitutional sections both appeal to a world that ought to be and acknowledge the world as it is. But Catherine nevertheless tries to create the conditions that would enable the circle to be squared sooner rather than later. Only through the creation of a consistent body of laws would commerce in goods and ideas flourish and subjects begin their apprenticeship as citizens. Political liberty, Catherine noted while still grand duchess, consists of the security in which a citizen "finds himself under the protection of the law, which causes one citizen not to fear the other." As to fearing one's ruler, however, Catherine is less forthcoming. She acknowledges the state's laws "must be sacred to a monarch, for they remain forever while subjects and kings disappear." Diderot would later drive home the very same truth, all the while driven to despair over the wiggle room Catherine left herself. It was, she concluded, the state—which does not entirely rhyme with ruler—that "has every interest in keeping strictly to the laws."[37]

When it came to the laws governing crimes and punishments, though, Catherine proved to be the most enlightened of rulers. Scarcely had she ascended the throne than she sent a generous amount of money to the family of Jean Calas, a victim of religious fanaticism in France. In 1761 the Catholic parlement in his native city of Toulouse had charged the Protestant merchant with the murder of his son. The cause, they alleged, was that Calas senior was enraged by his son's decision to convert to Catholicism. Because their case was based entirely on prejudice and innuendo, the city and church authorities, desperate for a confession, slowly and painstakingly tortured Calas in a public ceremony. And yet Calas, his body broken and bloodied on the wheel, did not confess. Finally, an exasperated executioner garroted the unjustly condemned man and had his body burned.

Soon after learning of the event, Voltaire launched a campaign to reverse the court's charges against Calas and revile those responsible for them. It was a decision requiring great valor and verve—of which Voltaire generally had much more of the latter than of the former. On this occasion, though, he summoned up both, making it his finest hour. In his many months of pamphleteering and corresponding, he galvanized public opinion and goaded royal officials with a single message: *Écrasez l'infame.* In his plea to stamp out the infamous thing, by which Voltaire meant religious fanaticism and superstition, Voltaire achieved his goal: the Toulouse Parlement's decision was reversed, Calas's innocence was restored, and his family, who had been forced to flee their home, reunited.

Voltaire's campaign enthralled the Republic of Letters, including its most recent and glittering addition, Catherine. Her financial gift to the Calas family was both canny and heartfelt. Canny in that it evoked, all too predictably, Voltaire's obsequious praise: The Republic of Letters, he declared, "is at your feet." Heartfelt in that Catherine, no doubt relieved by Voltaire's compliment, observed that she needed to thank him. When one enjoys great wealth, she wrote, it is easy to help another. But the Calas family and the world, she continued, owe you everything: "It is you who have battled the enemies of humanity: superstition, fanaticism, ignorance, and evil judges."[38]

The *Nakaz* was Catherine's means to join forces with Voltaire. Turning from Montesquieu to Beccaria, she deployed a series of principles based on the conviction that punishment should be preventive, not retributive. When it came to torture, Catherine found that while it served the latter purpose, it failed miserably to fulfill the former. In article 194, she declared: "The innocent ought not to be tortured; and in the eyes of the law, every person is innocent whose crime is not yet proved." The striking corollary to this axiom, one that looks back to Calas, is that torture must not be used to secure a confession of guilt. Catherine was no less appalled by the use of torture as a means for punishment. Its usage, affirms article

123, "is contrary to all the dictates of nature and reason; even mankind itself cries out against it, and loudly demands its total abolition."

Inevitably, the gap between legal principles and everyday practice remained great. The official practice of torture, as well as corporal punishment, seemed to have diminished, particularly in regard to nobles found guilty of crimes, but it did not disappear. This fact, ironically reflected in Catherine's many warnings to subordinates concerning torture, is not surprising.[39] An empire as varied and vast as Russia could not change over a generation or more, much less overnight. In 1765, when Catherine insisted to Voltaire that "toleration is established and persecution forbidden" in Russia, she was addressing the letter of her laws, and not the spirit in which they were, or were not, applied to and understood by her subjects.[40] There simply was not enough administration to ensure the application of these laws—or, for that matter, nearly enough liberty or literacy to cultivate them.

It was Catherine's determination to prepare the soil that led her, in July 1767, to convene the Legislative Commission. Inspired by the entry "Representatives" in the *Encyclopédie,* she oversaw an extraordinary exercise in state building. Her subjects, chosen to represent the kaleidoscope of social orders, convened in Moscow in order to debate the *Nakaz* and discuss how its principles could be translated into law. The unprecedented event captured the attention of Russians and foreigners alike. As a British envoy reported, the Russians "think and talk of nothing else, and in seeing the representatives of several nations, so very different both as to dress, customs and religion . . . assemble in their capital, they are apt to conclude that they are now the wisest, the happiest and the most powerful nation in the universe."[41] In a letter to Voltaire, Catherine echoed this upbeat account: "I believe you would enjoy this assembly, where an Orthodox Christian, heretic and Muslim listen to a heathen, frequently seeking amongst themselves a middle position." Having forgotten the habit of burning one another at the stake, she continued, they would never again contemplate the act. Instead, they would say to those who sought to burn a heretic, "He is a man, just as I am; and according to Her Majesty's *Nakaz,* we are obliged to do as much good, and as little harm as we can."[42]

Voltaire no more believed this account than we do, if only because it resembled his own description, thirty years earlier in his *Philosophical Letters,* of the tolerance shown one another by Jews, Christians, and Muslims in the London Stock Exchange. The sole difference is that Voltaire's walk-ons find common ground in enlightened self-interest, whereas Catherine's cast finds common ground on the stage she has artfully arranged. But the inflated, if not utterly invented, tableau they both offer is meant, not to distort reality, but instead to point to a better reality. This explains the dazzling pomp and circumstance with which Catherine opened the convention in late July 1767. Draped in a majestic imperial robe and flanked by court officials, the empress looked on while her vice chancellor, Alexander Golitsyn, delivered the official welcome. He reminded the representatives why they had been called to Moscow—to work toward "the common good, the felicity of mankind and the introduction of good manners and humanity, tranquility, security and felicity to your dear fatherland."[43]

These events simply enthralled Diderot. Not only had Catherine flown to his rescue, but she now seemed determined to do the same for all of her subjects. But rather than plying them with gifts, the empress would supply them with law. In a letter to his friend, the sculptor Etienne-Maurice Falconet, Diderot enthused: "Our Catherine is for now the only sovereign who, free to impose any form of government or yoke she wishes on her people, instead has the wisdom to tell them that 'We are all made to live under laws which are made for one reason: To make us happy.'" Diderot then imagines Catherine exhorting the representatives to speak with candor: "Come and teach me about your lives; come and converse with me. Do not fear displeasing me; I will listen to you with patience."[44]

As it soon became clear, however, the gathered deputies would, if not displease the empress, certainly disappoint her expectations, modest though they were. Along with Golitsyn's inspiring words, the deputies were treated to house rules: they were forbidden to interrupt or assault one another. Should a fight nevertheless break out, it would most probably not be fatal, because swords were also forbidden. But apart from the occasional scuffle, brawling turned out to be the least of Catherine's concerns. Each representative had, in effect, been deputized to present a list *(nakaz)* of proposals and grievances from their locality. Compounding the sheer number of *nakazy* was, in many cases, their excessive length and execrable quality, rendering nearly Sisyphean the task of reading and absorbing them. Moreover, as absolute beginners in public debate and policymaking, the deputies had to juggle foreign rules of decorum and order with equally foreign political and philosophical concepts.

Though she observed the opening sessions, Catherine had, like the god of Voltaire's imagination, deliberately removed herself from her creation. Unlike Voltaire's god, however, Catherine could not ignore the confusion that stymied the commission's activities. As she closely followed the proceedings, she sent to the invaluable and inevitable Vyazmensky, who was overseeing the proceedings, a stream of memos venting over the sluggish and meandering pace. Seeking to jolt the representatives, Catherine peremptorily moved the proceedings in the dead of winter from Moscow, a city she disliked, to her beloved Saint Petersburg. But the change of scenery failed to change the speed of the commission's deliberations. Tragically, the only subject that galvanized the aristocratic deputies was serfdom. Though Catherine had been in power for five years, she was shocked by the visceral opposition to even the slightest reform to the status of serfs. Here was a world over which even the Minerva of the North wielded little, if any, power. Twenty years after the commission, Catherine's response to these events was still raw: "You hardly dare say that the serfs are just the same people as we; and even when I myself say this I risk having stones hurled at me. . . . I think there were not even twenty persons who would have thought about this subject humanely and as human beings."[45]

By the end of 1768, as her enthusiasm dimmed and with her attention taken by imminent war with the Ottoman Empire, Catherine postponed the commission's sessions. She never reconvened the commission, even after Russia emerged the battered victor of the long and costly war. But the work of the commission, and promise of the *Nakaz,* was not forgotten by enlightened opinion in Russia and abroad. Whether it was fully understood, particularly by Diderot, was an entirely different question. In a letter to his friend Falconet, who had recently arrived in Saint Petersburg to undertake Catherine's commission for a monumental equestrian statue of Peter the Great, the philosophe declared his infatuation with the empress: "Our Catherine is, for now, the only sovereign who has told her subjects: 'All of us are made to live under laws. The laws are made only to render us happy. No one, my children, knows better than you which conditions can make you happy. And so, come to teach me, explain this to me. Do not fear to contradict me. I will listen to you with indulgence and swear that your candor will have no unfortunate consequences for you.'"[46]

Like Voltaire and nearly all the members of the Republic of Letters, Diderot enthused over the Legislative Commission's significance. Let us, he told Falconet, build a hundred monuments to the empress. Clearly Diderot had already erected a certain statue of Catherine in his mind—a statue that would not be exempt from the wear and tear of time and experience. Had it not been for his great distance from Russia, along with his deep adoration of Catherine, Diderot might have suggested fewer statues. Indeed, once he collapsed that distance and contemplated Catherine up close, the philosophe would insist that while statues honoring the empress were well and good, statutes limiting her rule and empowering a representative government would be even better.

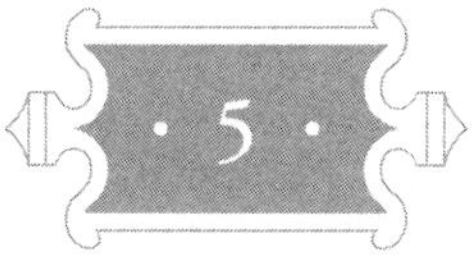

The Shadow Lands

THIS HAD TO BE BECAUSE IT WAS WRITTEN ABOVE.

–*JACQUES THE FATALIST*

DIDEROT HAD TOLD FRIENDS AND FAMILY that he would stay in Holland no longer than two weeks. But his friends and family, knowing their man, were not surprised as the two weeks stretched into two months. Speaking for many, Madame d'Épinay began to wonder if Diderot would ever push on to his destination or, indeed, ever return to Paris, so taken was he by the cascade of new places and people.[1] On the other side, the Abbé Galiani, for his part, still believed that Diderot would leave for Russia. "Or, more precisely, he will find himself one fine day in Saint Petersburg, unaware of how he got there."[2]

The Russian empress shared the French *salonnière*'s doubts, but not her good humor. In a letter to Falconet, an increasingly irritated Catherine noted that the philosophe "seems to be traveling slowly."[3] In her business-like fashion, Catherine had already dispatched her chamberlain, Alexis

Narishkin, then in Paris, to The Hague in order to collect Diderot and carry him back to Saint Petersburg. While Diderot was thrilled by his escort's character—a fine fellow, he announced, who "[though] from a barbarian land possessed the delicate qualities of a civilized nation"—he nevertheless fretted. Come the eve of his departure, on August 23, he confessed to Madame d'Épinay that his "heart was troubled." Suffering from the prospect of "putting half a terrestrial diameter between his friends and himself," he asked forgiveness for the wrongs he committed should be never return to Paris. Madame d'Épinay seemed less moved by her friend's melodramatic farewell than by his announcement that he would return to Paris in the following January. "Voilà," she observed drily, "the project of a man who has never traveled outside his country."[4]

It turns out, though, that Diderot had yet other projects, both more fantastic and more philosophical, than traveling through Russia in the dead of winter. When not entertaining the young and gobsmacked Russian by improvising ribald tales—"The Beautiful and Spiritual Mademoiselle of Memel" was a favorite—Diderot turned his hand to other genres, less ribald but more radical. Always aware of why, at the age of sixty, he was rattling across the continent in the company of a Russian court official, Diderot began to outline the discussions he wished to have with Catherine. Given the misleading title *Interviews with the Empress Catherine II,* Diderot's sketches identified and fleshed out the themes for their encounters. When not pelting the irrepressible Narishkin with questions about his country's economy, politics, and society, Diderot plumbed his own country's history to serve as a foil to his vision for Russia. Tellingly, the first "interview" he composed upon leaving The Hague was about the growth of royal power, climaxing with Maupeou's coup against the Paris Parlement in 1771.

Inevitably, Diderot also entertained himself by improvising, this time on paper, on the very act of traveling. Though he had begun his masterpiece *Jacques the Fatalist and His Master* as early as 1771, Diderot revised and added to the manuscript during his voyage to Russia and back. Like many of his works, including *Rameau's Nephew, Jacques the Fatalist* led a sequestered existence while Diderot was alive. Apart from a reading to a small number of friends, Diderot did not seek to publicize or publish the novel, in part or whole, in either France or Holland. He might have worried over the official reaction; as he wrote to his Dutch publisher Marc Michel Rey shortly after his return to France, "Intolerance grows greater here with each passing day. Soon the only works the censors will allow will be almanacs and, with corrections, the Lord's Prayer."[5]

In 1796, when *Jacques the Fatalist* was finally published, it was the Lord's Prayer—amended or not—that had been placed on the defensive. In the midst of the Revolution, and in the immediate wake of the Terror, a new dogmatism—based on the unquestioning belief in the power of reason and the state's ability to improve human nature—had taken root in France. Republican critics welcomed the novel as a "severe mirror of truth" that reflected the debased character of the aristocracy, a work based on "solid republican principles." Predictably, the periodicals published by a ravaged, but resilient, aristocracy assailed the novel as the disease for which it pretended to be the cure: a manifesto for philosophical determinism that had led France, awash in atheism and materialism, to its present sorry state.

None of this would have surprised Diderot. With *Jacques the Fatalist,* the philosophe was fatalistic, resigned to writing the novel not for his contemporaries but instead for future readers. The future extended even further in the English-speaking world; astonishingly, the first English translation of the book did not appear until 1959. And yet *Tristram Shandy*—the creation of the contemporary Irish-English writer Laurence Sterne—rambles across Diderot's work. Mischievously, the philosophe proudly claims he plagiarized certain scenes from Sterne's novel—unless, he suggests, his own novel came first, which would mean that Sterne had plagiarized Diderot's work! Indeed, Diderot's novel anticipates the work of another Irish classic (though originally written in French): *Waiting for*

Godot. (Unless, of course, Godot came first, which would mean that Diderot had copied Samuel Beckett.)

Jacques the Fatalist is a busier and bawdier Beckett. Like Gogo and Didi, Jacques and his nameless master are traveling companions who are making haste slowly toward an uncertain destination. Shackled to one another by the invisible chains of habit and familiarity, both pairs, when not sparring with one another, speculate about matters great and small. During their perambulations, they encounter odd characters, all the while posing questions to which no answers seem forthcoming. The bantering of these two pairs of friends, though smacking of the Borscht Belt, also burrows into the very bone of the human situation. But don't expect a reassuring diagnosis. When Didi blurts out that he understands nothing, Gogo tells him to use his intelligence. Didi does so, only to confess: "I remain in the dark." This exchange had, in effect, already taken place 200 years earlier between Jacques and his master. As they scratch their heads over the nature of destiny, the master demands to know what it's all about. When Jacques replies that he doesn't know, and the master demands to know why, Jacques answers: "I don't know that either."[6]

Of course, the parallels go only so far (though they certainly go farther than either Didi and Gogo, and Jacques and his master, go in their respective journeys). Whereas Beckett observes the fourth wall of theater—the imaginary barrier between the actors and audience—Diderot barges right through it and puts his arm through ours. There we are, his dear readers, walking along with him on the rims of the many *mises en abyme,* or stories within stories, that erupt over the course of the novel. Time and again the storyteller breaks off the telling of Jacques's loves, either by squeezing sudden and chance encounters *into* his narrative, or by squabbling with his reader *outside* the narrative. As the narrator warns, in this brilliant philosophical exploration parading as a shaggy dog story, he can do what he wishes with us. Having left Jacques and his master dozing off under a tree, he whispers: "So you can see, Reader, that I'm well away and it's entirely within my power to make you wait a year, or two, or even three years for the story of Jacques's loves, by separating him from his master and exposing each of them to whatever perils I liked." Having revealed so-called realism as anything but real, and instead as a literary mug's game for gullible readers, the narrator then shows us mercy: "But I will let the two of them off with a bad night's sleep, and you off with this delay."[7]

But the narrator's act of mercy risks being little more than a reprieve he can as easily revoke as retain. On a whim, he threatens to break off the story. When the innkeeper's wife has mesmerized Jacques, his master, and you, dear reader, with the riveting story of Madame de la Pommeraye, the narrator boorishly crashes the party: "Well now, Reader! What is there to stop me from starting a violent quarrel between these three characters, from having the innkeeper's wife taken by the shoulders and thrown out of the room by Jacques, from having Jacques taken by the shoulders and thrown out by his master, from sending one off in one direction and the other in a different direction so that you wouldn't hear either the innkeeper's wife's story or the rest of the story of Jacques's love life? But don't worry, I will do no such thing."[8] Caring not a whit about his slipshod craftsmanship, he offers two different versions to Jacques and his master's response to the story, and shrugs us off: "Tomorrow or the day after, when you have had time to consider more fully, you may decide whichever of these two versions suits you best."[9] Dogged by his relentless reader, who demands clear answers to reasonable questions, the narrator pushes back, complaining to us that we always have questions, but never gratitude. "If you are not grateful to me for what I am telling you, be very grateful for what I am not telling you."[10] When the reader again interrupts him, wishing to know the when and why to a particular tale, the narrator cannot contain himself: "Reader, your curiosity is extremely annoying. What the devil does it have to do with you?"[11]

Depending on your understanding of the rights and duties of a writer, it has everything, or nothing, to do with you as a reader. Or, more to the point, as Diderot's "reader," who is our make-believe stand-in: an advocate

I never met and I never consulted with, but who nevertheless represents my expectations as a reader of realist fiction. Most of us expect a narrative logic to drive the story, which should be peopled by recognizable characters acting on clearly defined motives. In short, we expect lives in realist fiction to be anything but real lives. Fiction, especially its realist variation, gives us what life cannot: sense and structure, coherence and clarity, beginnings and endings. Henry James neatly captured the paradox: "Really, universally, relations stop nowhere, and the exquisite problem of the artist is eternally but to draw, by a geometry of his own, the circle within which they shall happily appear to do so."[12] This is what the realism of Samuel Richardson gave his most besotted reader, Denis Diderot: fictional characters so endowed with autonomy and specificity, so embedded in events following a recognizable logic, that they seemed as real to Diderot as he did to himself.

By the time he left on his meandering route to Russia, however, Diderot was less smitten by the intense form of illusionism we call realism. It amounts to the way we never were, are, or will be, drawing a curtain over what really happens when we tell someone a story. (Take this very moment. The events that have punctuated today's bout of writing—waking my daughter, learning she had cramps and a headache, and giving her the day off from school so I could write in peace—have been written *out* of the words you now see before you.) Diderot was already on to this. In his aptly named short story "This Is Not a Story," he begins by way of introduction: "When one tells a story, there has to be someone to listen; and if the story runs to any length, it is rare for the storyteller not to be sometimes interrupted by his listener."[13] By way of illustrating this point, he then parachutes us into the gap where one story has just ended, and a second is about to begin, leaving us to gather up our chute and orient ourselves.

The standard historical model of the novel, perhaps the most distinctive genre in Western literature, privileges the realist tradition. In a sense, realism came to define the novel. In his groundbreaking work *The Rise of the Novel,* Ian Watt recognized that the novel raises more sharply than any other genre "the problem of the correspondence between the literary work and the reality which it imitates."[14] But, he continued, language in the novels of Richardson and Fielding, Balzac and Zola, is strictly referential, and not a source of interest in its own right. But Watt ignored the fact that language happened to be a great source of interest for Laurence Sterne as well as for Diderot. Ten years before he found himself on the road to Saint Petersburg, Diderot had met Sterne in Paris. The two men hit it off and Sterne, once back in England, sent his new friend the first six books of *The Life and Opinions of Tristram Shandy.* The novel electrified Diderot, who baptized Sterne the "English Rabelais" and revised his attachment to Richardson's novels. In essence, he found himself at a fork in the literary road. One path, paved by Fielding and Richardson, led toward the tradition of literary realism; the other path, blazed by Sterne, tunneled below the first path, finally bursting through the cracks in the guise of modernism.

Not surprisingly, Diderot wanted to keep his Clarissa and savor his Shandy too. On the one hand, prizing the emotional experience offered by Richardson's approach, he insisted upon the moral lessons contained within the realist frame. But he was increasingly fascinated by the very art of framing our stories and what happens when the writer takes the frame—and story within—and pushes his head through it. When we tell a story—or when we write about how others tell stories, as I have been doing today—the narrative seems seamless but in reality resembles Frankenstein's monster, scored and scarred by stitching and sewing. In *Jacques the Fatalist,* Diderot tells a story about the telling of the story—about the stitching and sewing required to give you, dear reader, the illusion that no such labor was required. As the narrator harrumphs, "I admit that it is not enough for a thing simply to be true, it must be amusing as well."[15] Turning down countless opportunities to introduce all sorts of coincidences, the narrator explains that while novelists would never miss such a chance, he refuses to stoop to such devices. "I disdain all these expedients.

I can see that with only a little bit of imagination and style, nothing is easier to rattle off than a novel. But let us stick to the truth."[16]

Of course, few things are less easy to rattle off than a novel, at least a good novel. But it is even more difficult to rattle off a rattling good novel that is not a novel, especially one as indifferent to reaching an end as its two travelers are to reaching their destination. (Like their creator, the travelers much prefer to talk about traveling from the comfort of an inn rather than face the discomforts of traveling from one inn to the next.) The reader not only interrupts the narrator but also often corrects his mistakes, reminding him that he could not have been at scenes as he claims to have been. Even his own characters, as they clamber over the ruins of the fourth wall, interrupt the narrator. When he, yet again, digresses in order to relate a particularly grim account of justice gone astray, the master pipes up: "That's horrifying."[17] Horrifying to be sure, though perhaps not nearly as much as were you, dear reader, to suddenly take control of my keyboard and offer your two cents about the story.

"Writing, when properly managed," Sterne wrote, "is but another name for conversation." Diderot could not have agreed more, but unlike the Irish minister-cum-novelist, Diderot used the novel's conversations as philosophizing by other means. With the works of Helvétius and Hemsterhuis fresh in his thoughts, Diderot decided to revisit the paradox of determinism. "Decided" is an odd choice of words, of course, since a deterministic world means that the past is not just prologue to the present, but in a fundamental sense *is* the present. What has already been, utterly "decides" what will be. While man can do as he wills, in Arthur Schopenhauer's clipped formula, man cannot will what he wills. Diderot's preoccupation with determinism spills across the novel's pages, splashing all the characters. Though they are soaking wet, they nevertheless insist they are perfectly dry; though they acknowledge determinism's inescapable logic, they act and speak as if they are exempt from its reach. Time and again, when events take unexpected turns, Jacques quotes the refrain of his former master—a military captain devoted to Spinoza and duels—

that it could not have been otherwise. It is, Jacques observes, "written on the Great Scroll above"—it is what it is because it was what it was.

And yet the novel's characters live their lives in superb defiance of such ironclad laws. To be sure, Jacques spouts his captain's Spinozism and has not just one but many masters. There is not just his former master, apparently killed in a duel but whose body sporadically turns up in a horse-pulled hearse, but also his current master, who often seems as lifeless as the dead master. Most important, there is the mastering presence of the past: the incalculable number of anterior events that have piled up to determine the present moment. Yet Jacques's sense of freedom is as irrepressible as his sense of panache, and it is only after the fact that he couches his acts in philosophical terms. The narrator concludes, "Like you and me he was often inconsistent, and inclined to forget his principles, except, of course, in the moments when his philosophy dominated him and then he would say: 'This had to be because it was written up above.'"[18] By turns courageous and mischievous, proud and practical, he is his own man to the point that he rebels, with hilarious success, against his master when the latter insults him. Everybody knows, Jacques tells his master, "that your orders aren't worth a fig unless they have been ratified by Jacques."[19] Ultimately, when the master reconciles himself to the fact that he will always be Jacques's servant, the two men reconcile with one another.

A similar reconciliation takes places between the narrator and reader—who, like Jacques and his master, are shackled to one another in a mutually irritating but mutually necessary relationship. Without the one, they both understand, the other would not be. As a result, they stumble as best they can toward a middle way. The narrator in *Jacques the Fatalist* boasts that he can do whatever he wishes with his characters, the reader be damned. But he also knows that he, too, will be damned, if only to eternal obscurity, if he follows through on his threat. His writ as writer is not absolute, but limited; if the author spurns the reader's desires, the reader will be in his rights to spurn the writer. He can, in a word, rebel—even if that means nothing more than closing the book and tossing it aside. As the narrator acknowledges, "I must either go without your applause or follow your taste."[20] But he also insists that the two of them can be, well, on the same page, and explodes angrily when the reader treats him like a "wind-up doll." It is no doubt necessary, he explains, "that I follow your wishes, but it is also necessary that I sometimes follow my own."[21] As to whether those wishes are willed, the narrator does not say. For a moment, all he can do is echo the master's irresolute response to Jacques's brief on behalf of determinism: "I believe I want when I want."[22]

What Diderot wanted above all else, as the carriage navigated the archipelago of monarchies large and small that then constituted Germany, was to avoid Prussia. Though Grimm and even Voltaire—remarkably, given his own experience as an orange squeezed dry by Frederick—prodded Diderot to visit Frederick, they also doubted the wisdom of their advice. Half dreading that Diderot would follow his counsel, Grimm begged Count Nesselrode, a friend serving in Frederick's court, to keep a sharp eye on the unpredictable philosophe. "I commend Denis to your charity. If you do not outdo yourself, he is capable of doing everything wrong. . . . Make him do what he ought to do and only what he ought." As frustrated as he was frantic, Grimm added: "Ask him why he has not written me even once."[23]

Neither Grimm's fears nor his hopes were realized. With the perpetually pliant Narishkin at his side, Diderot crossed the Rhine and came to a short rest at Dusseldorf. The four-day stay was long enough to meet with the city's native son, Friedrich Jacobi, in his magnificent summer residence in Pempelfort. However, it was written in the Great Scroll above that the meeting would sputter, as Jacobi was an anti-rationalist who spied the sinister presence of Spinoza behind every enlightenment ideal. Much more taken by the romanticism of Diderot's estranged friend Rousseau, Jacobi was ill at ease with his guest's unpredictable and unorthodox conversation. In his account of the visit, Jacobi's description of the Frenchman's "burning soul" and "audacious and lively mind" rings less as praise than as lament.[24]

Once their carriage left Pempelfort and a palpably relieved Jacobi, it swung far enough to the south to resist the gravitational pull of Berlin. Angered by Diderot's parabolic orbit, Frederick mirthlessly pushed the planetary metaphor in a letter to d'Alembert. "A great encyclopedic phenomenon," noted the Prussian king, "has, in its elliptical path, brushed the borders of our horizon. But the rays of his light have not reached as far as us." When d'Alembert, in a maladroit effort to excuse Diderot's itinerary by emphasizing how much he tried to persuade his friend to stop in Berlin, a dour Frederick replied: "As for the invisible Diderot, I have nothing more to say."[25] In case d'Alembert was not absolutely clear on Frederick's opinion of this "phenomenon," the Prussian king added (apparently with a straight face): "He keeps repeating the same things. What I know is that I cannot bear reading his books [which are] filled with conceit and arrogance that repel my instinct of liberty."[26]

A near-disastrous encounter on the road reminded Diderot of just how powerful Prussia's pull nevertheless was. On a road between the towns of Hamm and Lippstadt, the carriage carrying Diderot and Narishkin approached a second carriage further ahead. As the road was too narrow for the carriages to pass one another, Diderot and Narishkin shouted to the driver to sound his horn. Refusing to give warning, their driver plowed on, barely averting a tumble into the roadside ditch. When a frantic Diderot asked the driver why he didn't warn the other carriage to give way, the man, stunned, asked Diderot if he had not noticed the Prussian officers on the other carriage. "If I had done so, those officers would have made me pay, sooner or later." Even here, Diderot spied the crippling influence of Frederick: "Despotism is nothing other than a long succession of slaves, extending from the lowest of valets to the highest of officials, none of which dares to sound his horn in front of his superior. The horns sound only from top to bottom. While the ruler's horn sounds loud, what can we say about the others?"[27]

In a letter to his wife, Nanette, Diderot neglected to recount this particular episode. Still, he could not help but tell her that along with losing his wig during the journey, he had nearly lost his life from an attack of abdominal colic. The state of German roads hardly helped matters: "Try to imagine," he told his wife, "the state of a man who is suffering from violent stomach pangs and traveling on the worst possible roads. With each bump—and there was a bump, more or less strong, at every moment—it would not have felt any worse if someone had plunged a knife into my stomach."[28] As the novice voyager had discovered, abysmal travel conditions were one of the few constants across the motley collection of small states. Germany had neither a powerful and centralized state, like France's, to oversee its roads, nor the ancient Roman network of roads as did much of western Europe. As a result, traveling was always a dicey exercise, especially outside of winter, when heavy rains transformed the pitted and rutted roads into impassable swaths of mud. Travel inns, Diderot also discovered, rivaled in quality the roads they shouldered. Travelers habitually complained of bills as indecipherable as the food was indigestible, while others echoed a newspaper's warning that "a man may travel many days and not find a bed to lie upon." Indeed, a number of travelers found that they had no choice but to bed down on straw.[29]

Diderot reached Leipzig in early September, a stray straw no doubt clinging to the balding pate no longer hidden under a wig he no longer had. Clearly, the further Diderot plunged into unfamiliar lands, and the longer the relentless jogging and jolting of the carriage, the freer he felt from what remained of his usual philosophical restraint. He had become a Lui unloosed, a narrator unedited. In a conversation with Georg Zollikofer, the city's leading and liberal-minded Protestant minister, Diderot good-naturedly dismissed the existence of hell. A pity, he added, since it really ought to exist "for one class of human beings: bad princes and their teachers."[30] Remarkably, Diderot also waxed about atheism "with the fervor of a visionary," leaving the polite but perplexed Zollikofer to conclude that his celebrated guest's "sensibility and imagination are incontestably greater than his reason."[31] For his part, Karl Lessing, the younger brother of the renowned Enlightenment writer Gotthold Lessing, gave the dish to the equally celebrated Moses Mendelssohn about a public harangue Diderot delivered in Leipzig. With a mix of disbelief and distaste, Lessing recounted that Diderot, standing outside the house of his host and still in his bedclothes, instructed a crowd of merchants and professors on the reasonability of atheism. For good measure, Narishkin, by now utterly under Diderot's spell, was doing the same with a group of students nearby. Lessing concludes: "While one can be both a good philosopher and an atheist, it is the height of stupidity to speak so candidly in a city one doesn't know." He concluded: "May Russia keep this great philosopher!"[32]

Russia, however, had yet to welcome the great philosopher. In fact, even the empress of Russia was uncertain of Diderot's whereabouts. From the moment the philosophe made his theatrical exit from Paris, Catherine had tried to keep tabs on his progress. It was mostly for naught. After Diderot had finally arrived, much to the empress's relief, at The Hague, she was now wondering if he would ever leave the Dutch city. Catherine had her doubts, and not only because of Diderot's unpredictable character. Learning from Golitsyn about his guest's fragile state of health, she confessed: "I worry that his arrival in St Petersburg is still uncertain."[33] Her fears deepened when an ailing Diderot reached Duisburg, a city sandwiched between the Rhine and the Ruhr. "I was expecting Diderot at any moment," she complained to Voltaire in mid-September, "but I've just learned that he has fallen ill in Duisburg."[34]

Grimm knew his man, though. Being a long-suffering recipient of his friend's melodramatic intimations of his mortality, he sighed: "I expect to learn that he is now looking for a burial plot in Duisburg."[35] Perhaps he suspected that Diderot's terminus was the very reason for his repeated claims of faltering health. In the eighteenth century, Russia was far off the beaten tourist path. In the case of the English, only the most adventurous voyagers, keen on pushing beyond the well-established itinerary of the continental Grand Tour, traveled to Russia. When they did, many opted to make the trip by sea, despite its many dangers, rather than face the body-numbing trial of overland travel. For the sixty-year-old Diderot, the rigors of the trip were even greater. What was he thinking when he decided to set out? Nothing is more absurd, he wrote to Nanette, than an old man who acts and thinks like a young man. "An old man's mind should rest in his body, just as his body should rest in an armchair. . . . For everything to stay well, everything must stay at rest."[36]

By the time Diderot reached this realization, he was also reaching the end of his journey. Ironically, it was a journey he could have undertaken, when all was said and done, from the comfort of his study. In a work he wrote shortly before he left, Diderot had pirated a recently published book of Admiral Louis Antoine de Bougainville. While we now remember Bougainville for the flowering shrub named in his honor, the admiral galvanized France in the mid-eighteenth century with his sensational account of his circumnavigation of the globe. Beyond question, his portrayal of Tahiti, which he claimed for France, was the account's high point. In his *Supplement to the Voyage of Bougainville,* Diderot used Bougainville's descriptions as the raw material for his own imagination. In essence, he reinvented Bougainville's own invention of Tahiti, mixing the voyager's observations—already shaped by Western views of "primitive" societies—with his own observations. As with the *Persian Letters,* in which Montesquieu created a certain idea of Persia in order to critique French politics and customs, Diderot did the same with his Tahiti. A world free of priests and kings, sexual prohibitions, and material deprivation, Diderot's Tahiti did not reflect the actual island society nearly as much as it mirrored all the flaws and failings of French society.

Just as Europeans needed exotic Pacific islands to better understand themselves—and better misunderstand the ostensible subject of their reflections—so too did they need eastern Europe. Then as now, cartography was narrative by other means, one that blends fact and fiction, science and sensibility. This was especially the case with what the historian Albert Lortholary has called the "Russian mirage," the mostly fictitious creation that fastened its grip on the French imagination in the eighteenth century.[37] Indeed, it might well be that Russia is the greatest of all Enlightenment fictions. From the vantage point of Paris, pre-Petrine Russia was a bare and barbaric world. After Peter, it teetered between civilization and barbarism; with Catherine, it would become fully European. In effect, just as the West created "the Orient," so too did it create "Russia." Just as the Renaissance fashioned the "Middle Ages"—or, better yet, the "Dark Ages"—in order to underscore its cultural and intellectual preeminence, so too did western Europeans invent eastern Europe—which included the western reaches of Russia—as a means of emphasizing its own superiority. As the scholar Larry Wolff argues, Russia was "subjected to the same process of discovery, alignment, condescension, and intellectual mastery, was located and identified by the same formulas: between Europe and Asia, between civilization and barbarism."[38] In short, eastern Europe formed the shadowlands between light and dark, reason and superstition, hope and fear. It measured the gradation, in the words of the eighteenth-century American explorer John Ledyard, "between Civilization and Incivilization."[39]

No Enlightenment thinker was a more articulate or more audacious participant in the activity that Ledyard called "Philosophic Geography" than Voltaire. In his biography of Peter the Great, he conjured an image of Russia turned toward the West, if only because its head had been wrenched in that direction by its ruthlessly modernizing tsar. Before Peter, Russia had been a land, Voltaire announced, where "almost everything was still to be done."[40] He thus applauded Peter, who "wanted to introduce his subjects to neither Turkish nor Persian manners, but instead ours." As Voltaire never tired of telling Catherine, she was destined to continue the westward turn begun under her predecessor. "Under Peter the Great," he affirmed, "your academy of arts and sciences looked to us for light. Under Catherine the Great, we now look to your academy for light."[41] Turning from lights to swords, Voltaire styled Catherine's military campaigns against the Turks—as well as her machinations against the Poles, which led to their nation's dismemberment by Russia, Prussia, and Austria—as carrying the gospel of the Enlightenment into the benighted lands of Eastern Europe. "Due to your destiny and genius," he assured Catherine, "I humbly expect the sorting out of the chaos into which the world has plunged . . . and that light will overtake darkness."[42]

Voltaire's portrayal of Russia largely cut the prism through which French travelers saw Russia. This particular brand of cartography, which merged much imagination and little information, found a home in the *Encyclopédie.* In his entry on Russia, Louis Jaucourt notes that the vast country not only lay a nearly unfathomable "2,000 leagues from France," but itself, no less monstrously, spanned nearly that same length from its western to eastern border. Russia was so vast, Jaucourt marveled, that it spilled across two continents and encompassed an empire "as much in Europe as in Asia." It was as if the stark division between "European" and "Asiatic" elements transformed Russia and the rest of "eastern Europe" into a kind of cultural tidal basin, awash in the brackish waters formed by the influences from either direction. Prior to Peter's reign, "the usages, clothing and manners in Russia always had more of a resemblance to Asia than to Christian Europe." Yet, the planting of European practices remained so fragile that "some interval of barbarism might be able to ruin this beautiful edifice."

Just as in her *Nakaz,* where Catherine hauled Russia wholly and firmly into Europe, Jaucourt now tugged the map back toward the east. At the same time, he replaced the firmly drawn boundary between Europe and Asia with the equivalent of a dotted line. Jaucourt's hand at mapmaking, accomplished without ever leaving Paris, was hardly novel. It reflected the volatile and shifting shape of eastern Europe, and Russia in particular, in the minds of travelers and thinkers from western Europe. Not surprisingly, when Count Louis-Philippe de Ségur left for Saint Petersburg in the early 1780s to assume his new position as French envoy, it was as if

Voltaire and Jaucourt had arranged the landscape that jogged outside his carriage's window. Gazing upon the great expanses of land, Ségur could not help but think of Peter's "triumph over nature" and how he had imposed "the fecund warmth of civilization upon this eternal ice."[43] By the time he reached Saint Petersburg, the Frenchman's reflex of seeing this polar world in dramatic polarities had petrified. He was astonished to find united in the city "the age of barbarism and that of civilization, the tenth and the eighteenth centuries, the manners of Asia and those of Europe."[44]

Like his fellow philosophes, Diderot could not help but see Russia through the same prism. Along the final stretch of road to Saint Petersburg, however, Diderot could not see beyond the next inn. Both he and Narishkin were the worse for wear, and Diderot's efforts to keep up his companion's spirits with even bawdier ballads, like "The Servant Girl at the Cloven Foot Inn," could not compensate for their trek's sheer dreariness and seeming endlessness. As they approached the Narva River, Diderot was again felled by an attack of colic. Utterly drained, Diderot wondered if he should have Narishkin push on to Saint Petersburg and leave him behind, no doubt to expire alone in an inn. But, reassuring Nanette, he resigned himself to finishing the journey. *Hélas,* what choice did he have? If he stayed behind, he would have given his young companion the dilemma of either pulling into Saint Petersburg without the man he was supposed to accompany, or angering the tsarina by delaying yet again their long-anticipated arrival. But their trials were not at an end: Narishkin also soon fell seriously ill. The Russian aristocrat was brought so low, Diderot worried, that he either would need to "leave him dead in the hedge or bring him back to his country an imbecile."[45] Instead, he cheered Narishkin by dashing off another piece of doggerel. Playfully disputing Narishkin's attempts at stoicism—"It is better to suffer in silence," he announced, "or end it all"—Diderot instead declares, in the poem's last line: "I will instead scream bloody hell, and continue to live!"[46]

On a snow-swept afternoon on October 8, nearly fifty days after leaving Holland, Diderot and Narishkin's carriage lurched into Saint Petersburg. While Diderot was "more dead than alive," alive he nevertheless was, as he reported to Nanette.[47] Whether he was screaming bloody hell, he did not say.

The Hermitage

THE POINT IS NOT TO BORE HER MAJESTY.

—DIDEROT TO FALCONET

"Here's how our century passes by! We condemn, we judge, we mock and speak with spite of everyone and everything. But what we don't see is that we ourselves are deserving of laughter and condemnation. When our biases displace common sense, then our own vices are hidden from us, and only the mistakes of another are visible. In the eye of a neighbor, we can see a speck of sawdust, but in our own eye we don't see the plank."[1]

So concludes the climactic speech in the Russian comedy *O These Times!,* staged by Saint Petersburg's Imperial Theater in April 1772. Spoken by Mavra, a sharp-eyed and sharper-tongued servant, the words target the play's three aristocratic women, whose moral callousness is rivaled only by their intellectual shallowness. Mavra's comments underscore the great distance between the religious piety of her superiors and the casual cruelty they show to their serfs. By having a maid measure the work yet to be done by the Enlightenment, the anonymous author invites her audience to face uncomfortable truths about themselves.

"O these times, indeed," the playwright might well have sighed—times so extraordinary that empresses expressed themselves through comedies. It was a poorly kept secret that Catherine had penned not just *O These Times!* but three other plays in 1772 alone. Yet more extraordinary is that Catherine found both the time and the temper to write a comedy that gently poked fun not just at the aristocracy but at herself as well.

Most extraordinary of all, Catherine had few reasons to laugh, or make others laugh, during the five years that had passed between the closing of the Legislative Commission and opening of the play. When she told Voltaire that, of all the heads of state, she was the easiest to make laugh—"I am basically a very cheerful person"—Catherine was truthful.[2] Foreign observers frequently remarked on her keen sense of humor, especially among her closest friends and associates. Yet her jolliness was tested during this period. Her first military campaign, launched against the Ottoman Empire in 1767, had lasted longer than anticipated. When it finally lurched to an end in 1774, Catherine, despite her grand expectations, contented herself with claiming the Crimea and victory. Perhaps more disappointed was Voltaire, whose wistful hope was for Catherine to "exterminate [his] Turkish enemies" so that he could be carried into Constantinople on a litter.[3]

Events at home, however, were even more troubling. In the spring of 1771, plague arrived with the rains that transformed the streets of Moscow into sludge. Fatefully, the disease's source—whose nature was never fully diagnosed—may well have been cloth goods imported to Russia from Ottoman territories. No doubt worried that the news would damage her country's reputation as fully European, Catherine waited until October to tell Voltaire. By the time she wrote, as many as 800 Muscovites, covered with purple blotches, were dying every day. Not only did the epidemic strain the powers of the city's rickety administration, but it also shattered the city's veneer of civility. In her letter to Voltaire, Catherine recounted the fate of the city's archbishop, Father Ambrosius. Terrified by the relentless advance of the disease, growing numbers of Muscovites flocked to a well-known icon of the Virgin Mary, gathering in great numbers at the base in the hope of salvation. Worried that the icon had become a vector of the disease, Ambrosius ordered its removal. An enraged crowd, finding the icon gone, surged to the monastery where Ambrosius had taken shelter and ripped him limb from limb. Only the arrival of soldiers, who killed more than a hundred rioters, finally imposed order.

Catherine had few illusions concerning reason's reach in her adopted country. Yet she was stricken by the violent death of Ambrosius, a cleric she had herself appointed and who had acted on behalf of his people's best interests. "Clearly, our famous 18th century has so much to be proud of!" she wrote in despair to Voltaire: "How wise we've become!"[4] She was also increasingly terrified by the disease's canniness—retreating and advancing without warning, all the while eluding a clear diagnosis. Unprecedented quarantine measures were introduced in Saint Petersburg, and Catherine dispatched Grigory Orlov to Moscow in order to take command. With his usual courage and competence, he tightened the quarantine measures, giving vast powers to a newly formed plague commission that he chaired. By year's end the combination of these new prophylactic measures and the bitterly cold winter succeeded in breaking the plague's hold on the city.

But Catherine had little respite; in June, at the very moment the plague was building in Moscow, her son Paul fell ill to influenza at the Peterhof Palace just outside Saint Petersburg. As the limp seventeen-year-old hovered between life and death, Catherine confronted not just the mortality of her son but that of her reign as well. Russian and foreign observers had long commented on how little time Catherine spent with Paul, and her seeming lack of emotional attachment. What the mother did not lack, though, was a clear understanding of her son's role in her public life. Her legitimacy flowed through her son; were he to die, so would her hold on power.

As a result, whatever her maternal cares may have been, Catherine's practical cares mounted as Paul struggled against fever and diarrhea for nearly two weeks. In a palace that had become a hospital ward, Catherine devoted herself to nursing her son back to life. By the end of July she had won the battle: Paul had recovered sufficiently to walk around his bedroom. When she wrote to a friend that "on the subject of the grand duke we have had a severe alarm," Catherine was no doubt referring to more than her son's health.[5] The scare also served as a reminder that the sooner her son was married, the better for the future of her reign.

By mid-1772 another kind of quarantine, this time aimed at Grigory Orlov himself, had come to preoccupy her. Unfailingly faithful to the man who had brought her to power a decade earlier, Catherine learned that Orlov had begun an affair with a cousin much younger than the now forty-three-year-old empress. The news shattered the empress, who later confessed that Orlov's "betrayal cruelly tormented me and forced me from desperation to make a choice at random."[6] In this case, the "random choice" was Alexander Vasilchikov, a handsome though bland officer in the royal guard who had caught Catherine's eye. With typical decisiveness, she promoted Vasilchikov to Adjutant General, the very same post held by Orlov, and he soon assumed his place in Catherine's bed as well. At the same time, Catherine forbade Orlov, who had been handling peace negotiations with the Turks in Moldavia, to reenter Saint Petersburg. When the enraged Orlov failed to break through the quarantine, he informed Catherine he would abide by her decision, but at a steep price. Still deeply attached to Orlov, and deeply aware that she could not afford to alienate him, Catherine quickly agreed to the terms of the "divorce": a kingly pension, choice real estate in Saint Petersburg, and 10,000 serfs. In a letter of striking candor and warmth, she told Orlov that he was and would always be essential to her well-being: "I shall never forget how much I am obligated to all your clan and those qualities with which you are adorned and how much they can be useful to the fatherland." All she wished, Catherine concluded, was "mutual tranquility."[7]

Orlov accepted her terms and remained faithful as Catherine's subject, if not as her favorite, but tranquility remained elusive. While Vasilchikov cut a dashing figure, he paled in comparison to Orlov's canny, if uncultured, intelligence and humor. He could offer Catherine neither the great ardor nor good advice that Orlov did, and she felt the loss deeply for more than a year after the breakup. The poor man was alive to the deadness of Catherine's feelings toward him, complaining that she treated him "as nothing more than a sweet little thing *(cocotte).*"[8] Clearly, sweet little things could not begin to fill the gaping abscess left by Orlov's forced exile. As Catherine later confessed, "I have never cried so much since the day I was born as I have over the last eighteen months."[9]

As the Great Scroll would have it, at this same moment a much-awaited carriage carrying Diderot arrived in Saint Petersburg. His initial welcome, unhappily, failed to make him feel any more alive. Before leaving Paris, he had arranged to stay at the house of his friend, the sculptor Etienne-Maurice Falconet. Along with his assistant (and companion) Marie-Anne Collot, Falconet had gone to Saint Petersburg in 1766 in order to undertake, thanks to Diderot's enthusiastic recommendation, Catherine's commission for a monumental equestrian statue of Peter the Great. When he wasn't cheering on Falconet as he labored over his commission—"Work, my friend, work with all your force! Above all, give us a beautiful horse!"—Diderot was busy imagining their happy reunion in Russia. In fact, he scripted and staged the moment they would again see one another: "What a day! What a moment that will be, for both of us, when I knock at your door, enter the house, throw myself into your arms and we begin to cry out confusedly. 'It's you.' 'Yes, it's me.' 'Well, you finally made it.' 'Yes, I did.' Yes, we'll babble! And pity the person who, seeing again a friend after a long absence, can speak clearly and not babble."[10]

When Diderot arrived at Falconet's residence on the Millionaya, the aptly named street across from the Winter Palace, the only element from his imagined tableau was the babble. But it was babble bred of embarrassment. The weary traveler had barely stepped into the house when Falconet informed him that his son had unexpectedly arrived in Saint Petersburg. Indeed, Pierre-Etienne Falconet, who had been studying with Sir Joshua Reynolds in London, had in fact showed up without warning at his father's door. What he didn't tell the uncomprehending Diderot was that Pierre-Étienne had arrived nearly two months earlier. In a letter to Catherine, in which he announced that it was "raining Falconets," the less than pleased father allowed his son to take the bed he had prepared for his friend Diderot.[11] Oddly, though, he neither sought to find different lodgings for Diderot, nor seemed especially regretful over the turn of events. Stricken by his friend's news and seeming coldness, "the philosopher's heart," later wrote his daughter Angélique, "was forever wounded."[12]

Diderot did not have the time to tend to his wound. What was he to do, where was he to go? How could he, in his weakened condition, think of putting up at a hostel? Was this, then, to be the climax of his epic trek across the continent? "There I was," he reminded Nanette, "sick and a stranger in a city where I didn't understand a word."[13] At that moment, he suddenly thought of Narishkin. Penning a desperate note to his traveling companion, Diderot had his reply within the hour: a carriage pulled up in front of Falconet's door to carry the homeless philosopher back to the Narishkin palace, a snowball's throw from the Winter Palace and sharing the same wide square dominated by the Cathedral of Saint Isaac.

At his host's firm insistence, Diderot would remain there for the entirety of his stay. Tellingly, though, he almost immediately began to dream about his return to France. It would be a roundabout return, he mischievously tells Nanette. Continuing east to the Great Wall of China, he announces, he would push across Asia and the Ottoman Empire, pass through Constantinople and sail to Carthage. Once back in France, he would stop at several cities, lay over in Langres and, only then, come home. "But you will tell that it's hardly worth so much effort to find one's resting place; and you would be right. You will also tell me that I must return as quickly as possible by the shortest route; and you would be right. And so, that is what I will do, and we will have, after the torments of our long separation, the quiet joy of being together again."[14]

Just as the great distance now separating him from Nanette cast a golden haze over the realities of domestic life, the close proximity to Catherine began to clear away the comforting illusions Diderot had held about the Russian empress. He certainly had time to dwell on the matter, since a week passed between arriving in Saint Petersburg and meeting his host. Yet another bout of colic, which he blamed on the waters of the Neva, forced Diderot to spend several days in his bedchamber. The delay suited Catherine, who was attending to a crucial matter of state: Paul's wedding to Princess Wilhelmina of Hesse-Darmstadt, a marriage Catherine arranged following her son's recovery from his bout of influenza. Orchestrating the many festivities then unfolding in the city, Catherine had little time to think about her newly arrived guest.

As for the guest, barely strong enough to lift himself from bed, he had nothing but time to think about his still-unseen host. More precisely, Diderot had time to think about his proper relationship to Catherine. This was an unusual, if not unprecedented, situation for a philosopher. It was even more unusual in Diderot's case. He was, after all, someone who, when not being kept in prison by his own government, was kept at arm's length by *salonnières* because he was as careless in editing his conversation as he was his writings. But Diderot knew that Catherine already knew all of this, just as she knew—or so he assumed—that he had not made this cross-continent trip simply to express his gratitude for the gifts she had showered on him.

As soon as Catherine had bought his library, Diderot understood that she had also bought, if not him, at least his nonrefundable ticket to Saint Petersburg. That he would have to go one day was clear; less clear was how he should act once there. "How can Denis *le philosophe,*" he wondered, "deserve to be called a collaborator of Catherine's? How might he also work for the happiness of the people?" There was little modesty in these repeated self-interrogations, and why should there be? "I'm high-minded and, on occasion, come across great and powerful ideas that I convey in a striking fashion. I know how to captivate, move and touch the minds of others." Granted, d'Alembert is better at differential equations, Diderot allows, but his erstwhile colleague cannot match his gift in "elevating and inspiring the love of virtue and truth." But therein lies the rub! How could such a man survive at the imperial court? "I always wear my heart on my sleeve! I am incapable of lying, incapable of hiding my affection and distaste, and incapable of avoiding traps that others might lay for me!"[15]

Instead, he had explained to Nanette, his mission was to show Catherine, a ruler who could do so much good, her proper image. "Don't scold me for this trip," he pleads: "I had a duty to do."[16] But how would he reconcile this particular duty toward an empress with the philosopher's general duty to seek and tell the truth? In his *Pages contre un tyran,* Diderot did not hesitate to lecture Frederick: "To whom should a philosopher address himself frankly, if not to a sovereign?"[17] But even though Diderot had been able to give Berlin wide berth, he could not escape the gravitational pull of Saint Petersburg. Having resisted for so many years, he finally resigned himself to address his thoughts to Catherine; now, he had to find the means to gently couch his candor.

One rule was never to pretend that he knew better than the empress. This was the fatal mistake committed by his fellow philosophe, Lemercier de La Rivière, whom Diderot had the misfortune to recommend to Catherine in 1768, declaring that if the empress had the hankering for truth, then La Rivière was her man. So much her man, Diderot emphasized, that La Rivière is "our consolation for the loss of Montesquieu."[18] Catherine, however, decided she had been sold a false bill of lading. Though La Rivière met the empress just once, that was clearly more than enough for Catherine. The "beautiful soul" and "brilliant mind" that Diderot saw in La Rivière were quite lost on Catherine. While a solid economist—Adam Smith thought highly of La Rivière's work—the

Frenchman was a bumptious diplomat who had clearly come to Russia to lecture, not learn. During his shorter-than-anticipated stay in Saint Petersburg, La Rivière's imperious character so annoyed the empress that she dismissed him as "Solon-La Rivière."[19]

Diderot thus sought the role not of Solon, but of Socrates. Not only had others cast him in this role—Grimm liked to call his friend "our century's Socrates," while Voltaire dubbed him "Diderot-Socrates"—but Diderot believed himself to be suited to it.[20] He spied the same philosophical lineage in his dedication to virtue and love of dialogue, as well as in the same fates nearly shared by the modern Parisian and the ancient Athenian. In a letter to the royal censor Malesherbes, in which he lamented the relentless attacks on the *Encyclopédie,* Diderot compared his own imprisonment to Socrates's death: "For ten years, for thirty, I have drunk bitterness from an overflowing cup."[21] The Socratic reference is clear; among the occupations Diderot pursued to while away the time in Vincennes was a translation of Plato's *Apology of Socrates.*

Who can say whether Diderot saw Catherine as Alcibiades, the Athenian leader who had been one of Socrates's students and, depending on one's view, either spectacularly realized or rubbished the master's teachings. Diderot did see himself, though, in the Socratic role of gadfly, as a bringer of questions as much as truths. But crucially, he knew he was a gadfly that could be swatted away by the flick of an imperial wrist. In his preliminary notes for his sessions with Catherine, Diderot seems determined to remind himself as much as his imperial host that he is not La Rivière. The economist, he agreed, was someone who "rather ridiculously gave himself too much importance." Do not think, Diderot announces, that I will be the sort who, having just arrived and my bags still unpacked, declares: "Madame, stop what you are doing. Nothing good can be done until you hear me out. I alone know how to administer an empire."[22]

This led Diderot to embrace a second rule: gratitude always means saying you're sorry—sorry for unavoidable missteps and misunderstandings, sorry for the inevitable impression of not appearing grateful enough.

Far from being another La Rivière, Diderot exclaims, he is himself "nothing, really nothing at all." Everything he now has—"well-being, peace and security"—he owes to Catherine. Indeed, if he is anything at all, he is like a child whom Catherine will "permit to say all the stuff and nonsense passing through his head."[23] In another memo, he instead portrays himself as "Denis le philosophe"—a dreamer, one who "takes the liberty of addressing his daydreams to Her Imperial Highness." Yes, these reveries might well contain information, even insights on occasion. More important, though, is the light Diderot wants to throw on the utterly different worlds the two interlocutors inhabit. Their conversations, he proposes, will reveal "all that separates the thoughts that occupy the mind of a ruler and the ideas of a poor devil holding forth from his garret." Nothing is easier, Diderot admits, "than to run an empire while one's head rests on a pillow."[24]

Rarely has such a commonplace been given such uncommon force as, a week after his arrival, Denis *le philosophe* was well enough to raise, not just his head, but also the rest of his body in order to meet Catherine at a masked ball in the Winter Palace.

Fortunately, Melchior Grimm had preceded the Frenchman's arrival by a few weeks, more than eager to play an enlightened John the Baptist to the greatly anticipated coming of philosophy made flesh in the person of Diderot. While the immediate reason for Grimm's presence was the decisive role he played in the negotiations over the marriage contract between the Grand Duke Paul and Princess Wilhelmina, he had already made Catherine's acquaintance through his role as editor of the *Correspondance littéraire.* Ironically, the relationship that formed between Catherine and Grimm when they finally did meet in Saint Petersburg eventually eclipsed the one between the empress and Diderot.

Grimm's early years no more foretold such a future than did Catherine's own youth. Born the son of a Lutheran minister in Regensburg in 1723 and raised in Leipzig, Grimm seamlessly shed his provincial background, maternal language, and paternal religion upon moving to Paris in 1748. Having come as tutor to a German aristocratic family, Grimm stayed put in Paris after his young charge returned home. A prim and diminutive figure, his sharp-angled face softened with face powder, Grimm embraced the principles of the Enlightenment with enthusiasm but not excess. (His excesses were mostly found in his use of face powder, a weakness that earned him the moniker "The White Tyrant.") He proved more influential in Paris than his aristocratic patrons, thanks to his artful patter, spoken in flawless and unaccented French. (Years later Goethe rued that Germans learning French were all doomed to fail—with one exception, a certain "Herr von Grimm."[25])

Rousseau, who had first befriended Grimm, introduced him to Diderot—ironically, given that a few years later Rousseau would fall out in spectacular fashion with both of them. To Rousseau's annoyance, Diderot and Grimm fell madly in *amitié,* if not *amour,* becoming fast friends and collaborators. Diderot commissioned Grimm to write for the *Encyclopédie;* more importantly, Grimm brought Diderot on board at the *Correspondance littéraire.* In fact, when Grimm took over the journal from the Abbé Raynal 1754, he turned to Diderot for advice. Inevitably, the seasoned editor's advice morphed into a full-blown collaboration; though he was already overstretched by the *Encyclopédie,* Diderot began writing articles and reviews for the journal as well. Grimm was ecstatic; in the pages of the journal, the White Tyrant made clear who was the master. Addressing Diderot, he declared: "You are my friend and my master. You show me what I think, and you confirm me in thinking it."[26]

In 1764, having learned that Catherine had offered to subsidize the embattled *Encyclopédie,* Grimm thought the empress might be an easy touch for the *Correspondance littéraire.* "Since you have heaped favors on one of the most celebrated philosophes of France, all who cultivate literature and think, wherever in Europe they live, have regarded themselves as your subjects. . . . It is therefore with the most entire confidence that I present my homage at your feet." But while lathering Catherine with compliments, Grimm also keeps an eye on the journal's bottom line. With one of history's more florid provisos found in fine print, he adds: "If your exacting duties as sovereign permit you to satisfy the passion which all the great spirits have shown for literature throughout the ages, if you deign to cast a favorable glance at these sheets, you will bear in mind that the regular appearance of a periodical cannot always be guaranteed."[27] Grimm, who left the subscription rate to the discretion of his small, but powerful readership, was overjoyed when Catherine replied that she would pay 1,500 rubles a year in order to join the happy few.

From Catherine's perspective, the rubles were well spent. Under Grimm's guidance, the *Correspondance littéraire* brought Paris to the capitals and courts of European rulers. But it was a particular kind of Paris—namely, a philosophic Paris. As Grimm reminded his readers—including Catherine—in 1767: "Today everything is philosophe, philosophic, and philosophy in France."[28] In the *Correspondance littéraire,* Grimm announced his *parti pris:* "I believe in the communion of the faithful, that is, in the gathering of that elite of excellent minds, elevated souls, delicate and sensitive, dispersed here and there on the surface of the globe, nonetheless recognizing one another and understanding one another from one end of the universe to the other, and I believe in the unity of enlightened minds and of people of taste."[29]

Dedication to matters of good taste, however, was not quite the same as dedication to matters of good (and virtuous) philosophy. Moreover, Grimm was more aware than his friend Diderot that his particular elite was responsible to those above them. In 1767 he reported on the discourse that Antoine Léonard Thomas, a member of this self-appointed elite, gave at the Academie française: "Those who govern men cannot at the same time enlighten them. Busy with action, they are always on the move, and their souls do not have the time to reflect. A class of men has thus been established whose role is to use their minds in peace, and whose duty is to activate those minds for the public good."[30]

Yet Grimm grasped that such peace came only at the forbearance of rulers. As a literary correspondent, he understood that his subscribers were not to be trifled with. For his friend the Abbé Morellet, Grimm had become a "man who, for money, is hired to amuse a foreign prince every week—to whom he belongs."[31] Like Voltaire and d'Alembert, and decidedly unlike Diderot, Grimm was a fan of enlightened despotism. His ardent attachment to the person and station of ruler was a wedge that eventually separated him from the philosophe.

Yet Diderot did his best to ignore the advanced signs of Grimm's fatal weakness for kings and queens. Though critical of Grimm's efforts to ingratiate himself with Frederick the Great—to little avail, as Frederick declined to subscribe to the *Correspondance littéraire*—Diderot understood his friend's reasons for doing so. Yet, by the time he decided to visit Catherine, Diderot must have begun to wonder about Grimm's transformation into a cagey and cosmopolitan consigliere, a savvy and surefooted adviser on diplomatic and dynastic matters to the continent's aristocracy. He had, as Mme d'Épinay said of him, the "unique gift of inspiring confidences while giving none."[32] His friend Baron d'Holbach was more severe, telling Grimm: "You never say anything, and you never believe anything."[33] Yet it was these same traits that helped Grimm arrange the marriage between Grand Duke Paul and Princess Wilhelmina. Like an artist accompanying his finished work to his patron, Grimm's final task was to escort the princess from her home to Saint Petersburg. The superb results of his mission—the series of wedding celebrations in Saint Petersburg—were already in full swing when Diderot arrived.

When he made his decision to go to Saint Petersburg, Diderot did so knowing that his German friend would also be there. And yet, just as Falconet wounded Diderot, so too did Grimm; just as the frustrated artist failed to run to the philosophe with open arms, so too did the flourishing diplomat. Taken up by new responsibilities and new ambitions, Grimm did not immediately pass by Narishkin's to see "Socrates." As for "Socrates," he saw no reason to order a goblet of hemlock. He glossed over the slight, insisting that it was a "sweet pleasure" to see Grimm when he finally called. In the same breath, though, Diderot admitted that he rarely tasted the sweetness of this pleasure. "I almost never see Grimm; he's become a satellite of a planet he is obliged to orbit."[34] Indeed, Grimm increasingly sought to be the sole satellite circling the imperial sun—so much so that, in a letter to Mme Geoffrin, he complained that he had to share the solar system with Diderot. At Catherine's behest, the Imperial Academy of Sciences held a ceremony at which both men were made members. The empress, Grimm muttered, had played him a "bad turn": "It is the one time I'll be obliged to see my name alongside Diderot's. When I complain about this to Her Majesty, she either disagrees or mocks me."[35]

Grimm certainly had ample opportunity to complain: the afternoon hours that Diderot spent in Catherine's company were sandwiched between long tête-à-têtes between Grimm and the empress. More tellingly, while Diderot was never invited to join the small dinners at the Hermitage, Grimm soon became a fixture at the gathering (though as etiquette required even in this relaxed setting, the commoner was fixed at the other end of the table from the empress). Diderot would not have been surprised by this sudden complicity between Her Imperial Majesty and his old friend: not only did Grimm and Catherine share the same native language (though they mostly used French), but they also shared the same worldview. Grimm was not a world unto himself like Diderot, but instead a man of the world whose motto might well be "Make change, but slowly." Slowly enough, to be sure, to savor the unexpected pleasures of life in Catherine's circle: "It is unprecedented," Grimm blurted to Mme Geoffrin, "that a man of my station should have been treated by the sovereign of one of the most powerful empires with the kindness that I have experienced."[36]

In Catherine's memoirs, life under the Empress Elizabeth had at times seemed little more than an interminable series of court intrigues and masked balls. Often enough the balls were little more than intrigues and conspiracies by other means. Varying in size from 150 to 200 guests, these events littered the fall and winter seasons in Saint Petersburg. Especially intriguing was what Catherine called the "Metamorphosis" ball, when Elizabeth obliged her court to wear the clothing of the opposite sex, though without masks. The male courtiers dreaded this particular ball, Catherine noted, "because they felt that they were hideous in their costumes." As for the women, "most of them resembled stunted little boys, and the eldest had fat, short legs that hardly flattered them."[37]

Most, but not all: one exception was Elizabeth, who, Catherine noted, had "more beautiful legs than I have ever seen on any man and admirably proportioned feet." And though she doesn't say so, Catherine herself was the other exception. In her account, she remains on the sidelines, slyly commenting on the carnivalesque event, but not participating in it. In this world turned upside down, Catherine and Elizabeth alone are left standing right-side up. However, it is at another masquerade, given at the Winter Palace in 1750, that Catherine triumphed by hardly masquerading at all. Noting that Elizabeth frowned on overdressing, Catherine wore a simple white outfit, with a single rose placed in her hair. Her appearance riveted the entire court, leading Elizabeth to exclaim: "Good God, what modesty. What, not even a beauty spot!"[38]

"They said that I was very beautiful and particularly radiant," Catherine recalled. But, she added, this was not quite the case. "To tell the truth, I have never believed myself to be extremely beautiful, but I knew how to please and I think that this was my forte." To know how to please, of course, is to know how to act; when knowing how to act is one's forte as a teenager, it becomes one's second nature in adulthood. Empress of all Russia, Minerva of the North, Giver of the Laws, Cleopatra of the Dniester, and Scourge of the Turks: these are but a few of the many roles that Catherine had come to play with consummate skill. As early as 1764, the envoy George Macartney, who later led Great Britain's first diplomatic mission to China, marveled over Catherine's ability to perform her imperial role: "It is inconceivable with what address she mingles the ease of behavior with the dignity of her rank, with what facility she familiarizes herself with the meanest of her subjects, without losing a point of her authority and with what astonishing magic she inspires at once both respect and affection."[39]

Just as it was the practice of the imperial court to have a screen behind which the empress could listen in on interviews between her officials, Catherine in effect created a screen of words and gestures behind which she observed her audience. No doubt Catherine was touched in meeting the elderly man for whom she had done so much, but at the same time she was fully cognizant of her audiences. It may well be that her awareness of these situations was sharpened by reading Adam Smith. Leaning on the Russian translation of *The Wealth of Nations* by the Scottish-trained law professor S. E. Desnitsky, Catherine had incorporated certain elements from the book into the *Nakaz.*[40] But Desnitsky had also translated the earlier *A Theory of Moral Sentiments,* in which Smith describes how individuals, by naturally adjusting their expressions and words, become unnatural—and for good reason. Were we not to "tune" up or down our reactions to the world, the world would shun us; were we unable to properly display our sympathy, it would be for naught.

No one should have been more alive to these elements of public performance than Diderot himself. One of the works he wrote in 1773, perhaps during his time in Saint Petersburg, was *The Paradox of the Actor.* Inevitably, he cast the piece as a dialogue, one launched by the provocative claim that great actors must show much intelligence and great indifference to their characters. In order to persuasively exhibit a range of feelings, Diderot argues, an actor must be unfeeling. It would spell disaster if it were otherwise. "If the actor were driven by emotions, how could he play the same part twice in a row with the same spirit and success? Unable to contain himself at the first performance, he would be exhausted and cold as marble by the third."[41] Should the actor confuse pretending and being, channeling her character and acting out her character, the result would be disastrous.

For this reason, Diderot argues for the superiority of artifice over authenticity—or, better yet, for the need of artifice to give lasting expression to authenticity. Just as Vernet, at ease in his studio, recreates nature's passions on a canvas, an actor, at ease in his role, recreates human passions on a stage. Because an authentic emotion can, by definition, occur just once, Diderot asks what needs to be done in order to repeat it. Ideally, should you come upon a woman on a street corner, destitute and in tears, you would be disturbed and moved to respond. But the ideal rarely occurs in everyday life. Instead, in real life, stuff happens: a bucket of slop heaved out a window, an unexpected visitor at the door, or a child demanding attention. Indeed, you might have arrived a minute too soon, a minute too late to catch the woman crying. And so, if actors—on stage or a street corner—are to grip our heart, they must learn how to reenact those same emotions. It is not that actors no longer feel; instead, their emotions about the particular scene differ from those of the audience. In this respect, actors seek to defeat time and overcome chance; if they are good at what they do, they can repeat the same gesture time and time again, each time sparking an authentic response from the spectator.

Hovering over Diderot as he wrote his dialogue was David Garrick. In 1763, Diderot met the celebrated actor and director in Paris; a decade later he still carried a vivid memory of the encounter. In a private performance, Garrick claimed he could convincingly portray, strictly through facial expressions and wordless gestures, any series of emotions he should choose. Challenged to do so, Garrick grabbed a chair cushion and announced that it was his child. In Diderot's account, the actor proceeded to caress, cuddle, and kiss it—"all the tomfooleries of a father playing with his child." But suddenly the cushion slipped from Garrick's embrace and fell out the window. Garrick's face contorted in utter despair and the spectators, Diderot marveled, "were seized with such consternation and horror that most could not bear it and had to leave the room."[42]

In the dialogue, however, Diderot recalls a different tour de force by Garrick. His head jutting out between folding doors at a Parisian salon, the actor's face registered an astonishing series of emotions in just a few seconds: "From great joy to calm pleasure to simply tranquility, from surprise to shock to sorrow, from dejection and fear to horror and despair. Then he made his way back to the beginning. Is it possible for his soul to experience and express, in concert with his face, all of these emotions?"[43] For Diderot, there is no doubt over the answer: rather than sounding the depths of his soul, Garrick instead harnessed the powers of observation. "A great actor studies the world and uses the man of deep feelings as a model. Upon meditation and reflection, the actor then decides what he must add or remove in order to improve upon this model."[44]

The matter of acting fascinated Diderot, and not only because he was an avid playgoer and aspiring playwright. He grasped, as did Smith, that society was a stage. Echoing the Scot's remarks about the dangers run by those who, overcome by emotion, flout the spectator's expectations, Diderot warns that there "are a thousand circumstances" where the spontaneous expression of feelings "is as harmful in society as in a theater." By the same token, countless situations require that we exhibit emotions we do not feel deeply or at all. Hence the need to emulate—to *act* upon—commonly accepted rules of expression. "Do not people in society refer to a man as a great actor? By this, they do not mean that he feels, but that he shines in simulating these emotions, though he feels nothing."[45]

Who was the actor, then, and who was the audience when Diderot and Catherine finally met at the palace masquerade? When Diderot, stooping slightly and hesitant, was led to Catherine, who was surrounded by a knot of courtiers, the contrast could not have been more jarring. Not only had he crowned himself with a borrowed and ill-fitting wig—replacing the one he had lost in Germany—but he had also donned his philosopher's mantle: a plain black suit. Standing in the midst of more than a hundred brilliantly masked and garbed guests, Diderot's drab appearance sparked expressions of wonder and shock. "Everyone judges him on this [sartorial] singularity alone," observed L. H. Nicolay, an adviser to Grand Duke

Paul. For Nicolay, the Russian aristocracy's reaction to Diderot's appearance underscored "how terribly hard it is to maintain a great reputation, and how dangerous it is to leave one's study for a brilliant court."[46]

Yet Diderot was more aware of this "singularity" than Nicolay. Despite his nearly comic appearance and gestures, the philosophe was anything but naive. Shortly before he had left Paris, he sent a note to Madame Geoffrin, thanking her for the gift of a new dressing gown. Touched by her gesture, Diderot was also saddened. "Cursed be the miscreant," he exclaims in mock outrage, "who invented the art of rarifying a piece of ordinary cloth by simply dyeing it scarlet!" The new gown, he moans, is not only stiff and rigid, but conveys a public image at odds with its wearer's self image. While he now looks like a "mannequin," the old one's streaks of ink and layers of dust "showed me to be an author and honest laborer. But now I look lazy and rich, and nobody can tell who I am."[47]

No doubt as Diderot wished, everyone that night at the Winter Palace could tell who he was—or, rather, who he wished to be *seen* as. His "philosopher's coat" stood out as starkly among the masked Russian aristocrats as did Saint Petersburg's palaces among the military barracks and workers' hovels. It was the sartorial equivalent of Diderot's short story "This Is Not a Story," which both adopted and undermined the foundations of fictional realism. In short, it was a costume that was not a costume.

Catherine, perhaps, was alive to this particular masquerade and determined to play an equal role. Superbly indifferent to her guest's appearance, she asked him to sit down and recount his trip. Though they conversed for nearly an hour, Diderot later swore he was so "agitated and flustered" that he could not remember a single word he said. Whatever Diderot did say, though, "pleased her greatly"—so much so, he reported, that he could tell from Catherine's responses that she was "deeply affected." While we cannot plumb the depths of Catherine's feelings, she was no doubt moved. Standing in front of her, after all, was the man upon whom she had showered so much attention and money, and to whom she had issued so many indirect, yet increasingly insistent invitations. Have him come to Saint Petersburg, she instructed his friends, if only to show his gratitude. Voltaire was too old, d'Alembert too rude, and Diderot was the last great philosophe standing. And now, here he was: What greater claim to the applause of the Republic of Letters? Or, for that matter, what greater promise was there for conversation as entertaining as it was enlightened? As Catherine gazed on her visitor, his wig registering his frantic arm gestures while his words cascaded above the heads of a mesmerized audience, she admired the role she played in the spectacle as much as she did the role played by Diderot.

As she brought their conversation to an end, Catherine pointed to the door that led to her private apartments: "Monsieur Diderot, do you see that door? It will be open to you every day from three to five."[48]

How should we imagine this moment? Is Catherine gesturing with her hand, or perhaps with her mask, toward the door? Is Diderot's gaze following her gesture, or instead fixed on his benefactress? Are they sitting across from one another or side by side? Does the blackness of Diderot's coat, standing out against the glittering attire of the other guests, mark him as a figure to be pitied or admired? Indeed, what are the expressions of those in the audience? Are some of them smiling, while others frowning? Are there, in fact, some whose attention is focused elsewhere, on a lover or a competitor, and indifferent to the extraordinary event unfolding in their presence?

We do not know what was said—or, for that matter, *how* it was said—during this first conversation between the philosophe and the empress. Catherine did not commit a detailed recollection to paper, whereas Diderot gushed about Catherine but offered precious little detail in his rare letters to Paris. And yet, while we cannot re-create what took place, we can perhaps re-create what Diderot *believed* should have taken place. In his *Discours sur la poésie dramatique,* Diderot confides he often thinks in spatial terms, the way a painter would, when he is writing a dramatic scene. "One way of making up my mind," he explains, "is to gather the objects together in my imagination, to transfer them from nature to canvas, and to examine them at a distance where they are neither too close nor too far away."[49]

But distances are not just spatial; they are also moral. Any great work of art, be it on paper or canvas, begins not with a brushstroke but with a conceptual stroke. By arranging his characters—penciling in his mind a series of variations—Diderot was taking the measure of their relationships not just to one another but also to the moral lesson he sought to convey. "These people think that all one needs to do is to arrange the figures; they do not know that the first point, the important point, is to find a great idea; one must walk up and down, meditate, put down one's brushes and rest, until the great idea is discovered."[50]

The greatness of an idea, to Diderot's mind, was measured by its moral cogency. Indeed, as an art critic, Diderot was fascinated by the relationship between aesthetics and ethics. More precisely, Diderot believed that without the latter, the former was worthless. For this reason, few artists frustrated him more than François Boucher. When the great Rococo artist died in 1770, shortly before Diderot left for Russia, he had become the most successful artist of his age. Despite Boucher's great productivity, the demand for his bucolic idylls and fulsome nudes always outstripped the supply. All of this annoyed Diderot to no end. While he agreed that the Rococo master was unrivaled as a draftsman, he raged that this was precisely the problem. Boucher's palette of colors left Diderot dazzled, but the painter's palette of moral convictions left him deadened. The lush colors and voluptuous women were all fine and good, but only as wallpaper for an insular and artificial world. "Such colors! Such variety! Such wealth of objects and ideas! Boucher offers us everything, except truth."[51] A painting should be not just true to the nature of our world, Diderot believed, but true to the nature of those who inhabit it.

How different from the paintings of Jean-Baptiste Greuze, whom Diderot quickly took to calling "my man." Greuze's rendering of a sick man reclining in a chair and surrounded by his family, titled "The Paralytic" and displayed at the 1763 Salon, riveted Diderot's attention. He was particularly drawn to paintings, like Greuze's, that inspired him to tell the story, as well as the lesson, he believed they contained. From his very first Salon review in 1759, Diderot described the paintings in meticulous detail, but also shared his emotional responses to them. Works by his preferred artists encouraged him to weave stories about the figures portrayed, providing not just a commentary but also a narrative illuminated by moral concerns. Diderot had no qualms about his ethical preoccupation. In the chatty manner that defined his art criticism, Diderot shares his thoughts with the reader as he reflects on Greuze's canvas: "This kind of genre pleases me: it is moral art. High time, too! Hasn't the painter's brush been devoted long enough to debauchery and vice?"[52]

The moral ideals so dear to Diderot imbue the complexion, facial expressions, and body gestures of the gathered family members. It's as if Greuze, through his brushstrokes, allows us to hear voices—how the old man "can hardly speak with a voice so weak"—and relive the emotions of others: Upon seeing "how grateful he is for the help he's offered . . . the tenderness of his gazes and pallor of his skin, one needs to be heartless not to be moved."[53] If you had been with me at the Salon, Diderot tells Greuze, you'd have heard a young girl exclaim: "My God, how this old man moves me! If I look at him again, I fear I'll start to cry." Indeed, Diderot adds triumphantly, that young girl was my daughter! "When I gaze on this old man, so eloquent and sympathetic, I feel my soul is seized like my daughter's, with tears ready to fall from my eyes."[54]

Might not something similar have been the case, to Diderot's painterly eye, when he looked back on his tête-à-tête with Catherine? On one side, a stooping man, clad in a simple black coat, his face lined by his advanced age and adventuresome trek, approaching the empress. And on the other side, the empress, extending one hand to be kissed, while gesturing with the other to a seat next to her? The gathered masqueraders, meanwhile, having dropped their masks, their faces reflecting the anticipation and admiration they felt for this long-awaited moment? Could not have Diderot's man transformed this very moment in the Winter Palace into a similarly affecting tableau?

During his stay as Catherine's guest, Diderot certainly had good reason to ask himself this question: after all, Greuze's old man, still reclining and still declining, happened to be hanging in the Hermitage. In 1766, the same year Catherine bought his library, Diderot joined forces with Prince Golitsyn to serve as the empress's art agents in Paris. The purchase of Greuze's masterpiece was among their first in a series of coups orchestrated by Diderot and Golitsyn that astonished and eventually angered French art collectors. Along with helping the empress acquire Rembrandt's "Return of the Prodigal Son" that same year, then Bartolomé Murillo's "Rest on the Flight from Egypt"— a canvas upon seeing which, Falconet blurted out, you could only fall to your knees—Diderot outmaneuvered a gaggle of other buyers to secure the acquisition of the Thiers collection. Diderot's capture of this horde of 500 paintings, bristling with canvases by Rembrandt, Van Dyck, and Rubens, outraged French collectors. "The public truly hates me," he reported. "Art lovers, artists and the wealthy are all crying out."[55]

In a sense, Diderot's arrival at the Hermitage was a kind of homecoming. While it was not the house Diderot built, it was very much the house he decorated. More so than any other imperial agent, Diderot's sharp eye and business savvy shaped Catherine's binge buying of paintings and sculptures. His patroness more or less gave him carte blanche, both literally and figuratively. Catherine was willing to spend whatever it took in order to bring great art to Russia, just as she was glad to allow Diderot to define the precise greatness of that art. For the empress, the growing pile of masterpieces at the Hermitage was little more than imperial politics by other means. Nevertheless, certain works touched her deeply. In particular, she was drawn to Jean Huber's series of intimate paintings of Voltaire engaged in everyday activities at his estate of Ferney.

By Catherine's own account, she "burst out laughing" when she saw Huber's portrayal of Voltaire rising from bed, getting dressed, and dictating a letter all at the same time. To see the lord of Ferney furiously multitasking reminded her that "the vivacity of his character and the impatience of his imagination give him no time to do one thing at once."[56]

It's not certain if Diderot saw Huber's paintings at the Hermitage—though it is certain he never saw, despite Malcolm Bradbury's claim to the contrary, Jean-Antoine Houdon's famous statue of Voltaire. Commissioned by Catherine, the statue arrived in Saint Petersburg in 1781, seven years after Diderot departed. (And the statue nearly departed a few years later, when Catherine's son, the reactionary and short-lived Tsar Paul I, pointed to the marble Voltaire and commanded: "Get rid of this monkey." Happily, his staff ignored the order, hiding the statue instead.) Bradbury wrote a historical novel, of course, and not a monograph. Yet the scene when his Diderot spies the statue at the Hermitage and believes, if only for a moment, that he is facing the real Voltaire—"Is it possible his own journey has drawn the clever octogenarian fox out of his rich Swiss lair?"—rings with truth as well as laughter.[57]

But it is a particular kind of truth—one akin to *vraisemblance*—that Diderot has in mind. Unlike the historian, Diderot argues, the poet "requires that there should prevail throughout the texture of his work a clear and perceptible connection." Diderot believes that whereas the historian must remain true to the past's inability to offer ready-made truths, not so the fiction writer. In the latter's work, "there is less truth but more verisimilitude . . . than in the historian's."[58] In turn, the plausibility of a crucial scene, one skillfully shaped by the artist, can offer a moral truth that the chaotic cascade of actual events simply cannot. Rather than burdening the artist, the absence of historical documentation frees him to recreate an event that is both plausible and laudable. Diderot acknowledges that historians have informed us of some of what Henri IV said and did. But is that really enough? What about those countless, possible circumstances in which the good king "would have acted and suffered in conformity with his character, and in a more extraordinary way, which history does *not* offer us?"[59]

If the poet happens to be named Denis Diderot, he might well have us imagine the philosophe and empress sitting side by side that night, tasked with different duties, yet equal in importance and equally admired by the knots of guests to either side of them. Indeed, Diderot's sense of importance must have swelled when Catherine told him the doors to her private chambers would be open to him every day. Even this inveterate dreamer expected, or so he later insisted, that he would be accorded no more than a handful of meetings. After the official presentation, he thought a month would pass before a second visit, during which Catherine would ask him a few questions. There would then be, a month later, a third meeting, at which he'd say his farewells.[60]

That this was not the case embittered relations between Diderot and Falconet, whom Diderot had, more or less, packed off to Catherine along with the troves of paintings he had purchased on her behalf. In 1764 Catherine had decided to act upon Elizabeth's plan, still unrealized at her death, to raise a statue as monumental as its subject—her father, Peter the Great. Her decision was not just an act of piety to the memory of Elizabeth, but also an act of political symbolism aimed at her court and subjects. By commissioning such a statue, Catherine would reinforce her claim to a throne to which she had not even the most distant of dynastic claims.

There was yet another upside to the decision: it would reinforce Catherine's effort to haul Russia onto the European, and more particularly the French, stage. Paris was a sculptor's showcase, with the celebrated works of Jean-Baptiste Pigalle, Jean-Baptiste Lemoyne, and their many disciples scattered across the city's streets and squares. When Ivan Betsky, appointed by Catherine as director of the Academy of Fine Arts, announced a competition to choose a sculptor for the statue, all the contestants were French. All the bids were well over 400,000 livres, except for one: Falconet's. His entry won, but his request was so low—200,000 livres, paid out over eight years—that Catherine made it known she was prepared to pay an additional 100,000 livres.[61] Falconet's refusal to accept the upwardly revised offer—he insisted it was too high a price—should have warned the empress that she had just signed with an artist as pigheaded as he was principled.

Catherine was swayed less by Falconet's bargain basement bid than by his close ties to Diderot, who thought highly of the young artist's skill as a thinker as well as a sculptor. The very idea of statues had, of course, long obsessed the editor of the *Encyclopédie,* and he had commissioned the young artist to write the entry on sculpture. More important, the two men had launched an impassioned debate, carried out in letters, over the very raison d'être of the artist. Does he, as Diderot argued, make art in order to achieve immortality? It is the "respect for posterity that touches the heart and raises the spirit and is at the root of great accomplishments."[62] Or, as Falconet countered, should posterity be damned and the artist's only concern instead be the estimation of his contemporaries? "Fear of scorn, shame and humiliation," he told a disconcerted Diderot, is "all the incentive I need."[63]

By the time Diderot knocked at Falconet's door in Saint Petersburg, the sculptor had tasted from all three bitter dishes. But his prickly character—Diderot warned him that he was "quick to feel slights, easy to insult and always have sarcasm and irony ready at hand"—had helped in their preparation.[64] When Falconet had first arrived—with his young assistant (and lover) Marie-Anne Collot—in Saint Petersburg in October 1766, Catherine showered him with attention. Falconet soon saw that, for Catherine, he was far more than the artist hired for a particular commission. He personified the very club, the Republic of Letters, to which she wanted to belong. Within a matter of days, the subject matter of their conversations had become wide-ranging, and the tone relaxed and familiar. The following February, when Catherine left for Moscow to prepare for the Legislative Commission, she and Falconet remained in touch through letters that were striking for their easygoing and bantering language. Indeed, Catherine had more or less commanded Falconet to be informal: "Don't stand on ceremony, don't bother with formalities and, most important, don't multiply the titles which leave me indifferent."[65] When the Frenchman pursued flattery by other means, asking Catherine to read the letters he was sending to Diderot, she slapped him down: "For the last time, I neither want nor need to see your letters. But as you've asked me to correct this one, please forgo the praise you shower upon me which I don't deserve."[66]

At first, Catherine sought Falconet's advice on matters ranging from policy to philosophy. At the same time, she refused to impose her own idea of how the statue should look, telling Falconet that he must not "mind what I am saying, because I can be quite wrong. Hold fast to your opinions."[67] Considered little more than an artisan by the French court, Falconet was dizzied by the freedom and respect offered by the empress. Gobsmacked by Catherine's "constant attention," the fifty-year-old sculptor felt reborn in the icy reaches of the north: "If I had come to Saint Petersburg without a soul, this majestic miracle maker [Catherine] would have created one especially for me."[68] As for Catherine, she was clearly satisfied with her new Parisian import. Announcing Falconet's safe arrival to Mme Geoffrin, she reassured the *salonnière* that she was happy with her latest acquisition. Describing Falconet as "unique," Catherine concluded that while there might be artists of equal talent, "none, I dare say, is his match in intellect."[69]

But Catherine also soon became convinced that no artist was Falconet's match when it came to high self-regard (and correspondingly low regard for those who didn't agree with his high opinion of himself). For all the scorn he expressed for posterity's seal of immortality, the Frenchman clearly craved the applause and admiration of his contemporaries. Convinced that those who did not make art had no right to rate the works of those who did—a position that made Diderot bristle—Falconet repeatedly clashed with General Betsky. When the two men first met, Betsky grandly announced: “Well, my good sir, let us talk about our statue.” In reply, Falconet asked: “*Our* statue? Excuse me, but don’t you mean *my* statue?”[70] From then, their relationship went steadily south. The courtier, who treated Falconet as a hired hand, was furious when the Frenchman rejected his repeated efforts to influence the making of the statue. During one of Betsky’s visits to the atelier, Falconet slapped down the official’s advice: “Are you a smith, Sir, for that is what I need now. . . . Everybody must stick to his profession, and no one should be robbed of what is his.”[71]

By 1773 Catherine’s early enthusiasm over Falconet had been dampened by his bitter stream of complaints aimed at Betsky, as well as by his overbearing sense of destiny that she herself had encouraged. Rumors even began to make the rounds that visitors to Falconet’s atelier, offering criticism of the model of the statue, would be pounced upon by the sculptor, who had been hiding behind the curtains.[72] Their correspondence, so fast and furious the first three years, became a trickle that dealt mostly with business matters. Falconet must have also sensed that, for Catherine, he served as little more than an opening act for the long-awaited arrival of *Denis le philosophe.* After all, was Falconet not, as Catherine told Mme Geoffrin, “a kindred spirit to our friend Diderot”?[73]

While recovering at Narishkin’s from the intestinal distress caused by the waters of the Neva, and the emotional distress caused by the ingratitude of the sculptor, Diderot no doubt dwelled not just on his own state, but that of his friend as well. Was it not possible that Falconet’s harsh welcome had more to do with growing doubts over the worth of his sculpture and the judgment that Diderot would deliver? This was the very same man who had proposed Falconet’s name to Betsky and Catherine, who exhorted Falconet ever since he hit the road for Russia to live up to his expectations, and who tirelessly inquired about the statue’s progress: “And so, my friend: How far have you gotten along? Has the horse begun to breathe? And what about the Tsar? It’s as if I see him. Look how commanding he is! See how the obstacles retreat before him!”[74]

Yet Falconet's obstacles only seemed to multiply. Harassed by Betsky and his minions, humiliated by the city's elite, who stared impassively at the statue of Peter, humbled by an empress who had once treated him as an equal, Falconet might have had second thoughts about the upsides to posterity. His fears and doubts over the value of his work reached critical mass when—later than expected, but somehow still too suddenly—his patron and pen pal, the age's most influential art critic, who was expecting to see a bronze tsar and horse worthy of his imagination, appeared in his doorway. If such thoughts had, in fact, skittered across Diderot's mind, they help explain why, less than a week after Falconet had turned him away, he returned to the atelier. He told himself that his friend's cold shoulder was not aimed at him, but instead was the symptom of a suffering and self-doubting artist, alone for too long in a land too far away.

Wearing his habitual frock and woolen bonnet, Falconet was perhaps surprised by the visit. Yet he was undoubtedly also relieved: after six years of unremitting labor on this monumental project, Diderot would tell him if he had gotten it right. Leading his friend into the atelier, Falconet stood to one side while Diderot, stooped but steady, slowly circled the massive clay model of the horse and its rider. The former, modeled after Catherine's favorite steed, Brilliant, is rearing on its hind legs—a revolutionary rupture with the ancient equestrian statue of Marcus Aurelius, whose horse is stately and earthbound. With his vast torso draped in a simple Russian cloak, Peter rises above his mount, his right arm slightly bent and reaching toward the horizon. How much time passed as Diderot studied the realization of the model he had long dreamed about? Did he ply Falconet with questions as he examined this "centaur-like" creature the sculptor had wrought?

Neither man tells us, but once Diderot began to speak, his words falling over one another, Falconet's chest expanded to near-Petrine dimensions. "You sensed my anxiety when I first stepped into your atelier. But now that I have seen what you have done, I will never again speak about sculpture if you have not made a truly sublime monument."[75] These were the first words Diderot blurted—as he reminds Falconet in a letter that Falconet had himself asked Diderot to write. Who better than the man who had supplanted him in Catherine's favor to reassure her that, despite the countless obstacles thrown his way by court sycophants and mediocrities, Falconet had created "the most beautiful work of this kind in all of Europe"?[76] It now remained for Diderot to sculpt a very different kind of work than Falconet's, but one no less beautiful and lasting.

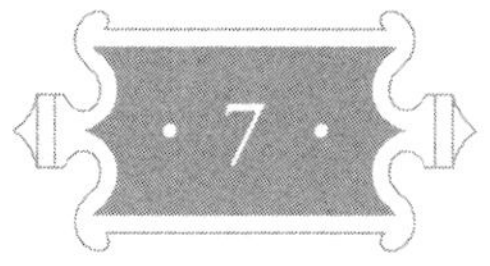

Extraordinary Men and Events

I AM PERMITTED TO SAY ANYTHING THAT GOES THROUGH MY HEAD. SANE THINGS . . . WHEN I FEEL CRAZY, AND CRAZY ONES . . . WHEN I FEEL SANE.

—DIDEROT TO PRINCESS DASHKOVA

In Saint Petersburg there was a time and place for masquerade balls, but there were also times and places to drop masks—if only by Catherine's command. Inscribed by the door leading into the Hermitage was a set of rules, written in Cyrillic, which managed to be both imperious and impish.

1. Leave all ranks outside, likewise hats, and particularly swords.
2. Orders of precedence and haughtiness, or anything however similar, must be left at the door.

3. Be merry, but neither damage nor break anything, nor gnaw on anything.
4. Be seated, stand, walk as you see fit, regardless of others.
5. Speak with moderation and not too loudly, that those present not have an earache or headache.
6. Argue without anger or passion.
7. Do not sigh or yawn, and do not bore or fatigue anyone.
8. Others should join in any innocent fun that someone thinks up.
9. Eat well, but drink with moderation, that each can always find his legs upon going out the door.
10. Disputes shall not be taken outside the isba [peasant hut], and what goes in one ear should go out the other before one steps through the doors.

Appended to this tongue-in-cheek Decalogue were the penalties that would be leveled at those who violated any of these rules:

> Whoever infringes the above, on the evidence of two witnesses, for any crime each guilty party must drink a glass of cold water, ladies not excepted, and read a page of the Tilemakhida out loud.[1]
>
> Whoever infringes three articles in one evening is sentenced to learn six lines from the Tilemakhida by heart.
>
> And whoever infringes the tenth article will no longer be admitted.

The dinners held in the Hermitage were both more unbridled and more unpublicized than Paris salons. Whereas the latter were overseen by *salonnières* who policed the conversations—with high points then shared through correspondence (and reported on by Grimm's *Correspondance littéraire*)—the conversations in the Hermitage had neither the same limits nor audience. Yet, rather remarkably, Catherine's relatively easygoing attitude toward free expression was not limited to the Hermitage's inner sanctum. In the *Nakaz,* Catherine questioned the near-universal practice among her fellow sovereigns of censoring free expression. She wondered how treason could issue from "words and punished as the very action itself," and warned against the "danger of debasing the human mind by restraint and oppression." Such a practice, Catherine concluded, would result in "nothing but ignorance and must cramp and depress the rising efforts of genius, and destroy the very will to write."

One practical consequence of Catherine's attitude, at least during the early years of her reign, was the absence of an official government censor. While a relaxed eye was kept on foreign books imported to Russia, the nascent literary scenes in Saint Petersburg and Moscow were largely unsupervised. On rare occasions Catherine ordered the suppression of certain foreign works, most notably the writings of Jean-Jacques Rousseau. Yet even here she was selective, forbidding translations of *The Social Contract,* but allowing a Russian edition of the revolutionary *Discourse on the Origin and Foundations of Inequality.*[2]

The state under Catherine not only ended its monopoly on publishing—anyone could now purchase a printing press, though it had to be registered with the local police—but it also began to subsidize journals that criticized social practices and manners. In *The Painter,* launched a year before Diderot's arrival, sharp satires of Russian aristocrats jostled with scarcely veiled attacks on the practice of serfdom. Not surprisingly, *The Painter*'s editor, N. I. Novikov, never criticized Catherine. More surprisingly, perhaps, the empress helped with the journal's shaky finances, quietly sending Novikov a few hundred rubles on at least one occasion.[3] It was with this paradoxical pattern of imperial patronage that, at least until the French Revolution, the Russian state maintained a more liberal attitude toward free speech than most other European nations.

When Diderot first met Catherine in the midst of the masked guests at the Winter Palace, he could not know that a very different masquerade, known as the Pugachevschina was unfolding 1,350 miles to the south. The guests at this particular event were Yaik Cossacks, one of the several Cossack communities that fished, hunted, traded, and periodically battled one another or the tsarist state, which was making slow but determined inroads into the steppes north of the Black and Caspian Seas. The Yaiks arrived at these events in their customary crimson dress and cascading moustaches, but their host, Emelyan Pugachev, had assumed a stunning disguise: displaying scars on his chest, which he asserted were the "marks of tsardom," Pugachev presented himself as Peter III. The reemerged "imperator" who was, in fact, a Don Cossack and Russian Army deserter, explained that he had escaped his treacherous captors in 1762 before they could kill him, and had since roamed the country to better understand his subjects. Pugachev's masquerade proved inspired: within weeks of his announcement, a popular storm gathered in the Urals that would reach and rock the foundations of Catherine's rule, even though the region was farther from Saint Petersburg than was Paris.

Astonishingly, Peter impersonators had long been a fashion. In the decade separating Peter's fall and Pugachev's rise, several other impostors posing as Peter had suddenly appeared, and just as suddenly disappeared, from the political scene. Driving this parade of charlatans were the worsening conditions of the enslaved peasantry, desperate enough to believe anyone who offered a solution to their plight. The serfs were the principal victims of the seemingly interminable war against the Ottoman Empire, in which every costly victory was followed by an equally costly defeat. More than 300,000 peasants were conscripted into the army, many of whom were so unhealthy that they died even before encountering combat. As for those who escaped conscription, they found themselves billeting and feeding troops who frequently pillaged their host villages and raped their wives and daughters.

As the state's war against the Turks ground on inconclusively, all the while grinding into deepening misery the serfs who worked the fields and mines, the Cossacks grew increasingly restless. In the short entry "Les Cosaques," the *Encyclopédie* described them as "warlike, cunning and prone to robbing." Not entirely inaccurate, the entry was nevertheless perfectly inadequate. Perhaps of Tartar origin, the Cossacks first arrived on the windswept steppes along the lower Volga and Don Rivers in the fifteenth century. Skilled horsemen, the various Cossack hosts supplemented their hunting and fishing by attacking trade caravans that plied the ancient routes stretching between Russia and Asia. Over the course of the seventeenth and early eighteenth centuries, Russian rulers sought to impose order on the Cossacks by suppressing their chronic marauding, but also by recruiting them to protect the frontier against nomadic tribes farther to the east. By the time Catherine assumed power, though, the Cossacks had begun to push back against growing interference from Saint Petersburg, especially when forced into military legions and ordered to shave their beards.

As cunning as he was violent, Pugachev quickly grasped the potential in this combustible mix of disgruntled Cossacks and desperate serfs. When he revealed his scrofula-scarred chest at the meeting with a small group of Yaik Cossacks, they no more believed Pugachev was Peter III than Pugachev himself did. But this was not the case for hundreds of other Cossacks, as well as the thousands of rebellious serfs who began to flock to his banner. Pugachev's performance as Peter was effective partly because he approached the role with the same skill and distance as Diderot expected from successful actors. No less important, though, there was a vast audience desperately keen for someone to reprise this role and deliver them from their miserable condition.

In mid-September 1773 Pugachev was on the march. His growing army swept through several towns strung along the Yaik River. Turning their attention to the regional capital of Orenburg, Pugachev's followers laid siege to the garrisoned city. A report of events, sent by Orenburg's governor, took nearly a month to reach Saint Petersburg, leading to a meeting of the Imperial Council on October 15—the very same week that Catherine and Diderot began their conversations. Finding the news worrisome, but not alarming, Catherine ordered a small punitive expedition, commanded by General Vasily Kar, to suppress "this godless turmoil among the people" and capture the "chief brigand, incendiary and impostor."[4] Ironically, Diderot's historical account of the French state, given that same week and through which he meant to underscore the catastrophic consequences of the seemingly irresistible growth of autocratic power, might have instead comforted Catherine's belief that Kar's small force would suffice to impose order.

As it turned out, nothing could have been further from the truth. In mid-November, Kar's force was crushed by the peasant insurgents, now numbering more than 10,000, leaving Kar himself to flee ignominiously to Saint Petersburg to report the news. Only now did Catherine grasp the magnitude of the problem. Ever since the coup that brought her to power, she had lived with the fear of a countercoup from rebels who considered her rule to be illegitimate. As the earlier frauds who masqueraded as Peter had reminded her, all it took was an especially skillful and daring impostor to topple her from power. Her unease was compounded by the knowledge that her liberalism, the raison d'être for the Legislative Commission, had encouraged the serfs to believe that their liberation, or at least the improvement of their lot, was in the offing. In 1768, when the Assembly's silence dashed these hopes, peasant disorders rippled across much of Russia.[5]

In response to the heightened threat, Catherine pored over maps of the distant region. Taking the full measure of the revolt, she sent General Alexander Bibikov, who had previously distinguished himself as the marshal of the Legislative Assembly, to quash the threat. Invested with full powers over military and civil administrations, Bibikov had a vastly more formidable force under his command than did the unfortunate Kar, who had by then been cashiered. Yet men and arms were not enough; there also had to be a text, written for the benefit of Pugachev's followers, defending Catherine's acts. Who better to write such a defense than Catherine herself? Portraying her rule as a force for social good and national greatness, she declared that her attachment to "enlightenment, philanthropy and clemency" had already prepared the soil for a "rich harvest" for all Russians. That a rogue like Pugachev had met success, Catherine added, underscored how greatly his followers, plunged into "profound ignorance" due to their great distance from the capital, required her guiding hand.[6]

No doubt Catherine's misconceived pronouncement, posted throughout the region, proved less effective than Bibikov's troops. In quick succession, the Russian general persuaded local landowners to form volunteer armies, launched inquiries into the treatment of serfs, mobilized the local clergy, and, in early 1774, shattered Pugachev's ragtag army. Though Pugachev managed to escape and raise yet another army, he was himself captured in September 1774, almost one year after he first launched his rebellion. He and his closest companions were carted back to Moscow, where they were questioned and executed. Tellingly, Catherine withstood the widespread desire for revenge against the Cossack rebels. Not only did she order her subordinates to "refrain from all questioning under torture, which always obscures the truth," but she also urged "moderation both in the number and kind of executions" to the judges overseeing the trials.[7] They dealt swiftly with their charge: Pugachev was quartered, a handful of collaborators were hanged, yet others sent into Siberian exile, thus dropping a blood-soaked curtain on the tumultuous run of the Pugachevsina.

The Pugachev uprising had terrified Catherine largely because an impostor had threatened not only to undermine her throne but also to remind both Russian and European opinion of the empress's tenuous legitimacy. But the nature of her response to the rebellion also made for sleepless nights in the Hermitage. What would the good citizens of the Republic of Letters, after all, have to say about the violence of the government's suppression? Pugachev and his crew, she told an official, "will end on the gallows, but what sort of ending is that for me, who has no love for the gallows? European opinion will relegate us to the time of Tsar Ivan the Terrible!"[8]

As Catherine knew, there were few embodiments of "European opinion" more celebrated than her recently arrived guest. The first private conversation between Catherine and Diderot took place the same week that his host had convened the Imperial Council to discuss the Pugachev rebellion. Did Diderot know about events in the distant Urals? While he makes no explicit reference to the rebellion in his memoranda, he later told his friend Jean-Baptiste-Antoine Suard that Catherine confided some lapidary thoughts on these events: "That fool Pugachev will be hanged by the end of three months," she predicted—wrongly, it turned out.[9] Regardless of what he knew and when he knew it, Diderot's choice for his inaugural imperial tête-a-tête was, quite tellingly, on lawlessness. Not that of a ruler's subjects, however, but instead the lawless behavior of rulers themselves. During his journey Diderot had begun to sketch a brief essay on the history of the French state. The idea, he explained to Catherine, was Narishkin's. While they were being jostled on the German roads like two sacks of potatoes, Diderot's traveling companion had suggested that he engage Catherine on "the great advantage enjoyed by a nation whose laws are ordered and obeyed" to one that, to its discredit, "acts on impulse and leaves in its wake foolish, absurd and contradictory institutions."[10]

Thus, at the very moment when the weakness of Russia's civil institutions had helped create the conditions for Pugachev's uprising, Diderot had chosen to lambaste the French monarchy's systematic repression of those same institutions in France. In his percussive account, Diderot portrays the French state as both overreaching and underachieving. Uninterested in standardizing the crazy quilt of regional laws and practices—creating "a code of simple laws which could be grasped by their subjects at a young age"—the Bourbons had instead busied themselves with undermining the limiting powers of the regional parlements. Through the exercise of powers and prerogatives that, over the course of long centuries, they had clawed from the monarchy, these intermediary institutions served as guarantors of certain fundamental freedoms. As long as this separation of powers existed without challenge, Diderot told Catherine, the State and people prospered.

But not for long: "Attacking this arrangement is the first step toward despotism; eliminating it is the final step."[11] With great deliberation and decisiveness, the state under Louis XIV neutered the nation's aristocracy, transforming an ancient and honorable caste dedicated to the nation's well-being into a "rabble of beggars, sycophants and ignoramuses" utterly dependent upon the generosity of the court. At the same time, Versailles's slow-motion seizure of the historical prerogatives of the parlements transmogrified a true monarchy into mere despotism.

More worrisome, though also more elusive, the court's creeping powers threatened not just the reality of liberty, but the very *illusion* of liberty as well. In his presentation to Catherine, Diderot took great pains to emphasize that the people, even if they are not truly free, must at least "believe themselves to be free."[12] Diderot compares this particular illusion to a "vast spider's web" stretched in front of the despot and on which "the people worshipped the image of liberty. Those with the eyes to see had long ago seen through the web's openings and understood what lay behind it. But tyranny has since sundered this web, showing its face for all to see. Even when a people are not free, the belief they have in their freedom is nevertheless precious. It would have been preferable for them to have kept this belief, but now they see and feel their enslavement."[13]

At this moment Diderot showed himself to be as keen a political realist as his host. In his image of the spider's web, Diderot perhaps had in mind the famous observation made by Cardinal de Retz concerning the tumultuous and murderous Fronde, the mid-seventeenth-century aristocratic uprising against the young Louis XIV that ultimately failed: "As they woke, they blindly sought the laws; they could not find them; stricken with panic, they cried out for them; and in all this turmoil the questions they raised . . . became a matter for doubt; and, as a result, for half of those concerned, odious. The people entered the sanctuary: they lifted the veil which must always conceal anything that can be said, anything that can be thought, concerning the rights of peoples and the rights of kings, which are never so much in harmony as when they are shrouded in silence."[14]

Along with Retz, John Locke might also have influenced Diderot on this score. Having written the entry on Locke for the *Encyclopédie,* Diderot knew and admired the Englishman's political writings, including his *Second Treatise on Civil Government.* The treatise, which had inspired Diderot's subversive entry on "Political Authority," may have left a rather tragic imprint on his thought. In a controversial passage, Locke allows that rulers must, at times, violate laws for the greater good of society. Prerogative, he declared, "can be nothing but the people's permitting their rulers to do several things, of their own free choice, where the law was silent, and sometimes too against the direct letter of the law, for the public good."[15]

Though such an allowance no doubt pained Diderot, he clearly found the alternative even more painful. Besides, he was also persuaded by the materialist basis for his position. In a sense, he borrowed from Locke's sensationalism in his claim that the sentiment of liberty—a feeling for what it is, and the capacity to miss it when it is absent—is as important as any theoretical or abstract affirmation of freedom. Without such visceral awareness of human liberty, we are unable to appreciate its loss. As Diderot's materialism insisted, a blind man from birth cannot appreciate a sunset in the same way as can a man blinded later in life. Hence Diderot's earlier claim that when a tyrant's subjects do not respond to their enslavement with violence, "there is no more resilience and the whole system is slackened and degraded." For this reason, Diderot tells Catherine, it is in her interest. no less than in the interest of her subjects, to raise their consciousness of freedom. Even if a legislative assembly amounted to nothing more than a "phantom of liberty," it would nonetheless "leave a positive impression on the popular spirit. A people must either be free—which is best—or at least believe itself to be free, for this belief has valuable effects."[16]

In the midst of his Delphic pronouncement on individual liberty and spider webs, Diderot expostulated: "Oh, unhappy nation! I cannot help but shed tears over your fate!"[17] No doubt he raised both his voice and arms as he made this melodramatic declaration. With this dash of histrionics, Catherine saw for the first time, though scarcely the last, Diderot's love of self-dramatization. At first Catherine seems to have been very much taken by her guest. Indeed, his friend Grimm, who had arrived in Saint Petersburg a few weeks before Diderot, more or less cast himself as his public relations flak. "The Empress is truly enchanted by him," he declared in one letter, while in another he announced the continued success of Diderot's appearances at the Hermitage: "Our Denis enjoys the most complete and brilliant success with the Empress" who continues "to shower him kindness."[18]

Was this success spurred by the contents of Diderot's conversation? This must have been one reason, given Catherine's abiding intellectual curiosity. In the midst of one conversation, when Diderot seemed astonished by her familiarity with so wide a range of subjects, his host replied: "I owe this to the two excellent teachers I had for twenty years: unhappiness and seclusion."[19] Whether Diderot's insights into politics—human nature itself—were altogether new to her, or instead insights she had long ago acquired, but now heard couched in language that was admirably provocative, remains unclear. Much clearer, though, was Catherine's response, veering between admiration and astonishment, to these sessions. With her front row seat—indeed, with the only seat—to Diderot's expositions,

Catherine marveled over the variety and originality of her guest's flights of oratory. "Diderot's imagination, I find, is inexhaustible," she told Voltaire. "I place him among the most extraordinary men who have ever lived."[20] Echoing her wonder, Voltaire lamented that he had "never had the consolation of meeting this unique man, who is the second person in the world with whom I have always wanted to converse."[21] (No need, of course, for Voltaire to remind Catherine who was first on his list.)

"His head is most extraordinary," Catherine had earlier observed about Diderot, "and all men should have the same heart he does."[22] Yet at times Diderot proved too extraordinary. His originality, in both his ideas and his gestures, was so bold as to border on lèse-majesté. Diderot suggested this himself in the midst of one heated discussion. Impatient, Catherine burst out that neither was following what the other was saying: "We are both too hotheaded, and are constantly interrupting one another." Wryly, Diderot replied: "The difference, though, is that when I interrupt Your Highness, I am being foolish." Catherine dismissed Diderot's remark with polished candor: "And would this be foolishness if it was man to man?"[23]

Foolish or not, Diderot could not help but be himself. As Grimm excitedly reported to Mme Necker, their mutual friend behaved with the empress as he did, well, with old friends like Mme Necker. "With her he is just as odd, just as original, just as much Diderot, as when with you. He takes her hand as he takes yours, he shakes her arm as he shakes yours, he sits down by her side as he sits down by yours." But, Grimm added, "In this last point he obeys sovereign orders, and, as you might imagine, a man does not seat himself opposite to her Majesty unless he is so obliged."[24] Catherine soon realized her mistake in allowing Diderot to sit anywhere that was within arm's reach of her. In a letter to Mme Geoffrin, the empress marveled—or perhaps muttered—over the liberties Diderot unwittingly took in her presence. "I cannot get out of my conversations with him without having my thighs bruised black and blue. I have been obliged to put a table between him and me to keep myself and my limbs out of range of his gesticulation."[25] Rumors flew about Diderot taking even greater liberties in Catherine's presence. From Naples, the Abbé Galiani related Diderot's latest excesses to their mutual friend, the philosopher Antoine-Léonard Thomas: "What do you think about our philosophe? One hears frightful things about his behavior in the Empress's presence. It's said that he dared to throw his wig at her and pinch her knee. Our Diderot is unique; his head is the world's storehouse; he knows everything, yet at times seems to know nothing."[26] Catherine herself echoed this sentiment, exclaiming how "at times he seems to be one hundred years old, but at others he doesn't seem to be ten."[27]

Scarcely had his conversations with Catherine begun when Diderot was sharply reminded of his sheer vulnerability, regardless of his perceived maturity, to the whims of individuals far more powerful than he was. When he left France for Russia earlier that year, Diderot's departure was hardly a cause for regret or remorse along the corridors of Versailles. Indeed, a cruel witticism making the rounds claimed that the court, when asked by Diderot if the king had any objection to his trip, replied that not only had he no objection to his going, but that he could stay in Saint Petersburg for all that Louis cared.[28]

Versailles's indifference toward Diderot's Russian trip, compounded by scornful ignorance, was not universally shared, however. The French ambassador to Catherine's court, François-Michel Durand de Distroff, soon took an interest in Diderot's activities. Recently arrived from a posting in Vienna, the Frenchman found himself in the unenviable position of representing a nation increasingly desperate to counter Russia's growing military and diplomatic ambitions across the continent, as well as overcome Catherine's chronic mistrust of French designs. So desperate, in fact—at least to the minds of some of Catherine's officials—was France to parry a rising Saint Petersburg that it was rumored to have lent a surreptitious hand in stoking the peasant rebellions in the Urals.[29]

While the notion of Durand conspiring with Pugachev is too preposterous for words, the actual conspiracy in which the diplomat tried to enmesh Diderot was only slightly less so. In mid-November, Durand paid a visit to the philosophe in his quarters at the Narishkin palace. The diplomat had been impressed—and irritated—by Diderot's unreserved access to Catherine. The empress, he reported to the foreign minister, the Duc d'Aiguillon, "takes a particular pleasure in conversing with Diderot. She has given him the same hour everyday at which she wishes for him to visit." To his visible annoyance, Durand added that their "conversations take place without witnesses, and are often very long."[30] Yet Durand also saw possibilities in this intimate rapport between the wayward Frenchman and the Russian ruler—so much so that he decided to visit Diderot. The reason for the visit, he explained, was to remind Diderot of his patriotic duties. Invoking the greater glory of the fatherland to his no doubt gaping interlocutor, the ambassador told Diderot "what I expect from a Frenchman"—namely, to persuade Catherine (Durand knew that he himself was despised by her) to reconsider her foreign policy and persistent hostility to the prospect of a Russo-French alliance. To that end, Durand pressed upon Diderot a list of proposals that the ambassador had the flair and foresight to set down on paper. All Diderot had to do, Durand concluded, was present these proposals to Catherine during their next tête-a-tête.[31]

Faced by the prospect of being used by a state that had never wished him anything but ill, against a woman who had always wished him nothing but good fortune, Diderot panicked. He protested that he was not qualified to carry out Durand's request, but to no avail: force majeure prevailed. When Durand reported to Versailles that Diderot had agreed to "eliminate, if possible, the prejudice the Empress feels for us," he seems to have raised the specter of the Bastille if Diderot refused. This was certainly the gist of Aiguillon's response to Durand's idea. Given Diderot's unorthodox political and philosophical positions, Aiguillon believed that Durand should not "count on [Diderot's] sentiments to rightly conduct himself." It would be better, he advised his emissary, to remind their man in the Hermitage that we "do not have a good impression of his love of the fatherland." Behind this remark was a scarcely veiled threat that Diderot, upon his return to France, would be welcomed not with open arms but instead with a *lettre de cachet* and another stay in prison. As the British envoy in Saint Petersburg, Sir Robert Gunning, reported to London, Diderot "feared being thrown into the Bastille when he returned home, should he have refused to comply with the French Minister's request."[32]

Fear does not begin to reflect the depth of Diderot's anxiety following Durand's visit. Impossibly distant from his friends and family in Paris, an isolated foreigner in a strange and snowbound city where there was no one to whom he could turn for advice, Diderot must have felt unbearably alone and vulnerable. Quite suddenly, it appeared that unless he executed Durand's demand, he would be sentenced to spend the remainder of his days as Catherine's guest. No doubt this grim prospect heightened Diderot's already crippling longing for home. In a letter to a confidant, Grimm worried about his French friend's worsening case of "Swiss sickness"—a common phrase for homesickness—which was serious enough to make Grimm "anxious sometimes."[33] Grimm was not alone in worrying about Diderot's morale. The Swedish ambassador, Baron de Nolcken, also glimpsed the depths of Diderot's Swiss sickness. Upon meeting Diderot, he wrote, he was utterly "disabused" of the popular belief that great philosophers were superior to "bourgeois virtues like paternal love, conjugal care and friendship." The "amiable old man," Nolcken observed, "talks only about his wife, daughter, his granddaughter and friends, and his extreme desire to see them again."[34]

The news that Angélique had given birth to a healthy girl was both heartening and heartrending. In a letter to his wife, Diderot lamented the pointlessness of an "overly active old age." The place of an old man was at home, in the midst of "children who continue to look for their grandpa even after he has passed away and whose sense of loss and regret make for his elegy."[35] As for Angélique, Diderot strove to maintain a sense of humor—"Well, my girl: You're a mother. God knows what a serious and wise person you will now become"—but his desperation nevertheless bled into his letter: "Believe me, I will spare absolutely no effort—none at all—to speed up my return." In the midst of the honors that Catherine has shown him, Diderot confides to Angélique, he is nevertheless surprised to find himself "unexpectedly longing for all of you, and the pain grows with each passing day."[36]

Diderot concluded his letter to Angélique by marveling over the baby's first cries. "Have you ever," he asked, "heard more agreeable music?" That music might well have been echoing in his thoughts as he considered the dilemma he now confronted. He certainly had occasion to recall Catherine's own humanity when, in late October, he had accompanied the empress to the Smolny Institute, a school for girls that Catherine had founded in 1764. Diderot was overwhelmed by the welcome the empress received from her young charges, excitedly recounting the experience to Nanette: "I wish you could have seen her in the midst of fifty or so girls taking her by the arms, throwing their arms around her neck and covering her with kisses. You would have wept with joy!"[37]

In the end, Diderot threw himself on Catherine's mercy. He could do nothing other than bare his soul to the empress and bear the consequences of his truth telling. But the truth-baring required a certain preparation. At his next session with Catherine, who seems to have been unaware of Durand's antics, a jittery Diderot introduced his topic by describing it as the "dream of Denis the philosophe." But though a dream, he continued, it was utterly true. "I am going to subject myself," he informed a puzzled empress, "to the law of being truthful, because one must be an honest man before being a good citizen or patriot."[38]

Given Catherine's close personal and diplomatic ties to Frederick of Prussia, Diderot's vow of candor bordered on the suicidal. While there are few subjects on which the French court and the philosophes agree, he tells Catherine, there is one notable exception: "All of us sincerely hate the Prussian king." While Catherine knew this claim was dubious—after all, didn't her good friend Voltaire, despite his difficult moments with the

Prussian ruler, still praise Frederick?—she allowed Diderot to continue. The two groups, he observed, had differing reasons for their animosity. "The philosophes hate him because they regard him as an immoral and ambitious politician for whom nothing is sacred; a prince willing to sacrifice everything, even the happiness of his subjects, to his quest for power." As for Versailles, however, the reasons are more practical: the court hates Frederick because "he is an obstacle to their designs." The implication Diderot seems to make is that Catherine has reason to hate, or at least distrust, Frederick for both philosophical and political reasons. Turning to the Russo-Turkish War, which was slouching into its fifth year, Diderot suggests that Russia and France, unlike Prussia, have a common interest in bringing it to an end. He laments the war's length, and suggests that a negotiated settlement is preferable to the hope for a decisive battle. As long as the war lasts, Diderot warns, it will be "impossible for you to pursue your grand aim of securing the happiness of your people."[39]

Having put paid to Frederick's pretensions as an enlightened ruler, Diderot proceeded to demolish any pretension that Louis XV might have to such a title. No doubt enjoying the empress's full attention, Diderot was blunt: "Madame, it is over for our monarch. While the end of a great king's long reign often diminishes its beginning, it is rare that the last years of, to put it kindly, a mediocre king will repair his early disasters. We still have a way to go to bottom out in our decadence. But who knows our fate under the next king? Personally, I'm pessimistic, but let's hope I'm wrong!" While Diderot's brutal candor about Catherine's fellow ruler is arresting, what is truly astonishing is that his observation voided the very argument he had just made for an alliance. If the aged French king was, in fact, a mediocrity, and his successor hardly more impressive, why would Catherine ever entertain the prospect of a Franco-Russian understanding?

As if aware of the contradiction, Diderot showed not just all of his cards, but also the document given to him by Durand. Throwing aside any remaining pretense as a worldly and wise advisor, Diderot exclaimed:

"This role does not suit me. I know too well that this document can spell the end to my own life, as well as to my legacy." Pausing to allow his words to have their full effect, Diderot then added: "But I also know to whom I have the honor to speak, and the sacred sanctuary in which I am deposing my thoughts." With a mixture of genuineness and genuflection, Diderot emphasized the sacredness of this particular sanctuary: "My fellow Frenchmen believe they know you! Yet, no matter how elevated the idea they entertain in your regard, they do not know you. I will teach them who you truly are . . . that you unite the soul of a Roman with the seductiveness of Cleopatra." Gazing across Catherine's private chamber as if he were addressing a great throng of luminaries, Diderot expostulated: "Ah! My friends! Suppose this woman on the throne of France! What an empire! What a terrifying empire she would create, and in so short a period of time!"[40]

Terrifying must have also been Catherine's reaction when she realized that her celebrated guest, enjoying unprecedented access to her Imperial Highness, had been turned into a diplomatic valet for the Bourbons. According to Gunning, Catherine reassured Diderot that she would not hold him responsible for Durand's brazen effrontery on one condition: that Diderot would faithfully report to the French envoy the use she made of his document. With that, she mashed the paper into a ball and tossed it into the fireplace.[41] As he watched the paper flare and crumble, Diderot reflected on his host's theatricality, all the while digesting how helpless he, or any man or woman, was in the presence of a monarch—or perhaps more accurately, the presence of a despot.

"I have never known myself more free than living in what you call this land of slaves, and never known myself more enslaved than living in what you call the land of the free."[42] When Diderot made this paradoxical observation to Catherine, he underscored that Russia was, quite simply, a land of slaves. In a few memoranda the Frenchman, with his visceral hatred of slavery, could not help but raise the subject of serfdom. Striking a practical stance, in one memorandum he argued that Russia needed citizens, not serfs. "Either free them or allow them to purchase their freedom." These newly freed men and women would then form a "third estate," without which Russia could never pretend to modernize.[43] More fantastically, he proposed to Catherine that she "plant in the middle of Russia a colony of free men—very free—such as the Swiss." This community, which would continue to enjoy its traditional liberties and practices, would serve as a kind of "yeast," a social leaven that would slowly, but surely, raise the character and customs of the peasants.[44]

But Diderot's remark about freedom and slavery also pointed to the unusual nature of his situation. Even if it was only within the walls of the Hermitage, and at the pleasure of his host, he could speak so much more freely about so many more subjects than he ever could in France's halls of power. On the topic of religion, Diderot spoke with a degree of candor that would have been striking even at the freewheeling salon of his friend Holbach. He undoubtedly felt encouraged by Catherine, who saw in Christianity—in particular, the Eastern Orthodox Church—the gospel of social order, not personal salvation. Unlike Frederick, who paraded his religious skepticism, Catherine shouldered without complaint the many burdensome religious duties imposed upon her as titular head of Russia's Eastern Orthodox Church. But in turn she imposed a policy of religious toleration that was both hardheaded and heartfelt, extending to her empire's Muslim and (though to a lesser degree) Jewish populations. As she declared in the *Nakaz,* "The human mind is irritated by persecution, but the permission to believe according to one's opinion softens even the most obdurate hearts."[45]

For Diderot, mental irritation was the least of the evils spawned by intolerance. In a conversation with Catherine devoted to the topic of tolerance, he seemed to luxuriate in his litany of ills caused by intolerance. Breeder of lies and foe of truth, source of injustice and spiller of blood, "intolerance has been one of my nation's great plagues." The most embattled of its enemies, Diderot continued, were he and his fellow philosophes. "When a nation is enlightened, the government does not dare carry out whatever stupidity it wishes." But a "stupefied" population results from an intolerant government that has carried the day. In a remarkably prescient, nearly Orwellian insight, Diderot observed that when intolerance is instilled in a nation, not only are the people brutalized, but so too is language. "It seems to me that language is the thermometer of a nation's state of mind. If I were to return to France in a century and wished to know its condition, I'd ask to see the most recently published book."[46]

Clearly, a single session at the Hermitage was not long enough to exhaust Diderot's thoughts on this subject. His following memorandum, titled "First Addendum on Tolerance," suggests that Diderot returned to the topic at his next meeting with Catherine. This time he fingered religion itself, and not merely religious excess or enthusiasm, as the culprit. History reveals, he announced, that a persecuted religious community touts tolerance only so long as it remains persecuted; the moment it comes to power, it turns into the persecutor.[47] How could it be otherwise, given the absolute, yet incompatible, claims made by all religious sects? While each sect has its particular god and its particular truth, each of them also claims the indivisibility and universality of its system of belief.

Even the absence of religions does not offer a completely satisfying solution to this state of affairs. Diderot allows that "neither fanaticism nor intolerance is incompatible with atheism"—a remarkable concession from someone who had, just moments earlier, confessed that he himself was an atheist. While he might change his position on his deathbed—"It's a crick that can occur in even the firmest of heads"—for now he knew his mind: "I don't believe in God."[48] But even his personal convictions were irrelevant. Whether he believed or didn't believe, Diderot insisted that were he king, he'd banish the very notion of God from his law code. In God's place, he reassured Catherine, "I would relate everything to simple and natural causes which are as invariable as humankind."[49]

Had Catherine read the September issue of the *Correspondance littéraire,* which arrived by diplomatic pouch shortly before Diderot's carriage, she would not have been surprised by Diderot's claims. She would have found the first installment of a curious piece titled *Supplement to the Voyage of Bougainville.* Curious not because she had not heard of Bougainville—had not the French admiral published a best-selling account of his just-completed circumnavigation of the world? The work's popularity was largely due to Bougainville's description of his encounter with the native people of Tahiti. Instead, the reason the piece was curious is because it was couched in a series of dialogues, spoken by characters either unidentified or who did not figure in Bougainville's own account. More curious still, the *Supplement* sat below the rubric "Suite des contes de M. Diderot" (Sequel to M. Diderot's Stories), and picked up the themes of two earlier stories published by Diderot, including one, "Ceci n'est pas un conte," that insisted, as the title blared, it was not a story.

In a word, the *Supplement* was not a supplement—at least not one the good admiral had himself tacked onto his original account. Instead, Diderot had again stolen into someone else's work and, for all intents and purposes, hijacked it. The result is a darkly comic work that repeatedly upends European assumptions about religion, morality, and sex. Sandwiched between the so-called supplemental material—a speech by a Tahitian elder and a series of dialogues between the expedition's chaplain and a Tahitian named Orou—are dialogues between two Frenchmen identified as "A" and "B." In a spirited conversation about Bougainville's account, B quickly shows himself to be older and wiser than the inquisitive and inexperienced A, who peppers his friend with questions about the "supplement." Indeed, B reveals himself to be none other than our Parisian homebody Denis Diderot when he confesses to A that, until he had read Bougainville, "I had always thought that a person was never so well off as when at home."[50]

Of course, Diderot never set sail to Tahiti; with his voyage to Saint Petersburg, he lost not just his wig but also the remains of his wanderlust. That was hardly an obstacle, though. As B happily insists, just as Bougainville needed nothing more than a "plank" to circle the world, he and A "can make a tour of the universe" in their chairs.[51] In fact, what better way to make a foreign land one's own than by *not* visiting it? Long before Frank Herbert designed Dune, or James Cameron proffered Pandora, eighteenth-century thinkers re-created uncommon countries from the comfort of their studies, mostly in order to critique their own countries. In his *Persian Letters,* Montesquieu trawled travel accounts of Persia in order to create a personal Persia. His Persia's principal purpose was to serve as a scalpel with which he could dissect and decry French politics and practices. So too for Diderot, who, stirred by Bougainville's account of the island, excitedly willed into being his very own Tahiti.

At first Diderot contented himself with a simple review of the *Voyage* that Grimm published in 1771. Instead of being an end to the matter, however, it was merely the start. Like a curious passerby who steps uninvited into someone else's house and, dissatisfied with what he sees, builds new rooms and floors, Diderot transformed the account into what he believed it should have been. The resulting exchanges between Orou and the chaplain reads at times like a literary collaboration between Jean-Jacques Rousseau and Abbott and Costello.

Thus, Orou encourages the chaplain to sleep with his nubile and willing daughter. Protesting that his religion and holy order prevent him from doing so, the perplexed priest nevertheless surrenders to his desires. The following morning, after the young girl thanks him for having lain with her, the confused priest tries to find his conceptual ground. Baffled by the unbound sexual mores of his hosts, he asks his beaming host if Tahitian fathers can sleep with daughters, brothers, with sisters, and husband with others' wives. Without losing a beat, Orou replies: "Why not?" Shocked by the answer, the man of God shouts that such acts amount to incest and adultery. This elicits a shrug from Orou, who confesses he doesn't know what these words mean. By way of clarification, the chaplain exclaims: "They are crimes, horrible crimes for which people are burned at the stake in my country." Probably after a puzzled pause,

Orou observes: "Well, whether they burn or don't burn in your country is nothing to me."[52]

While Rousseau had little to say about sex in his revolutionary *Discourse on the Origin and Foundation of Inequality among Men,* he had a great deal to say about civilization and its discontents. Rousseau believed this work was "more to Diderot's taste than any of my other writings," and rightly so: until the end of his life, Diderot kept returning to Rousseau's tragic portrayal of the collision between our civilized and natural selves.[53] By the time he wrote the *Supplement,* Diderot had long since fallen out with Rousseau, but he remained fascinated by his erstwhile friend's depiction of man in a state of nature. Rousseau's "savage man"—happily bereft of language and self-awareness—bears little resemblance to Diderot's self-aware and socialized Tahitian, but the two thinkers share an equally ominous view of Western civilization. In his account of the civilizing process, Rousseau deplores our material rise and moral decline: the origin of society "gave new fetters to the weak man and new forces to the rich man, irreversibly destroyed natural freedom, forever established the law of property and of inequality, made an irrevocable right out of a clever usurpation, and henceforth subjected the entire human race to labor, servitude and misery for the profit of a few ambitious people."[54]

With the arrival of Bougainville's ship, Diderot foresees that the Tahitians will be subjected to the same suite of sorrows revealed by Rousseau in his *Discourse.* Already, in his review of Bougainville's book, he had lamented the corruption of this apparently primitive and pure people by the arrival of Bougainville's ships. Breaking away from his critique in order to deliver a dramatic, if empty, plea to the admiral, Diderot exclaims: "Ah, Monsieur de Bougainville, take your ships far from the shores of these innocent and fortunate Tahitians: you will only destroy their happiness."[55] But Diderot was dissatisfied with this entreaty. In the *Supplement* he thus creates a memorable character (an old Tahitian), a mesmerizing setting (the beach from which Bougainville's crew and ships are departing), and a magnificent (though rather classical) oration. Watching the French sailors depart the island, the old man declaims: "Weep, wretched Tahitians, weep—but rather for the arrival than for the departure of these wicked and grasping men!" The sailors will one day return, the elder warns his fellow islanders, but they should be worried, not consoled, by this prospect. For when the sailors do return, he announces, they "will load you with chains, slit your throats and enslave you to their follies and vices. Someday you will be slaves to them, you will be as corrupt, as vile, as wretched as they are."[56]

For Diderot, chief among the follies Europeans brought to the New World was their old god. Diderot makes this clear in another dialogue between Orou and his French guest, when they take up the subject of religion. The chaplain matter-of-factly explains that the world, and everything in it, is the work of a maker. With sly naiveté, Orou replies that this maker, like any maker worth his salt, must have hands, feet, and a head. But he then discovers that this particular maker not only has none of those attributes but also is both everywhere and invisible. Increasingly puzzled, Orou declares: "He sounds to me like a father who doesn't care very much for his children."[57]

But Orou's mystification turns into indignation when the chaplain tells him that the maker has ruled that a man and woman must remain together their entire lives. This maker also gives men and women total freedom to break this rule, and does not hesitate to punish them for all of eternity if they break it. Angered over what he believes to be the sheer perversity of such an arrangement, Orou, having asked permission to speak candidly, launches a devastating attack against the moral and rational basis for the chaplain's claims. These precepts, he announces, "are admirably calculated to increase the number of crimes and to give endless annoyance to the old workman—who made everything without hands, head or tools, who is everywhere but can be seen nowhere, who exists today and tomorrow but grows not a day older, who gives commands and is not obeyed, who can prevent what he dislikes but fails to do so."[58]

Upon reciting these many logical and ethical absurdities—all the more subversive because they are taken, word for word, from the chaplain—Diderot has Orou turn to the subject of sexual mores on Tahiti. Basing his account on Bougainville's remarks about the island's polygamous practices, Diderot fashions a society where women and men freely exchange partners when both parties so desire. But far from being an island hothouse overrun by a lewd and lascivious people—an eighteenth-century version of Club Med—Diderot's Tahitians are principled and practical. They are principled, Orou explains, because they obey the laws of nature by pursuing such pleasures. "Is there anything so senseless," he asks, "as a precept that forbids us to heed the changing impulses that are inherent in our being, or commands that require a degree of constancy which is not possible, that violate the liberty of both male and female by chaining them perpetually to one another?"[59] Yet they are also practical, he observes, because this pursuit of sexual desire increases the island's prosperity, at least when measured by the health and size of its population. A eugenicist *avant l'heure,* Orou cuttingly concludes: "Just because we are savages, don't think we are incapable of calculating where our best advantage lies."[60]

Predictably, Diderot concluded that it was to his philosophical advantage to tie the laws that govern society to those that govern nature. Once A and B step back into the dialogue, the latter does not hesitate to make this very point. The needs and desires, pleasures and pains, we bring into the world, B reminds A, constitute the "code of morality appropriate for men to rest on." For this reason, he suggests "the most backward nation in the world, the Tahitians, who have simply held fast to the law of nature, are nearer to having a good code of law than is any civilized nation."[61] With a flourish worthy of Rousseau, B proclaims that our failure to follow the laws of nature instead of those espoused by potentates and popes is the source of humankind's unhappiness. When A asks if it is better to civilize man or allow him to obey his instincts, B does not hesitate: "If you want to become a tyrant, civilize him; poison him as best you can with a system of morality that is contrary to nature." But if we want natural man to be happy, B's advice is lapidary: "Keep your nose out of his affairs."[62]

While Diderot's attack on Christianity would have angered Rousseau, another of Diderot's influences, Spinoza, would no doubt have approved. Indeed, the opening line of the Dutch thinker's *Theologico-Political Treatise*—"The great secret of the monarchical regime is to deceive men and color with the name of religion the fear that is to master them, so that they fight for their servitude as though it were their salvation"—seems to be the starting point for Diderot's assault on how civil and religious institutions "devise all sorts of hobbles for him, contrive a thousand obstacles for him to trip over, saddle him with phantoms which terrify him, and arrange things so that the natural man will always have the artificial man's foot on his neck."[63]

Perhaps, as one biographer suggests, Diderot was in "one of his more anarchical moods" when he wrote the *Supplement.*[64] If he had been, though, the mood had largely evaporated by the time he ended the piece. Proving to be a diffident sort of anarchist, Diderot once again echoed Rousseau, who had waffled on this very same issue in his *Discourse on Inequality.* In that work Rousseau pulled back, by way of a long and serpentine footnote, from the upshot of his blistering critique of civilization. Did he truly wish, as critics like Voltaire claimed, to return to the woods and live with bears? Nothing could be sillier, he replied. We cannot return to a diet of nuts and berries, he observed, much less recover our original innocence. We are, in effect, what we have become. As a result, his reader's duty is to "respect the sacred bonds of the societies of which they are members . . . and scrupulously obey the laws and the men who are their authors and ministers."[65]

In a similar fashion Diderot veers sharply away from the consequences of his philosophical claims. Rather than looking forward to the day, as he did in his birthday limerick, of strangling the last king with the innards of the last priest, he instead looks to the laws and customs of one's own country. Steering his fictional alter ego toward the path of reform, not revolution, Diderot has B insist that we should protest foolish laws until they are changed. But in the meantime, he also reassures A—along with any powerful men or women reading his words—"we should obey the laws as they are."[66]

Colic and Constitutions

I HAVE DONE A HUGE AMOUNT OF WORK,
AND SO EASILY THAT I AM ASTONISHED.

—DIDEROT TO NANETTE

At the end of the *Supplement to the Voyage of Bougainville,* B urges A to follow the good chaplain's example: "Be monks in France and savages in Tahiti." To which his young friend excitedly replies: "Put on the costume of the country you visit, but keep the suit of clothes you will need to go home in."[1] Well, that might work for Tahiti, but what was one to do when in Russia? Was Diderot to put on the costume of Catherine's educator or her entertainer? Don the garb of a latter-day Seneca or a simple jester?

In the swirl of political and personal factions in Saint Petersburg, Diderot's plain black coat served both purposes. While it conformed to his own conception of the philosophe, it advertised his dangerous nonconformity at Catherine's court. When it came to certain subjects, though, the coat and its wearer relayed far worse than mere nonconformism. As he did in his impromptu speech in Leipzig to an unsuspecting crowd—with the important difference that in Russia he was not wearing his sleeping gown—at a succession of social gatherings Diderot rattled on about atheism's superiority to religion. Yet his claim—as he wrote in his short story "The Conversation between a Philosopher and the Maréchale de XXX"—that the "atheist may nevertheless be a man of probity" provoked rather than persuaded. At these gatherings, reported one guest, Diderot "constantly plays the role of a proud atheist." The consequence was sadly predictable: "Everyone abhors him."

Not quite everyone, however. With the empress, the philosophe continued to find favor; the doors to her private apartment were still open to him every day. In her letters to Voltaire, Catherine continued to wax on about the extraordinariness of their mutual friend. Afraid that Diderot was growing bored in Saint Petersburg, she admitted, "I could speak to him for the rest of my life and never grow tired of him."[2] Was Catherine ever bothered by his more provocative remarks? To his wife, Diderot insisted this was never the case. The empress, he exclaimed, "loves the truth with all her soul, and although I have at times told her truths that rarely reach the ears of kings, she has never been wounded." Indeed, having forthrightly contradicted her when she told him about a policy she planned to enact, the empress suddenly took Diderot's hand and told him: "You are right."[3]

Of course, Diderot understood that he was utterly dependent on Catherine's high regard. "Her Imperial Majesty still holds me in her favor," he reassured Sophie Volland toward the end of the year.[4] Echoing this sentiment to his wife and daughter, Diderot reminded them he was still free to enter Catherine's "private quarters from three o'clock to five or six o'clock every day."[5] Tellingly, when warned by an acquaintance that he was alienating the entire court by his unorthodox pronouncements, Diderot grinned: "I do not care about the servants; the only favor I seek is with the woman in charge."[6]

In a lapidary phrase to a friend, Grimm captured the darker side to Diderot's quip: "Apart from the empress, Denis has not made a single conquest here."[7] As for foes, Diderot had made them in droves. His unbridled candor in conversation, coupled with his unprecedented access to the empress, made him an object of intense fear and loathing among courtiers. But it was a fear shared by Diderot. "I am afraid of enemies," he confided to Nanette and Angélique, "jealous of the marks of distinction and favor given to me by Her Imperial Majesty."[8] From his privileged position at the Hermitage, Grimm watched the court's several factions unite, if only in their dislike for Diderot. Unlike Catherine, he noted, her courtiers "are neither sympathetic with nor accustomed to genius and its train of eccentricities."[9] The resulting intrigue spawned by Diderot's presence, Grimm fretted, was no less extraordinary than Diderot's brilliance. "You would not believe," he divulged to a friend, "all of the subtle and insidious persecutions to which Denis has been subjected."[10] Grimm was not the only observer to report on the web of intrigue that enmeshed Diderot. Reporting that the philosophe was "exposed to the most venomous jealousy," the Swedish ambassador Baron de Nolcken attributed it to the slavish character of the court.[11]

But Diderot did have a handful of allies in Saint Petersburg. While most of the courtiers treated the philosophe as they would a leper, he was welcomed by a small coterie of liberal thinkers. General Betsky, who had overseen Catherine's purchase of Diderot's library in 1765, led the group. He was joined by his daughter Anastasia Sokolova, one of Catherine's closest maids of honor, and Vice-Chancellor A. M. Golitsyn. The group's attachment to Diderot was in part Parisian—along with the Betsky, whose ties to Diderot dated to the purchase of his library, the vice-chancellor was the cousin of Dimitri Golitsyn, Diderot's old friend from Paris—but also partly philosophical. Timid reformists who were disappointed by the failure of the Legislative Commission and worried over Catherine's absolutist tendencies, they rightly believed that Diderot sided with them. Although they provided an admiring audience for Diderot, the group offered little by way of influence at the Hermitage. Outside of educational policy, which had long been Betsky's bailiwick, his group's views weighed little in Catherine's deliberations and court politics.[12]

Nevertheless, Diderot was grateful for any attachments at all in a place so foreign and frost-bound. Though his orbit hugged the Hermitage, he was strangely weightless. Free to visit Catherine every afternoon, Diderot knew that Grimm was her guest every evening, joining her small circle of friends and intimates. How else to explain the rarity of the visits he received from his great friend? With some bitterness, Diderot saw how his friend had changed over the years. He who had once been a *lumière,* committed to the same selfless goals and ideals that drove Diderot, had become a broker of dynastic marriages and a sounding board to rulers. Mme d'Épinay's sharp insight into Grimm's character—"He is perhaps unique in having the gift of inspiring confidences while giving none"—guaranteed his success as a courtier and confidant.[13] Reluctantly, Diderot told Nanette that what Grimm most sought, perhaps even at the expense of friendship, was "a brilliant life filled with admirers, honors, and distractions."[14] Though he himself was no stranger to such desires when he was younger, Diderot worried that Grimm had become a stranger now that he was older.

As Diderot's ties to Grimm and Falconet frayed, so did his health. The colic that fell him during his voyage had, since he crossed (and drank from) the Neva, become chronic. In November a prolonged bout led him, with little regret, to turn down Catherine's invitation to accompany her to the imperial estate at Tsarkoe-Selo in order to celebrate her name day.[15] His colic again erupted in December, keeping him in bed and away from Catherine for ten days. When he returned to the Hermitage, Catherine joked: "And so, Monsieur Diderot, quite some time has passed since we last saw one another."[16] Indeed, as late as January, Catherine reported to Voltaire that their mutual friend's health remained "shaky."[17]

When he was not shuttered at Narishkin's palace or shuttling to the Hermitage, Diderot made occasional forays into Saint Petersburg. Though persona non grata at the city's cluster of palaces, he found he was welcomed in less regal neighborhoods. Not surprisingly, given his attachment to the world of artisans, this self-described "son of a smithy" toured an iron forge one day. While he admired the men who worked the furnace, he confided to Catherine that the furnace itself could be better made.[18] No less unsurprisingly, given his attachment to the world of artists, Diderot agreed to sit for Russia's leading portraitist, Dmitry Levitzky. As in Van Loo's earlier portrait of Diderot, Levitzky's Diderot is without his wig; unlike the Van Loo version, Levitzky's Diderot is also without the tools of his craft—pen, paper, and desk. Although less than a decade separates the two portraits, they seem to hail from different eras. Worn and balding, wearing a red robe and thin smile, the Russian Diderot has little in common with the Paris Diderot. About the Levitzky portrait, Diderot could never say, as he did about the Van Loo, that it portrayed him not as a writer but as a grinning flirt made to look younger than his years.[19] With Levitzky, and with his Russian experience, Diderot is now taking the measure of his mortality.[20]

He had accompanied Catherine to the Smolny Institute, of course, but he also attended a session at the Imperial Academy of Sciences, occasioned by his election in November to that august body. In his formal address to the dozen or so other members, Diderot did not offer a grand speech, but instead plied them with a long list of questions on Siberia. His inaugural appearance, however, turned out to be his final appearance: Diderot skipped the following session, though it was devoted to answering his questionnaire, along with the subsequent sessions. (Grimm was also elected to the Academy that day. In a taste of what was to come, he harped bitterly to Mme Geoffrin on Catherine's decision to have him share this particular honor with his friend.)[21] Diderot also visited Falconet and Collot a few times at their studio, and though he urged his wife to forgive the sculptor for his earlier rudeness, the damage done to their friendship was irreparable. In the letter to Falconet commending his sculpture of Peter, Diderot tellingly ended the missive by twice repeating "adieu." As he signed off, he confessed: "I fear the arrival of this dreaded winter."[22]

The winter soon arrived. By mid-November the frozen Neva had become a racecourse for sled dogs and the temperature hovered slightly above zero.[23] Even with the fur-lined coat and muffs that Catherine had ordered for Diderot, her guest must have found the weather too forbidding, and his health too fragile, for sightseeing. Yet he had seen enough of Saint Petersburg to conclude that it simply wouldn't do as Russia's capital—or, more to the point, as Catherine's capital.

According to the city's lore, when Peter the Great banished his first wife, Eudoxia, to a convent, she cursed the city he was raising from the swamps: "St. Petersburg will stand empty!"[24] If Diderot had heard this story, he might have given Eudoxia's curse some credence, struck as he was by the contrast between the city's grand architectural gestures, from the vast Nevsky Prospect to granite-lined banks of the Neva, and the few people who passed along them. He was convinced that despite Peter the Great's herculean efforts, the city he founded as a second Paris had not only failed to become Paris, but also failed to be a city. Instead, it was a boggy stage dotted by clusters of palaces and rows of barracks across which flickered only the barest signs of commercial and civil society.

Walking from Narishkin's palace to the Hermitage, Diderot was inevitably reminded of this odd state of affairs. For a man who had spent his entire adult life in the capital of Europe, Diderot must have found the empty squares and prospects of Saint Petersburg a bizarre and gloomy sight. This explains, in part, his obstinate insistence on addressing the issue with Catherine. He devoted one of their sessions to the geographical aspects, in addition to the swampy soil, that undermined Saint Petersburg's role as capital. It was, quite simply, irrational to situate the imperial capital on the outermost fringes of the empire. It was an affront both to everyday reason and effective rule. A capital, Diderot argues, is like a heart: a nation's commercial veins and social arteries best function when they are all equidistant from the pump that allows them to subsist. Hence, building a capital "at the extremes of an empire is like an animal whose heart is found at the end of its finger or, as Monsieur Narishkin suggested, the stomach in one's big toe."[25]

Catherine might have arched her eyebrows when Diderot cited the impressionable Narishkin; she might have furrowed them when Diderot next cited her own words. In a previous discussion, the empress had told Diderot that, not unlike the reason for Louis XIV's decision to quit Paris for Versailles, Peter built Saint Petersburg because he worried that Muscovites disliked him. Yet Catherine, Diderot continued, need not worry: "Just as she loves all her children, all of her children love her." Diderot, who was effectively an inmate of the Hermitage and never strayed from Saint Petersburg, follows that debatable claim with another. While mutual love between a ruler and ruled is not, perhaps, a reason to reestablish Moscow as the imperial capital, there is also the matter of climate. As Moscow is further south than Saint Petersburg, he observes, its weather is more clement.[26] Except that it wasn't and isn't: Diderot again confused cartography with reality. Moscow is, indeed, four degrees latitude south of Saint Petersburg, but it is a difference without much distinction: its average temperature is more or less the same.[27]

Oddly, the respect for reality that imbues Diderot's approach to the making of iron is largely lacking from the attention he pays to the making of cities. Still, he was attentive enough to grasp that Catherine was not persuaded by his arguments. The empress, it seems, told him that the transfer of government from Saint Petersburg to Moscow would take not years, but decades, even a century.[28] In a subsequent conversation, he thus turned to his Plan B. Quite simply, if the capital could not be moved to where the people were, the people would be moved to the capital. Would it not be possible, he asks, to "thicken St. Petersburg with more people, to enliven and energize it, to quicken its commercial activity by attaching the many isolated palaces with private houses?"[29]

Yet even an empress would be hard-pressed to act on such a proposal—especially if she were rash enough to follow Diderot's advice. He suggests that Catherine free the country's artisans—"workers of all sorts, like cartwrights, carpenters, masons and rope-makers, like those in Paris." Unlike their Parisian peers, of course, the Russian artisans are serfs, tied to the country estates of their Russian masters. But imagine, he suggests, the tremendous civilizing potential of this workforce. By having them move to Saint Petersburg, they would form the equivalent of France's "third estate," making the capital denser and livelier. In a different memorandum, he again hammers at this theme: "I don't like men when they are spread apart, and I don't like palaces when they are isolated."[30] At times Diderot turns to geology to underscore his point: "When the angles of stones rub against one another, they are rounded and polished."[31] At other times, he turns to sociology, assuming that increased contact among human beings leads to increased goodness: "The proximity of men binds them together, while their interaction civilizes them."[32]

All of these turns, however, imply a beneficent yet despotic power—a power great enough to uproot and transplant entire towns. Diderot in fact urges Catherine to graft, into the "middle of Russia," a colony of Swiss citizens. Though planted in the midst of this strange and feudal land, these "free—very free—men" would conserve their privileges. Slowly, yet surely, he insists, this "precious yeast" will raise the surrounding population to their level: "Their particular character will spread and become generalized."[33] When not leavening the Russian heartland with Swiss artisans, Catherine should be lining the cities with streets. And what, he asks, should Catherine do once she has made streets? "Make more streets."[34] Obviously Diderot's goals are utterly dependent on there being a powerful hand to carry them out. And what that hand must do, quite literally, is *squeeze*. Diderot exhorts Catherine to force her subjects together. "Press them tightly together"—perhaps he reaches across the table separating him and Catherine and makes fists of his hands—"and by this one operation you will have an empire."[35] Ultimately, like Orou and his Tahitians, Diderot wants to grow the Russians; unlike Orou, he wants to grow them in—in fact, move them there, if necessary—Saint Petersburg. He cannot depend on a volcanic explosion or tsunami to shift great masses of people where they need to be, and thus turns willingly to the vast powers of a despot.

Yet those same powers also terrified Diderot. While they quicken the early stages of the civilizing process, they threaten the later stages. While the building of city streets and budding of artisanal activity are critical to a nation's well-being, they require laws to make them lasting. From the very first memorandum, devoted to what is effectively a lawless French monarchy, Diderot urges Catherine to bind herself to law. It is the nation, not a ruler, "that must be the source of law from one age to the next."[36] Catherine's greatest achievement would lie, not in amassing art or territory, but in making the nations, and her own person, subject to a single legal code. "It is certain she can do nothing better than to establish lasting laws that would pose an insurmountable authority to future despots."[37]

While Diderot's brief for the supremacy of law is uncontroversial, he teases uncomfortable corollaries from it. He thus warns Catherine that arbitrary rule, even the most enlightened, is necessarily evil. No matter how benevolent a despot, if she remained exempt from the laws to which her people are subject, a despot she remained. Indeed, he continues, there is a perverse logic to enlightened despotism: the more compassionate its character, the more catastrophic its consequences. A well-disposed despot ineluctably disposes the nation to the fundamental lawlessness of his rule. Such a ruler, he declares, "accustoms his subjects to respect and cherish rulers, regardless of their character." Such a reign, in turn, "takes from the nation the right to deliberate, the right to desire or not desire, and the right to be opposed—even to what is right and good for it."[38] It reduces citizens to lackeys whose servile relationship to their ruler is little different from that of Rameau's nephew to his patron. When he adds yet another twist to the paradox, telling Catherine that had England been ruled "by three sovereigns like Elizabeth, she would have been enslaved for centuries," the empress replied: "I believe it."[39]

To make his case, Diderot cites a passage from what he called Catherine's "breviary," *The Spirit of the Laws.* Diderot's attitude toward Montesquieu—the man who had become a monument, as well as the monument that was his book—was predictably complicated. In the early stages of the *Encyclopédie,* Diderot approached Montesquieu and, with typical chutzpah, invited him to write the entries on "Démocratie" and "Despotisme." The distinguished but diffident old man demurred, instead offering a literary scrap—an unfinished piece on "Goût." As a result, rather than landing a literary coup, Diderot had been fobbed off with a forgettable fragment on taste. Though Montesquieu, with his death in 1755, managed to fend off further requests from a persistent Diderot, this did not prevent the enterprising editor from transforming *The Spirit of the Laws* into a literary Trojan Horse. Not only did Diderot use it as cover for controversial passages on political theory, but he also turned Montesquieu's funeral into a cudgel with which to beat the royal court. Toward the end of an article dedicated, rather aptly, to "Eclecticism," Diderot abruptly informs the reader: "I wrote these reflections on February 11, 1755, upon my return from the funeral of one of our greatest men, devastated by the loss to the nation and the world of letters and disturbed by the persecutions he had known." The hostility shown by throne and altar to Montesquieu, Diderot lamented, was "the sad reward for the honor he had brought to France and the important service he had rendered to the universe!"[40]

Diderot thus enlisted the baron in his case for constitutionalism. On the one hand, this alliance between the two men made sense. Montesquieu had, after all, famously compared despots to the "savages of Louisiana." When they desire fruit, he observed, "they cut the tree to the root and gather the fruit. This is an emblem of despotism."[41] Would Catherine become yet another such emblem? The danger certainly existed, which is why Montesquieu, or so Diderot insisted, had the empress in mind when he penned such passages. "It is for her, and for her alone, that Montesquieu wrote," he reassured Catherine.[42] Implying that the empress would not dare fall short of her breviary's aspirations, Diderot repeatedly invoked the spirit of Montesquieu no less than the laws. Would not Catherine embrace Montesquieu's political lodestar, the English Constitution, were it to somehow be introduced into Russia?[43]

Better yet, would not Catherine embrace Montesquieu himself, were he to appear at the Hermitage? Worried he was not up to the task history had thrust upon him by bringing him to Saint Petersburg, Diderot insists Montesquieu would have fared better. "O Montesquieu, if only you could take my place! How you would speak! How she would reply! How you would listen! And how you would be heard!"[44] That Montesquieu would speak firmly against despotic rule was, for Diderot, beyond doubt. Did he not identify fear as the only principle of despotic government, and self-preservation as the only goal?

On the other hand, Diderot disputed Montesquieu's position on the critical question of where the ultimate source of political legitimacy resided in a monarchy. Was it located with the ruler or, instead, with the nation's intermediary bodies that stand in the way of despotism? To Catherine's great satisfaction—and Diderot's equally great agitation—Montesquieu's answer could not have been plainer: "In a monarchy, the prince is the source of all political and civil power."[45] Alive to the potentially despotic consequences his axiom entails, Montesquieu also insists that monarchs, unlike despots, rule according to fundamental laws. Yet Montesquieu himself hints at his claim's flaw, acknowledging that a monarch's power scarcely differs from a despot's. "In whatever direction the monarch turns, he prevails by tipping the balance and he is obeyed."[46]

This, in turn, proved to be Diderot's tipping point. As early as the first volume of the *Encyclopédie,* Diderot opposed Montesquieu's claim (which certainly did not help persuade the latter to write the articles on democracy and despotism). In his article "Political Authority," Diderot declared that the prince derives his power not from nature or God but instead from his subjects. "In a word, the Crown, the power of government, and public authority are all goods of which the nation is proprietor, and of which princes have the usufruct, as its ministers and trustees." While avoiding such blunt language in his memoranda, Diderot makes little secret of his disagreement with Montesquieu. Far from the source of power, the monarch becomes the spring of intolerance; far from being the foundation of enlightened government, arbitrary power undermines even constructive policies. In the end, a sovereign ruler will trade the duties of justice for the delights of Jupiter—a god, Diderot sighs, who rules the world in odd fashion. "Awakened by the world's commotion, he opens his trap door and observes: 'Hail in Scythia, plague in Asia, a volcano in Portugal, revolt in Spain and misery in France.' With that, he closes the door, puts his head back on the pillow and falls asleep. That is what I call governing the world."[47] For a sovereign struggling to subdue not just the Turkish infantry and Cossack rebels, but also her own emotional needs, Diderot's observations could only have raised a smile, if not the eyebrows.

"The trouble," Catherine confessed later in life, "is that my heart would not willingly remain without love for one hour."[48] By the time Diderot had arrived in Saint Petersburg, Catherine's experiment with the unfortunate Vasilchikov was a miserable failure. Wearied almost at once by Vasilchikov, the empress moaned: "I feel suffocated by him. . . . He is a bore."[49] In effect, she regarded him as little more than a *pis-aller,* or stopgap, ready to be sacrificed when necessary. To Vasilchikov's credit, he was sharp enough to understand his situation. "I was nothing more to her than a kind of male *cocotte,*" he complained, "and was treated as such."[50]

The moment for the *cocotte*'s sacrifice arrived in December. It was not just Vasilchikov's attentions in their private quarters, but Pugachev's depredations in the Urals that suffocated Catherine. Though she dismissed, in a letter to Voltaire, the rebellion as mere "foolhardiness," Catherine's unease was palpable.[51] The insurrection in Orenburg, the British emissary Gunning reported, has left "the Empress a good deal out of order."[52] Moreover, the war against the Ottoman Empire, launched with such optimism six years earlier, was mired in a bloody stalemate. At this pivotal moment in her reign, Catherine needed astute advice as well as great ardor, a discerning counselor as well as a desirable lover.

Grigory Potemkin checked all these imperial boxes. An ambitious and audacious offspring of a family that, for centuries, had served the tsars as officers and diplomats, Potemkin had left an early but deep impression on Catherine. Joining the rebellious horse guards who had rallied to Catherine in 1762, the gallant officer offered to the grand duchess the tassel she tied to her sword's hilt for the march on Peterhof. There followed a series of appointments, both in government and the army, and Potemkin consistently distinguished himself in war—he led a cavalry division against the Turks in 1769—and in peace. Fluent in Greek and Latin, and fascinated by religion—as a student, he had plunged into theology—Potemkin became an invaluable intermediary for the sprawling empire's many religious communities.

Given Potemkin's inspiring deeds and Catherine's insistent needs, it was perhaps only a matter of time for her to turn to him. In early December, when Potemkin was serving on the southern front against the Turks, she finally did so. "Since I very much desire to preserve fervent, brave, clever and skillful individuals," she wrote to him, "I ask you not to endanger yourself. . . . Upon reading this letter you may well ask: why was it written? To which I can offer the following reply: so that you had confirmation of my opinion of you, for I am always most benevolent toward you." Potemkin had no need of hermeneutical skills acquired as a theology student to interpret Catherine's missive: within weeks he was galloping back to Saint Petersburg.

That same month marked the beginning of the end to another intimate relationship. In a report to Paris, written on December 31, Durand de

Distroff excitedly observed that the meetings between the empress and Diderot "follow one another without letup, and get longer by the day."[53] But the Frenchman, kept at arm's length by both the court and Diderot, was not the most reliable observer. His claim was all the more dubious because Catherine spent part of the month celebrating her name day in Tsarkoe Seko, while Diderot spent part of it battling his colic at Narishkin's. In a letter to Nanette written at month's end, Diderot protested, perhaps too much, that he still "enjoys the favor Her Imperial Highness had deigned to show me."[54] How can we reconcile this claim, though, with a letter he had written just a week earlier, in which he wrote about his twice-weekly conversations with Catherine in the past tense?[55] Or, more revealingly, there is the title page of the collected memoranda, on which Diderot inscribed the date "3 décembre." Is it possible, as Arthur Wilson suggests, that Diderot was "himself aware that after that date their conversations had not been of a nature that could change policy?"[56]

As Diderot knew all too well, showing him the same favor did not mean that Catherine was showing him the same attention. By this point he could have told friends that when Catherine praised, as she so often did, her guest's "extraordinary" presence, this most likely meant she found his conversation captivating but unconvincing. But this did not mean he had given up the hope of inflecting certain aspects to Catherine's rule, if not inventing it from top to bottom. This, in part, explains why he devoted several of his memoranda to educational and not legal or political matters. His visit to the Smolny Institute in Catherine's company impressed upon him, in dramatic fashion, the empress's heartfelt attachment to the education and well-being of her young charges. He was sincere in his claim that even though Angélique had the most loving of mothers and most caring of fathers, she was nevertheless "raised more severely and less carefully" than the girls at Smolny.[57] (On the other hand, Diderot pressed Catherine to introduce a course on human anatomy at Smolny, singing the praises of the same Mlle Biheron who had taught Angélique.)[58]

The result of Catherine's passion for education, the Smolny Institute represented one of Catherine's most enduring commitments to the cause of the Enlightenment. This was to be expected; more so than any other subject, education channeled what Peter Gay calls the "logic of enlightenment"—namely, that even if most women and men are not yet capable of self-rule, "they must be *made* ready for it."[59] Education was the means of making a people—at least a people deserving of a monarchy or republic. The goal of education, said the empress, was "the making of the ideal man and perfect citizen."[60] Despotism alone, as Catherine's mentor, the Baron de Montesquieu, declared, rendered education meaningless. "Why should education take pains in forming a good citizen, only to share in the public misery?"[61] To be sure, the *Nakaz* touched on education only briefly. This glancing attention reflected Catherine's fear that the task of educating a "numerous people . . . in houses regulated for that purpose" dwarfed her government's capacity, at least in the short term, to create the needed school system. Nevertheless, the Legislative Commission created a committee to prepare such a system.[62] But as with most every project launched by the Commission, this particular committee failed to reach port. A final report was never submitted, and the committee was disbanded in 1771.

Yet Catherine pursued educational reform by other means. Shortly after taking power, she appointed General Betsky as her adviser on educational policy. Though found tiresome by his political foes, Betsky proved tireless in pursuing the enlightened goals he shared with his employer. He quickly issued his *General Plan for the Education of Young People of Both Sexes,* a document more focused on shaping citizens than scientists. One of the plan's recurrent themes is the shunning of corporal punishment in the classroom. In a line that might well have been written by Catherine, the plan announced: "The example of cruel punishments by mindless and savage schoolmasters must not be followed, since by such punishments children are humiliated and abased."[63]

Stirred by his visit to the Smolny Institute, Diderot urged Catherine to build upon—or, more accurately, build *out* from—this accomplishment. Rather than educate only well-born children, he asked the empress to turn her attention to her other subjects. The "tender mother to some children," he observed, "certainly does not wish to show herself as an unkind stepmother to others."[64] From this bold (if not foolhardy) comparison, Diderot moves to a bald assertion, claiming that almost everyone who has been anyone in the arts and sciences has been a commoner. The obscurity of their births and difficulty of their youths, he argues, drives men to distinguish themselves in a hostile and unforgiving world. As a result, "in all empires the arduous conditions of society serve as the testing grounds for manners, knowledge, talent and national glory."[65] The conditions in Russia, as Diderot learned from Betsky, were more arduous than most elsewhere in Europe. When Catherine came to the throne, primary schooling, overseen by parish priests, was a hit-or-miss affair, and two dozen or so grammar schools taught about 6,000 students.[66] As to the effectiveness of these schools, given the significant space that Betsky's Plan gave to condemning its practice, physical beatings seem to have been a common pedagogical tool.

By the time of Diderot's visit a decade later, little progress had been made in building a national school system. With the mounting financial and political costs of the war against Constantinople, Catherine's government had neither the means nor the motivation to tackle educational reform. In effect, that would entail opening a second front, where the enemies would be religious obscurantism and bureaucratic immobilism. The sharp contrast between Catherine's pedagogical ideals and the grim Russian reality—a reality brought home to Diderot by the Betsky circle—certainly caught the philosophe's eye. He cautioned Catherine that without a national school system, neither talent nor virtue would be rewarded, leaving Russia mired in mediocrity and misery.[67] The consequences, he warned, would be catastrophic. In a comparison perhaps as jarring as the evil stepmother, Diderot likened Catherine's coup to an earthquake, one that had left Russians in a state of uncertainty and unease. Hence the need for Catherine to impress upon her subjects that she wishes only their well-being, a stance to which she could lend substance "by the spurring of public education."[68]

What Diderot either failed to grasp or chose to ignore were the consequences of a system of national education based on the cultivation of reason, inculcation of knowledge, and incitation to civic-mindedness. For an absolutist state like Catherine's Russia, Diderot embodied the disease for which he pretended to be the cure. With near inevitability, the democratization of knowledge would, sooner or later, lead to the democratization of society and politics. None of this surprised Catherine. She was, after all, then considering a Russian edition of the *Encyclopédie* and was fully aware that the work's goal, like Diderot's pedagogical goals, was not just to change the common way of thinking, but also to enlist commoners into the ranks of the Enlightenment. But all of this was at best an irrelevance and at worst an annoyance to an empress who, ten years into her rule, was concerned with cementing, not a constitution, but Paul's succession.

While we do not know the order in which Diderot presented his memoranda, we do know that Diderot shared his hero Jacques's obstinacy even in the face of daunting challenges. It is not hard to imagine that, even toward the end, the philosophe continued to push his favorite subject: the primacy of law. While displaying his appreciation for Catherine's generosity was a powerful reason for his visit, his determination to make her an exemplar of enlightened rule was his true motivation. What better way to express his gratitude to Catherine than by helping sculpt her own statue, one firmly placed on a pedestal of law—one that would dwarf the great boulder on which Falconet's statue of Peter would rest? When he tells Nanette that he has not stopped working since his arrival in Saint Petersburg, we can nearly see him standing in a rubble-strewn studio, wearing a leather vest, hammering at a great block of marble from which his idealized Catherine would emerge. Diderot's prediction for Falconet's statue of Peter echoed his hopes for his own statue of Catherine: "He will make a great thing and he'll come back covered with glory!"[69]

But Diderot's tools differed from Falconet's: rather than a hammer and chisel, he employed his voice and reason. His skill with these instruments is especially striking in a pivotal conversation in November. By then, several meetings had already taken place, allowing Catherine and Diderot to form an idea of each other.[70] In those meetings, Diderot observed, he had spoken in his own voice. Now, however, he would be akin to an ancient bard, serving as nothing more than the vessel for divine inspiration. But his muse was not poetry, but instead reason. He would become, he told Catherine, the "passive voice of reason"—a voice that carried a warning.[71] While reason commended her efforts to introduce enlightened ideals to Russia, it declared that these efforts were doomed if they were not codified. "To create is not enough," Diderot intoned; it is "also necessary to conserve one's creations in their original state."[72] The making of laws, in effect, is tantamount to shaping a model from clay. Just as the sculptor uses a chisel to eternalize his vision, the legislator uses his reason to eternalize the law. And reason dictates that the legislator must surrender to the laws she has created. The legislator "must respect the law"—an imperative guaranteed by her creation of independent institutions devoted to defending the integrity of those laws. "If the ruler destroys one of these laws with her own hands," he warns, the entire edifice would be undermined.[73]

By the memorandum's end, however, Diderot shifts from the voice of reason to the voice of Catherine. Not only must a truly enlightened ruler subject herself to the law, but she must also be subject to her word. How remarkable, he exclaims, if Catherine, tempted to flout an earlier declaration, declared that she would not do so. "I made a solemn promise and I will not teach my subjects to distrust my words."[74] Is it possible that Diderot thus warned Catherine against breaking the promise contained in the *Nakaz*? Or, more broadly, counseled her against betraying, in the eyes of the philosophes, the great promise of her rule? At the very least, he revealed how crucial this matter was by refusing to do in this conversation what he repeatedly did in earlier discussions—namely, denigrate himself as an irresponsible dreamer or stuttering fool each time he pronounced a truth. This time, the truth would stand unadorned.

The Road Not Taken

THERE IS NO FITTER ROLE IN HIGH SOCIETY THAN THAT OF FOOL. FOR A LONG TIME THE KING HAD AN APPOINTED FOOL. AT NO TIME WAS THERE AN APPOINTED SAGE.

—*RAMEAU'S NEPHEW*

By the turn of the new year, Diderot, crippled by his bouts of colic, rarely ventured from his refuge at Narishkin's. Even there, though, a sudden spasm of pain would often force the plume from Diderot's hand, leaving him to shuffle from desk to bed. One such spasm no doubt led him to end his memorandum on the school for military cadets. Rushing matters to a conclusion, Diderot tells Catherine that he is too weak to continue. "Allow me to wish good night to Her Imperial Majesty, and be allowed to retire, as I sorely need to rest."[1]

Diderot nevertheless persisted in gathering what information he could about Russia. "I am making every effort," Diderot assured Nanette, "to educate myself here."[2] The obstacles, though, were many. Even had the ailing Frenchman escaped ice-bound Saint Petersburg to visit an estate and encounter its residents, he could not have escaped his ignorance of the language. Diderot never spoke to a representative from the very social class about which he cared most: the serfs. No less consequential, he was utterly dependent on a mere handful of sources for his knowledge of the country—Betsky and his unhappy few, of course, along with the smattering of French expatriates. What he learned from these circles was, by and large, their disillusionment with their employer's rule.

Indeed, even Catherine found herself interrogated by her guest. At his desk at Narishkin's, Diderot compiled a detailed questionnaire on Russia's economic conditions, which he then sent to the empress. She returned it in short order, revealing a mastery of frequently arcane matters ranging from property law to rhubarb cultivation. And on those occasions when she had no facts at hand, she always had great flair. Confessing her ignorance of Russia's annual grain production or beef exports—"I've no idea," she would off-handedly tell Diderot—Catherine deflected other matters with a *bon mot.* "God preserve us from them," she replied when Diderot asked if Russia had veterinary schools, and sighed "Rare and rarely obeyed" when he grilled her on the general regulations for the timber industry.[3]

When Diderot managed to quit his bed, he socialized with the small community of French expatriates—he refers with particular warmth to Nicolas-Gabriel Clerc, a military physician Diderot found "very congenial," and Mme Sophie de la Font and her daughter Wilhelmine, both of whom taught at the Smolny Institute—along with Betsky's circle.[4] But the circle's tight circumference reminded Diderot of his isolation, subject to a climate as harsh inside the Winter Palace as outside. By January the court was relishing a review, passed from hand to hand, of an unauthorized edition of Diderot's collected works. Though anonymous, the review's author appeared to be Frederick, still smarting from Diderot's earlier stiff-arm when he directed his carriage to give Berlin wide berth. He lambasted Diderot's plays, harrumphing that they "are not written so that they can be acted and are scarcely better suited to be read"—the first claim is not inaccurate, while the second is invidious—and sniggered over the "sublime tissue of nonsense" found between the covers of his early philosophical essay *Pensées sur l'interprétation de la nature.*[5]

More sublimely nonsensical, it would turn out, was Frederick's expectation that Diderot, in Grimm's tow, would nevertheless honor him with a visit on his much-anticipated return to Paris. As his homesickness deepened, Diderot had begun to make plans for his return to Paris. Determined to make the trip with Grimm, he was no less determined to avoid a layover in Berlin. Torn by his devotion to Diderot and his debt to Frederick, Grimm's predicament seemed without issue. "I am more than a bit embarrassed over Denis's intentions," he confided to Nesselrode at year's end. "As you can imagine, the last thing in the world I want is to cancel Berlin, but the last thing Denis wants is to place his foot there."[6] Two days later, after again appealing to Diderot to reconsider, Grimm reported the dreary result to Nesselrode: "As for Denis, I've lost hope. He absolutely does not want to pass by Berlin, and I am upset for both his sake and my own." Two weeks later, in mid-January, the accomplished diplomat conceded failure: "I believe that Denis will not travel with the prophet [i.e., Grimm] and the prophet will not travel with Denis, leaving both of them very much put out."[7]

Grimm and Diderot were not the only ones who were put out. In early 1774, threats to Catherine's throne simmered not just on the fringes but also at the center of her empire. In January she learned about an improbable conspiracy to force her to share power with her son, Paul. The man behind the plot, a freelancing German diplomat named Caspar von Saldern, fled the country upon being discovered, and his phantasmagoric plans fizzled. But that such plans were made at all, and with the apparently innocent collusion of Paul himself, outraged Catherine, who swore to have Saldern "tied neck and heels and brought back to Russia" for trial.[8] Though her vow went unfulfilled, Catherine was reminded that threats to her life or rule, whether issuing from the wintry steppes of the Urals or the hallways of the Winter Palace, would continue. Unable to extinguish the Pugachev rebellion, uncertain about the rumors of unrest among her own Guards, and unhappy with Valichikov, Catherine found little time to pay attention to her Parisian visitor. Indeed, careful observers like Gunning detected deepening signs of distraction: "The Empress's Temper is much altered of late; there does not appear the same Affability and Condescension about her that she has hitherto been remarked for."[9]

During the last two months of his stay, from early January to early March, Diderot makes no mention of the decline of imperial affability. This silence was not because he failed to see the empress's moods as clearly as Gunning, but because he rarely saw the empress at all. When they did meet to converse, Diderot nevertheless sensed the general futility of the exercise. Perhaps for this reason, in his final memorandum—it is not at all clear if it served as the basis for a conversation at the Hermitage—Diderot offered a nearly abject apology for his "indiscrete and inconsiderate" behavior, but also insisted upon a mild *apologia,* or defense, of the ideas he had espoused since the previous October. On the one hand, he asked for a "thousand pardons" for his "political brashness," yet on the other hand he insisted he had been neither "dishonest nor malicious." To be sure, he had been nothing more than a "spectator who takes it into his insignificant head to govern a great empire."[10] Nevertheless, he asked for forgiveness if only because his observations had been inspired by the sincere desire to aid the empress. In the end, Diderot seems to have deliberately echoed Catherine's remark that at times he seemed a hundred years old, but at other times like a ten-year-old. He was, he confessed, like "any other philosopher, which is to say a child who babbles about important matters."[11] Diderot was so taken by this phrase, or perhaps believed Catherine would be, that he inscribed it in Latin on the title page of the collected memoranda he gave her before he left.[12]

Diderot now grasped that his conversations with Catherine would not lead to anything more than fodder for gossip with friends, mockery from enemies, and speculation among diplomats. This explains the state of torpor into which he had slid, unwilling to socialize with his small circle in Saint Petersburg or correspond with his family and friends in Paris. To the Comte de Crillon, a newly arrived acquaintance, Diderot confided that he had stopped writing letters altogether. Both the great distance and his growing despondency had defeated him. "I am too far from friends to chat with them, though I have tried twenty times. After I tell them, 'Family and friends, I want to leave, I want to leave,' I've nothing more to write."[13]

Moreover, Diderot had nothing more to say to Catherine—apart, that is, from again expressing his gratitude. The empress had already seen to the arrangements for Diderot's return, providing him with a new carriage—an exquisite "English coach" designed to allow the frail passenger to lie down, but not designed, as it would soon become clear, for rutted and icy roads—and a devoted and dependable subordinate, Athanasius Bala, to accompany him as far as Holland. Worried that Catherine also planned to shower him with money and gifts, and thus compromise his desire to appear to his peers as uncompromised and unsullied, Diderot asked only to be compensated for the cost of his voyage. When Diderot returned, after prolonged absence, to the Hermitage in mid-February to see Catherine, they both knew it would most probably be their last meeting. There ensued a strange and poignant exchange, one that spoke not just to their sentiments toward one another but also to their presentiments about posterity's judgment. Upon greeting the philosophe, Catherine asked what she might do for him. Responding to this grand gesture with yet another *coup de théâtre,* Diderot unrolled a document he called "Peace Treaty between a Great Sovereign and a Philosopher." When the amused and astonished empress asked to sign the text, declaring she had no need to read the fine print, Diderot refused. Glancing at the gathered courtiers, he announced: "No, Madame, I cannot accept that, though it is true that your fellow rulers have frequently broken treaties they have read. But have the kindness to listen."

Tugged between exasperation and expectation, Catherine gave her assent; toggling between melodrama and comedy, Diderot cleared his throat. Announcing "Article 1," he declared he did not wish for money or gold: "I don't want others to think my praise has been bought."[14] (In a subsequent letter to Sophie Volland, Diderot explained that while he could have "filled both hands with gold from the imperial treasury, I preferred to silence the gossips in Saint Petersburg and convince the incredulous in Paris.")[15] As Catherine's smile broadened, Diderot moved to his second article, a request that his voyage be reimbursed. But not a ruble more than the actual cost: "A philosophe," Diderot announced, "does not travel in the style of a nobleman."[16] Catherine happily bestowed on him 3,000 rubles—much more than such a trip's true cost, but also a clean profit since Catherine had already provided the carriage and companion. Finally, article three proposed that Diderot receive from Catherine a memento of his visit. But the keepsake, rather than being grand and expensive, had to be an everyday object Diderot associated with Catherine. Looking up from his "treaty," Diderot suggested the empress's breakfast cup and saucer.

Proving yet again she was more practical than her guest, Catherine refused: such a gift was too fragile for the long haul back to France. Instead, she removed from her finger a cameo ring on which her portrait was engraved. "Here is such a token," she declared to her entire court as much as she did to her guest.[17] Unable to ask for more, Diderot did not: his silence was exemplary. He had completed the sort of moral tableau he always treasured—a sight not lost on the audience. Recounting the exchange to Nesselrode, Grimm exclaimed: "Such a charming woman, such a great man."[18]

Diderot understood there was no need for an encore—at least one performed in person. Instead, on February 22, two weeks before his departure, he drafted a farewell letter to Catherine. Upon reading the draft at Diderot's request, Grimm was relieved to find that his friend exhibited a different kind of greatness—namely, the greatness of an imperious thinker who lowered himself for an imperial occasion. The writing of the letter,

Diderot explained, would save Catherine the pain of seeing him overcome by emotion had he appeared in person. Leaving her, he insists, will be as painful as was leaving his own family the previous year. But the pain of departure, he declared, will be soothed by singing Catherine's praises to the world—or, better yet, Paris. "I tell myself that if you stop seeing this great sovereign, you will at least have the satisfaction to speak often of her. It seems I suffer less when I think about this."[19]

As to what he would say about his host, Diderot cites Catherine's willingness to lower herself to his level. "All of my life I will recall the moments when Your Majesty forgot the infinite distance separating us . . . in order to make me forget my own smallness."[20] After several jabs, some of them a bit awkward, at his arch-nemesis Frederick—"If we knew where the Fredericks are hatched, a good man would break all the eggs and replace them with Catherines"—Diderot again apologized for the "unheard-of stubbornness with which he tried Your Majesty's patience." With great panache, he finally swore that if his praise of Catherine ever rang hollow, he would agree to be declared the worst of ingrates.

Soon enough, though he was not alive to hear it, this is precisely what Catherine would call him.

Over four months of conversations, Diderot had donned a variety of guises at the Hermitage to express his brash political views, in particular his repeated exhortations to Catherine to acknowledge the supremacy of law. At first glance, his tour de force rivals David Garrick's performance for the Parisian audience of salon habitués, where he careened from one emotion to the next. Of course, while Garrick rifled through these various guises in a few minutes, Diderot acted them out over a few months. In both cases, the audience was awed; in neither case was it altered. The audience of Parisians that applauded Garrick's extraordinary performance afterward returned, without missing a beat, to their ordinary lives. As for the imperial audience of one in Saint Petersburg who praised Diderot's performances as extraordinary, she too returned seamlessly to her ordinary life. Catherine continued to rule after Diderot's presentations as she had ruled before.

As Diderot must have known, Garrick succeeded because he was a consummate actor: he assumed the words and gestures of a character created by a Shakespeare or Marlowe, all the while keeping a critical distance. The philosophe, on the other hand, failed in part because he was a terrible actor who could not help but bring his own emotions into play. In *The Paradox of the Actor,* he asked: "Can we laugh or cry when we wish?" The answer, he thought, was obvious: "Our success matches the degree to which we are more or less Garrick."[21] For this reason, the one role he had practiced his entire life—the man of sincerity—was poor preparation for the demands of his performance at the Hermitage. Regardless of the role, he remained Denis Diderot. That he recited from his own writings—which amounted to so many variations on the theme on the primacy of law—did not help matters. Hobbled by his scripts and hamstrung by his sincerity, Diderot was a hopeless actor; he could never become "a trickster who, reciting an author's tragic or comic lines, fools you completely."[22] For this reason, by the time his English carriage left Saint Petersburg on March 5, Diderot had already begun to reconsider the character of his audience, as well as the contents of his script.

Unlike the relaxed pace of Diderot's journey from Holland to Russia the preceding year, the return trip was rapid and relentless. The travelers, at least in Diderot's telling, barely survived their crossing of the Dwina River, where ice flows threatened to crush their coach, and by the time they reached Holland, they had left three broken carriages in their wake. For the monthlong duration of the voyage, Diderot wore only his dressing gown under his fur overcoat. With a dramatic flourish worthy of her father, Angélique later remarked: "He would stop neither to sleep nor to eat. He regarded his carriage as a house."[23] Diderot nevertheless stopped long enough in Hamburg to contact the city's well-known music composer Carl Philipp Emmanuel Bach, one of the great Bach's many progeny. He would have called in person, he explained to the Kapellmeister, but because he had only a sleeping gown to wear, he thought better of it. Still, with his thoughts focused on Angélique, Diderot inquired if he might purchase the sheet music for a few piano sonatas? But only at a reasonable price, he added. My reputation, the letter writer explained, "is greater than my wealth, which unhappily conforms to what I share with most men of genius, without sharing their same title."[24]

When he reached the home of the Golitsyns in The Hague on April 5, the exhausted traveler entered a period of hibernation. For several days Diderot mostly slept, leaving his chambers only to dine with his hosts. He insisted the trip had not been tiring, but it had clearly marked him. Back in Holland, his cherished "land of liberty," Diderot was not back to his former self; he was much talked about because he now talked so rarely at public gatherings. Famed for his gregarious nature, the philosophe became the talk of the town mostly because the town rarely saw him. "His existence at the Hague," the French emissary reported, "is scarcely felt. He is not to be seen anywhere."[25]

As Diderot slowly emerged from his seclusion, observers were struck by his changed bearing. The excitable thinker who rarely met a provocative idea he didn't like (and express) had disappeared, replaced by a diffident and dramatically aged man. According to one Dutch savant, Diderot was now "very reserved in social groups, carefully avoiding speaking of religion and other sacred subjects."[26] His philosophical foe Hemsterhuis, struck by the transformation in Diderot's character, improbably insisted that the Frenchman had *always* been a sad and subdued person: "Gaiety never resided in that somber spirit."[27]

The Batavian Socrates misunderstood Diderot's character as severely as he had Spinoza's writings. Nothing could be further from the truth than the claim that Diderot was a stranger to gaiety. But almost despite himself, Hemsterhuis glimpsed Diderot's changed demeanor; the Parisian betrayed a greater solemnity and deeper reserve. It seemed as if a shadow now stretched across Diderot's understanding of both himself and the world. If so, it was cast by Catherine, who ruled not just Russia, but much of Diderot's future. This future was not just public and political, but also personal and material.

In Saint Petersburg, Catherine had reminded Diderot that he had once proposed to her publishing a new edition of *Encyclopédie*. Diderot would serve as editor, Catherine as banker, and the project would serve both of their ends. Diderot would be able to heal a wound he had borne for nearly a decade. In 1764, André Le Breton, the publisher of the *Encyclopédie,* had committed an irreparable act. Worried that the censors would again impound the work and threaten his investment, he excised dozens of controversial passages from the last ten volumes of the work. Diderot was staggered when he uncovered the deed, but helpless: when he confronted Le Breton with his discovery, he learned that his editor had destroyed the proofs. The shattered man retreated to his home, where he penned a letter to Le Breton: "I wept with rage in front of you . . . in front of my wife, my child and my servant. . . . I shall bear this wound until I die."

For that brief moment in Russia, it seemed the wound would heal with the publication of a revised *Encyclopédie*. Moreover, the second edition would set to rest his persistent fears over his family's financial well-being. As Diderot excitedly told Nanette, he would earn 200,000 francs in advance as the work's editor. With this windfall, they could quit their cramped home on the Rue Taranne. Instructing Nanette to start looking for a roomier and better-appointed apartment, Diderot exulted that this *Encyclopédie* "will be worth something and will not cause me heartache."[28]

Yet heartache did follow. Catherine had tasked Betsky with the contract negotiations, but a frustrated Diderot told Catherine that the old man continued "to swing between yes and no" even as he was packing his bags for Paris.[29] Unable to nail him down, Diderot turned to Catherine, using his farewell letter to remind her that he was waiting to "build this pyramid" on her behalf. Despite Diderot's ploy, he would never build the pyramid. In the end, Betsky's elusiveness may have reflected Catherine's diffidence, or even indifference, toward the project. So much had happened at home and abroad since her original offer to publish the *Encyclopédie,* and her earlier motivations—in particular the desire to win the esteem of the Republic of Letters—had lost their urgency. Had not Diderot's voyage to Saint Petersburg, after all, been evidence enough of such esteem?

Loath to accept these changed circumstances, Diderot kept delaying his return to Paris. In June he launched a salvo of inquiries to Betsky, archly noting that despite "the cries of my wife, my children, and my friends," he remained at his post in Holland, gathering men and material for the *Encyclopédie.*[30] Failing to receive a positive reply, a dejected Diderot promised Sophie that he was doing everything possible to return to Paris, money be damned.[31] Yet as hope lingered, so too did Diderot. By early August, Diderot reassured Nanette and Angélique that he was on the "verge of leaving" Holland—an assurance he repeated a month later, promising that the day of his return "is not far."[32]

At the same time, Diderot was also preparing a different kind of return. Shortly after his promise to his family, Diderot composed a long letter to Catherine. The ostensible reason was to congratulate her on the peace treaty signed between Russian and Turkish representatives on July 23. "What a peace! What a glorious peace!" Diderot proclaimed. The peace's significance was not lost on Diderot: a long and costly war ended, and a new phase in Russia's military and political dominance began. The treaty allowed Russia to establish a powerful land and naval presence in the Crimea and the Black Sea, laying the foundations for the bloody territorial disputes that have erupted in our own time. Hence his message to Catherine—"The best and most zealous of your subjects does not rejoice from this news more sincerely than me"—was only to be expected.[33]

But when it came to her recently departed guest, Catherine had learned to always expect more. She knew Diderot would not content himself, like Voltaire, to sing hosannas to her martial genius. And she was right:

Diderot's zeal, she discovered, was not for the person of the empress, but for an ideal he still hoped she personified. To this end, he immediately qualified both the reasons for his joy and the glory of Catherine's victory. While military triumphs make for a brilliant reign, Diderot warned, they do not make for a happy people. "Thanks to reason's progress, our admiration is reserved for virtues other than those of the Caesars and Alexanders. We find it more glorious to make men than to kill them."[34] Military conquests are, at best, a means to enlightened policies; they become, at worst, ends in themselves. "You have a young nation to form," he reminded Catherine.

A difficult task, to be sure, but not as difficult as rejuvenating an old nation like France. Diderot's native land was a lost cause, while his "adopted country" remained a cause to stir the hearts of all enlightened peoples. "May the heavens," Diderot beseeched, "not distract you from this task."[35] But all too predictably, Diderot was unwilling to trust the heavens alone. And so, he decided to thrust himself into the fray. He told Catherine that he had taken the liberty to reread the *Nakaz*—moreover, he "had the insolence to do so with plume in hand."[36] Upon reading that line, Catherine no doubt frowned, perhaps dropping the letter from her own hand. Insolence, indeed. That this "most extraordinary man" had taken it upon himself to annotate the work to which she devoted so much time and invested so much hope, a work that had established her reputation as an enlightened ruler, could only have been for her a source of disquiet, not satisfaction. When Catherine finally read, several years later, the result of Diderot's annotations, her vague sense of unease would combust into molten umbrage.

Shortly before he had sent his fateful letter to Catherine, Diderot had written to his great admirer Mme Necker, a powerful *salonnière* and wife of the reformist finance minister, Jacques Necker. Eager to learn about Diderot's experience in Russia, Necker had urged him to return posthaste to Paris. He could not report on his travels, Diderot replied, since he had scarcely traveled at all. He never left the confines of Saint Petersburg, he confessed, and saw few people apart from the empress. In essence, Diderot came, didn't see, and left. But as for his dealings with Catherine, Diderot did have a remarkable insight he wished to share only with Necker. "Between us," he began, "let me observe that our philosophes who think they know despotism have only seen the tip of the iceberg. What a difference between seeing a tiger painted by Oudry [an artist famous for his animal portraits] and seeing one in a forest!"[37]

The time Diderot spent with the imperial tiger at the Hermitage perhaps gave special urgency to his flight from Saint Petersburg to The Hague. As he battered four successive carriages while barreling across the continent, Diderot turned to Tacitus to make sense of all that he had seen and heard. The Roman historian's severe account of the recklessness of emperors and fecklessness of senators struck Diderot anew. Once he arrived in The Hague, he turned to Tacitus as a means to distill his Russian experience. In a letter to Catherine, Diderot told her about his renewed interest in Tacitus, which had inspired a pamphlet he had just dashed off: *Notes marginales d'un souverain sur l'histoire des empereurs* (*A Ruler's Observations on the History of Emperors*).[38] The pamphlet, as the original title suggests—it was eventually retitled as the *Principes de politique des souverains*—(*Political Principles of Rulers*) pretends to be written by a sovereign.

Just which sovereign, though, Diderot deliberately leaves unclear. The work strikes a bloodless and Machiavellian pose—one easily attributed to Diderot's great bugbear, Frederick II. Yet this same cynical perspective can often be associated with Diderot's great benefactor, Catherine II. While some of the work's observations seem to be little more than winding footnotes to Tacitus's time in Rome, others are cutting aphorisms honed from Diderot's time in Russia. Perhaps he was thinking of the now-blighted hopes, originally encouraged by Catherine, for the new *Encyclopédie* when he wrote: "Regardless of the access granted to us by the powerful, regardless of their permission to have us forget their rank, one must never take them at their word."[39] Or, more importantly, Diderot regretted his blighted hope for something far grander: an enlightened ruler acting on his progressive political ideals. But did he have anyone to blame but himself for this misunderstanding? After all, as he bitterly notes, "Men of letters are so easily corrupted: lots of warmth and attention, and a bit of money, does the trick."[40]

The time spent with Tacitus was, in essence, a rehearsal for the *Observations on the Nakaz.* "Lacerations" might be a more accurate description, though. Far from being "mild mannered," as one biographer insists, Diderot's *Observations* veers from the candid to the confrontational.[41] The work is revelatory insofar as Diderot throws off any remaining hopes for enlightened despotism; it is revolutionary insofar as he unflinchingly draws the consequences. His revolutionary impulse, suppressed during the five months spent in Saint Petersburg, resurfaced in republican Holland. But the Dutch allergy to despotism was not the only prod. Writing to Sophie from The Hague on September 3, Diderot declared that he had, at best, "ten years at the bottom of my bag." He reckoned his growing collection of physical ills would claim his attention for two or three of those years, leaving him no more than seven years to do all that remained to be done.[42]

Diderot proved prophetic, dying thirty-six days shy of ten years later, on July 31, 1784. In the case of the *Observations,* he also proved prophetic: his analysis of monarchic regimes anticipated the revolutions to come on both sides of the Atlantic. Indeed, the opening lines of his declaration of principles—"There is no true sovereign except the nation; there can be no true legislator except the people"—foreshadow the opening lines of another declaration, written two years later, that begins with the words "We the People."[43] With those same lines, Diderot circles back to his article "Autorité politique," published in the first volume of the *Encyclopédie* nearly twenty-five years earlier. In that entry, miraculously gone undetected by the censors, he identified two kinds of authority. One issues from a powerful individual who wrested it from others, while the second flows from "the consent of those who bind themselves to it, by virtue of an actual or presumed contract with the person to whom they have given it."

The difference, twenty-five years later, is that Diderot now gives a name to the individual who claims authority by force. "The Empress of Russia," he declares, "is certainly a despot." No longer the jester or dreamer he played at the Hermitage, Diderot becomes, in the quiet of the Galitsyn residence, an inquisitor. He addresses Catherine in a language drained of caution, posing questions to which, he makes clear, there is but one right answer. "Is it her intention to maintain the despotism and transfer it to her successors," he asks, "or to abdicate it?" If the former, let her do what she wills with the Code, for the Code will have no more solidity than the "villages" that Potemkin will, in a few years, build to please her. But if she does intend to abdicate, she must bind not only herself to the law, but her successors as well. "If in reading what I have just written and listening to her conscience, her heart beats with joy, then she no longer wants slaves. If she trembles, feels weak and goes pale, then she has taken herself for a better person than she really is."[44]

Having drawn the full consequences of his initial claims, Diderot announces that the people, should they find their natural right to equality and liberty threatened by a ruler, have the right to depose him—or her. Indeed, the ruler's oath of office declares that when these rights are infringed, the people even have the right "to condemn us to death if the case demands it."[45] Should that death sentence require an intestine with which to strangle the wayward ruler, Diderot predictably suggests using one from the nearest priest. He blasts Catherine for invoking religion to justify her legal code. For good measure, Diderot also lashes out at Montesquieu for having done precisely the same in *The Spirit of the Laws.* Such a move risked making the rule of law hostage to the reign of fanaticism. "I do not like to give weight and consideration to those who speak in the name of the Almighty. Religion is a buttress which always ends up bringing the house down."[46] How could the very same ruler who seemed to share her religious skepticism during their private conversations countenance, much less cultivate, the decisive role of religion in public institutions? "No man of reasonable intelligence, casting an impartial eye over all the religions of the earth," Diderot exclaims, "would fail to see in them a tissue of extravagant lies." He thus urges this woman of exceptional intelligence to "suppress as much as you can a system of lies which will suppress you."[47]

As for pivotal passages in the *Nakaz* itself, Diderot is equally scathing. He slams as utterly irrelevant the opening line to which Catherine had given so much importance. Does it really matter, he asks, whether "Russia is a European power," as Catherine declared, or an "Asiatic" power as Montesquieu suggested? Not at all, Diderot replies. "The important point is that it should be great, flourishing and lasting."[48] The rule of laws, not men, is essential if Russia is ever to realize these goals. Diderot returns to the themes he had emphasized during his conversations with Catherine, but now does so with stunning bluntness. It requires the "heroic action of a good despot," one who will "bind one arm of his successor" in order to guarantee the people's happiness. Without the primacy of law, Russia will become prey to the whims of rulers and ways of fortune. Had he not told Catherine, during one conversation, that if England had had "three sovereigns like Elizabeth, she would have been enslaved for centuries"? And did she not reply: "I believe it"?[49]

As he did at the Hermitage, Diderot urges Catherine to establish a legislative body that shares power with the monarch and does not merely serve at her pleasure. What guarantee can Diderot offer that these representatives will rule wisely? Or, for that matter, what guarantee is there that they will be chosen wisely? Citing one of Catherine's most deeply held convictions, Diderot answers that the best of guarantees is education. The mortar of "public knowledge or instruction" will fasten citizens to one another, building a civic foundation strong enough to weather most political crises.[50] Crucially, the education of a people is not just the work of schools but also of laws. Driving his elbow once again into the *Nakaz* and *The Spirit of the Laws,* Diderot argues that legislation should not reflect a nation's spirit, but shape it. For this reason, he advises not "to stick to the best laws that a people can accept. You must instead give them the best laws possible."[51]

No subject better illustrated the moral imperative behind this axiom than serfdom. Its elimination was not just a moral necessity, but a political necessity as well. Taking up the *Nakaz*'s suggestion that more humane treatment will help "avoid the causes which have so often led to the revolt of serfs against their masters," Diderot offers what he deems a more effective solution: "There should be no serfs."[52] What better way to prevent the rise of future Pugachevs, after all, than by removing the source on which such impostors feed? What quicker way to create a solid and thriving third estate, the foundation for a true civilization? Though he never strayed from Saint Petersburg, Diderot perceived the vast array of social institutions and classes opposed to the emancipation of the serfs. The abolition of this peculiar institution, he recognizes, is hard in a country "where you cannot make the masters aware of the abuses of serfdom . . . so long as they are despotic."[53] Yet at the same time he bluntly demands to know if the empress "wants the nation to carry on in slavery?"[54]

Diderot also calls for an end to censorship: "In every well-ordered society there should be no subject which cannot be aired freely. The more serious and difficult it is, the more important that it be discussed."[55] Only an uncensored voice like Diderot's can list all of the critical subjects, ranging from the need for village schools, where he would "like the children to find food and instruction," to the need for financial reform. As if grading the paper of a bright but lazy student guilty of plagiarism, Diderot concludes that the Instruction would be truly instructive only by including all of these matters. Only then, he adds with a blistering flourish, would the *Nakaz* "become a work of originality, a set of principles made in good faith, instead of being an extract."[56]

In the concluding section of the *Observations,* Diderot tackles another of Catherine's sleights-of-hand—namely, her claim, inspired by Montesquieu, that a "great empire places sovereign authority in the person who governs." Catherine's airbrushing of Montesquieu's original "despotic authority" for "sovereign authority" did not slip past Diderot unseen. With honesty that slides into effrontery, Diderot confronts Catherine on this deliberate and dangerous misrepresentation: "I see in Her Imperial Majesty's Instruction a plan for an excellent Code, but not a word on the means of ensuring its stability. I see in it the name of the despot abdicated, but the thing itself preserved, and despotism called monarchy."[57] Having called Catherine out on her misuse of Montesquieu, Diderot recalls the uses of Socrates. With a panache that he failed to conjure at the Hermitage, Diderot casts himself as speaking truth to power, regardless of the consequences. "If the philosophe were asked what use is the advice which he stubbornly gives to nations and those governing them, and he replied sincerely, he would say that he was satisfying an unconquerable urge to speak the truth, on the off-chance of arousing indignation and even drinking from the cup of Socrates."[58]

Of course, by the time our Socratic disciple wrote these lines, he was safely ensconced with the Golitsyns in The Hague, drinking from glasses of wine rather than cups of hemlock. He was also trying to convince the empress, if not himself, that she enjoyed few things more than being told the truth. In December, Diderot reminded Catherine that having reread the *Nakaz,* he had "the audacity to write a few reflections in the margins." While the comments were candid, a sovereign who—as he tirelessly reminded friends and family—"loved the truth" would surely welcome them. So certain was he of Catherine's attachment to the truth, Diderot added, that he would "willingly condemn to eternal torture anyone who would not dare tell her the truth."[59]

Catherine might have replied, in jest, that her attachment to Becarria's *On Crimes and Punishments* would force her to condemn such a condemnation. She might also have replied, in seriousness, that at the very same time Diderot was scribbling in the margins of his copy of the *Nakaz*, she was busy overseeing the drafting of the Statute of Local Administration. Promulgated in 1775, the statute sought to reform Russia's centralized yet feeble administrative system by shifting a range of responsibilities, judicial as well as administrative, from the country's provincial centers to the localities under their control. In its effort to rationalize the ramshackle character of the tsarist courts and bureaucracy, it marked, as one prominent historian argues, an effort to encourage the growth of those *"pouvoirs intermédiares"* (intermediary powers) cherished by Montesquieu. Moreover, the statute sought to civilize and humanize these same institutions. With a nod to the concept of habeas corpus, for example, Catherine instituted a Conscience Court, a tribunal to which those detained more than three days without being charged could appeal.[60]

In the end, Catherine did not tell Diderot in her letters about the statute, and Diderot seems never to have learned from others about its existence. But Catherine had, of course, learned about the existence of Diderot's *Observations.* Though she never asked to read them, the empress took extraordinary measures to prevent others from doing so. Seemingly determined to outdo the strange episode when Durand de Distroff enrolled Diderot as a clandestine agent, Catherine instructed Golitsyn to purloin his guest's copy of the *Observations.* The prince, whose loyalty was first to his empress and not to his friend, rifled through Diderot's bags and took what he believed to be the only copy. When Diderot returned to Paris, he dared Nanette to count his belongings: "Wife, you'll have no reason to reprimand me for I have not lost even a handkerchief."[61] But once he resettled into his home, he discovered that although all his handkerchiefs were accounted for, the original copy of the *Observations* was not.[62]

Convinced that Golitsyn was responsible for the theft, Diderot's reaction was not surprising: apart from a business-like letter sent in 1780,

Diderot never again wrote to prince and princess. But given Diderot's long experience of hide-and-seek with French censors, he had taken care to have a copy made of the *Observations.* Rather like the sly Jacques, who was always several steps ahead of his master, Diderot had outwitted his own masters in The Hague and Saint Petersburg.

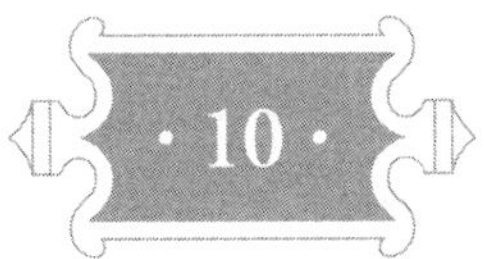

Send for Seneca

REMIND THE POWERFUL OF THEIR DUTIES FROM TIME TO TIME, NOT SO THEY CHANGE THEIR WAYS, BUT SO THEY KNOW THAT THEY TOO HAVE A MASTER.

—DIDEROT, *PRINCIPES DE POLITIQUE DES SOUVERAINS*

Upon his return to Paris, Diderot seemed to return to his former self. At the salon of Julie de Lespinasse, he regaled his friends with his experiences in Russia. He more than met the great expectations of Mme Necker. So compelling was his storytelling, so captivating were the stories, that she felt as if she "lived through, in fifteen minutes, the four months spent in Russia by this extraordinary man."[1] Still astonished that he was the subject—the hero—of this epic, Diderot spoke glowingly of the country he never saw and the inhabitants he never met.

But that was in public. In private, while his praise for Catherine was effusive, his observations on Russia were much less so. In fact, he was uncharacteristically circumspect; as he confided to Mme Necker, "I would be an ingrate if I spoke ill of it, and I would be a liar if I spoke well of it."[2] Tellingly, after the initial spasm of visits, Diderot retired to his home, taking on the appearance to outsiders of a bear in winter. "Our Russian . . . is de-Russifying himself," explained Mme d'Épinay to their mutual friend Ferdinando Galiani.[3] If so, he was de-Russifying himself into near invisibility. Henri Meister, the newly appointed editor of the *Correspondance littéraire,* remarked that his celebrated contributor "has never lived in a more solitary fashion than he has since returning to Paris."[4]

In one important respect, Meister's report was misleading; Diderot kept away from his usual haunts, but his life was far from solitary. Making up for his absence during his daughter's pregnancy the preceding year, he spent much of his time in the company of Angélique and her family. In fact, along with his granddaughter, Marie-Anne, Diderot now had a grandson, Denis-Simon, born in 1774. He thrived in the company of the children, and even formed a closer bond with his son-in-law. One of Vandeul's brothers, visiting for a week, observed that Diderot dined with them nearly every night. As for Nanette, she was as "touchy as ever" and preferred to remain at home, grieving for her old lapdog, which a visitor had sat on and killed.[5] But Angélique remained far more concerned about her father, whom she found "thin and changed." His journey, she later wrote, "shortened his life."[6]

Perhaps. What is clear, though, is that the journey had not just physical but also profound philosophical consequences. Diderot's historical sensibility lengthened and his political views grew sharper as he reflected on his experience in Russia. These changes were registered in one of the eighteenth-century's best-selling and forbidden books, the *Histoire philosophique et politique des établissements et du commerce des Européens dans les deux Indes,* or the *Philosophical and Political History of the European Establishments and Trade in the Two Indies.* The work, better known as the *History of the Two Indies,* was the brainchild of Guillaume-Thomas Raynal, a former Jesuit priest who had quit the order and rallied to the

Encyclopédie. Raynal was now the editor of *History of the Two Indies,* and he and his team of collaborators assembled vast amounts of data to gauge the economic consequences of European colonization, and marshaled the vocabulary of natural rights to rage over the human consequences. The result was revolutionary. Upon its publication in 1770, the cascading statistics and cutting strictures in *History of the Two Indies* galvanized the salons of Paris and terrified the court at Versailles.

Diderot had played only a minor role in the work's first edition, but he threw himself into the second (1774) and third (1780) editions following his return from Russia. In 1777 Vandeul reported that his father-in-law had already devoted four months to "revise and correct the work of a friend who is an abbé."[7] Yet Vandeul's description was slightly misleading. Just as he had done with Shaftesbury, Chambers, and Bougainville, the philosophe was up to his old tricks, doing far more than merely editing the abbé's work. Instead he transformed it and made it his own. Raynal, for one, was thrilled to have Diderot hijack his book. When Diderot asked him whether his "digressions" were not spoiling his work, the abbé replied: "I know the public's taste better than you do. Your words will make up for my boring and endless calculations."[8]

Raynal was right: Diderot's additions—which, Meister insisted, accounted for a third of the final editions—turned the *History of the Two Indies* into a veritable *"machine de guerre"* which remained of one of Europe's best-selling works across the final decades of the eighteenth century.[9] As Robert Darnton notes, the work "contained something to offend practically everyone in authority under the Old Regime and at the same time appealed to the broadest range of readers."[10] The Paris Parlement's public burning of the book in 1781 inevitably increased sales—a lesson learned by present-day governments that seek to prevent, say, the publication of inside accounts of their activities—and turned Raynal, who had prudently slipped out of France, into a global celebrity. It also turned the "Defender of Humanity, Truth and Freedom"—the caption Raynal inscribed under his portrait in the book's frontispiece—into an insufferable showboat.

After meeting him in 1785, Edward Gibbon sighed: "You would imagine that he alone was the Monarch and the legislator of the world."[11]

Raynal's fame left Diderot conflicted. How could it not? By assuming authorship of the work, the abbé had brought down on himself the shafts of lightning hurled by the Parlement and court. This act of self-sacrifice—which, given Raynal's subsequent lionization, was also an act of self-advertising—provided vital protection for Diderot and his fellow unnamed contributors. But Raynal's act also reminded Diderot that, ever since his stay at Vincennes twenty-five years earlier, he had never again dared to publish his controversial writings under his own name. This realization cut even deeper in the wake of his Russian experience. Had he spoken as honestly and truthfully to Catherine as he wished to believe? No less important, did others believe he had done his duty as a philosophe? This was an especially unsettling question in light of the unstinting generosity Catherine continued to show him. In fact, in mid-1779, while he was busy with the third edition of the *History of the Two Indies,* Diderot asked for, and received, a gift of 2,000 rubles from Catherine, probably to help his son-in-law in one of his business ventures.[12]

Perhaps it was his moral queasiness over these issues that gave even greater heat to his contributions to Raynal's work. Mining passages from his *Supplement to the Voyage of Bougainville,* Diderot lambastes the European claims to lands in the New World. He channels the voice of the Old Man, demanding to know the moral or logical grounds to claiming another's land as one's own: "And why does it belong to you? Are you as unjust and stupid as some primitive men who are accidentally carried to your shores, where they write on the sand or on the bark of your trees: *This country is ours?*"[13] He also presents a simple code for the colonization of other lands. While one has the right to claim uninhabited lands, should the "discovered" land already be inhabited, all the "discoverer" can claim is "the hospitality and assistance which one man owes another." Should he be refused this assistance, he can take what he needs to survive. "But should he take an iota more, he becomes a thief and murderer, deserving of no more pity than a tiger."[14]

Crucially, Diderot does not neglect the evils visited by the powerful on his native land. In an address to Louis XVI, Diderot is merciless: "Cast your eyes over the capital of your empire," he announces, "and you will find two classes of citizens. Some, wallowing in wealth, flaunt a luxury that provokes indignation among those not corrupted by it. Others, overwhelmed with need, make their situation worse by the pretense of a prosperity that they do not have. For such is the power of gold, when it has become the god of a nation, that it takes the place of all talent and replaces all virtue." As for the countryside, the situation is even more dire, where "the person who makes our prosperity is condemned to die of poverty." This "unfortunate laborer scarcely has enough straw from the land he cultivated so as to cover his cottage and make himself a bed."[15]

In his apostrophe to Louis, Diderot uses the familiar *tu* rather than the formal *vous*—an act of lèse-majesté. This crime, though, is dwarfed by what Diderot dubs *lèse-société*—an act that violates not the king's privileges, but the people's rights. Prophetically, he calls for an "assembly of the estates of a great nation and restoration of original freedom" which is based on natural right of "every man to dispose of himself as he wishes." Liberty means, in effect, the "property of your body and the enjoyment of your mind."[16]

As for despotic rule, Diderot savages the notion still upheld by Voltaire and his crowd: enlightened despotism. Marked by his experience at the Hermitage, Diderot jettisons his earlier ambivalence concerning this particular enlightened despot, concluding that the term is, quite simply, oxymoronic. No matter how well intentioned or high-minded, a despot necessarily violates the liberty of his—or, indeed, *her*—subjects through the exercise of untrammeled power. Even if he acted on behalf of the general good, Diderot declares, the despot stands, by his very nature, as a violation of the general will. However virtuous he might be, "any prince who did good contrary to the general will would be a criminal, for the simple reason that he had exceeded his rights."[17] Ultimately, however, the future of the Enlightenment would play out, not, as many of his contemporaries still believed, in the steppes of Catherine's Russia, but instead on the farms of Jefferson's America. In a soaring peroration to the revolutionaries of 1776, Diderot exclaimed: "May the news of your happiness bring to your homes all the unfortunate people of the earth. May all tyrants and oppressors, either political or religious, know that a place exists in the world where people can cast off their chains; where persecuted humanity has raised up its head again; where the harvest grows for the poor."[18]

While hailed by most enlightened thinkers, the book's publication in early 1781 nevertheless left one *lumière,* a confidant of Catherine as well as friend of Diderot, with a bad case of dyspepsia. Whereas Diderot grew into a political radical in his final years, Grimm had wizened into a political reactionary. Counselor to German princes, broker of dynastic marriages, and even for a short while the road manager for the young Amadeus Mozart, Grimm was outraged by the work's assault on enlightened despotism. In March, when he met Raynal at a literary salon in Geneva, Grimm made his displeasure known. With a flourish, he declared: "Either you believe those you attack cannot revenge themselves, which makes it an act of cowardice to attack them; or you believe that they can and probably will take revenge, which makes it madness to have made yourself vulnerable."[19]

Delighted by his *bon mot,* Grimm repeated it a few days later to, of all people, Diderot. Like Raynal, who had been left nonplussed by Grimm's sally, Diderot was speechless—at least at first. But once past the initial shock, Diderot grew furious over the flimsiness of his friend's faux dilemma. Compounding Diderot's fury was his conviction that Grimm had, in fact, aimed the barbed remark at him. After all, Grimm must have known that he, Diderot, had penned the book's most trenchant and provocative sections. Clearly, anger had been mounting inside Diderot ever since the visit to Russia, where it was Grimm, and not he, who won Catherine's confidence. He had not forgotten, upon telling Grimm that he saw the empress every afternoon, the German's nonchalant reply: "And I see her every night." The old philosophe's resentment, thickening with the passage of time, became the tinder that now burst into flames. In a long and impassioned letter, Diderot dismantled Grimm's logic and denounced his cravenness. Not only is it right to attack someone who holds foolish ideas, he proclaimed, but it is also right to attack those who, holding foolish ideas, are in a position to avenge themselves. Isn't this, when all is said and done, the duty of a philosophe?

The writing of *History of the Two Indies,* Diderot announced, had made Raynal and his collaborators worthy of the "mantle of Socrates." Does such a claim, he asked, make his old friend laugh? If it does, it confirms Grimm's tragic transformation. "You have become one of the most hidden, but most dangerous anti-philosophes. You live among us, but you hate us." Then, with a phrase sharper and crueler than Grimm's original sin, but also more accurate, Diderot concludes: "Ah, my friend, I see that your soul has shriveled while loitering at the keyholes and in the antechambers of the great in St. Petersburg and Potsdam."[20]

Having written his denunciation, Diderot thought twice about delivering it. In the end, either unwilling or unable to break publicly with his old friend, Diderot decided to keep the letter in his drawer. But that did not keep from him the realization that Grimm's words sliced closer to the bone than he wished to admit. Diderot had long since learned to balance the urge for provocation with the need for subordination, to measure his attachment to moral ideals against the need for mundane deals, and to qualify his duty to tell the truth with the threat of another prison spell. While Raynal's reasons for broadcasting his authorship of *History of the Two Indies* were not entirely selfless, it also required courage. As for Diderot, he felt a frisson of fear upon hearing voices below his window—as he told Grimm in the postscript to his unsent letter—announcing the Parlement's condemnation of the abbé.[21]

But the postscript does not end there. Diderot cannot help but deliver one more sally, informing Grimm that one is "incapable of heroic actions if he denounces them, and one who denounces heroic acts is incapable of them."[22] Diderot's logic is as shoddy as Grimm's dilemma is phony—nothing prevents a hero, after all, from discriminating among heroic acts—but it is also revealing. The high dudgeon of Diderot's postscript was fed by his fear of the low dungeons of Vincennes. Grimm had become, in effect, a proxy for his own self-examination, one that made him wonder if he was truly worthy of the Socratic legacy.

Diderot himself had, from time to time, cultivated his resemblance to Socrates, but ultimately he knew that the resemblance was mostly skin-deep. He wanted to be worthy of the Socratic mantle, but was he truly willing to turn it, through a heroic act, into his funeral shroud? Diderot already knew the answer. In mid-1769 he recounted to Sophie a debate he had just had with the Baron d'Holbach and Jacques-André Naigeon on the subject of Helvétius's humiliating public disavowal of *De l'esprit* several years earlier. How admirable, Diderot exclaimed, the philosophe who stood his ground and defended his writings! Standing before his judges, such a man would declare: "Yes, I am the one who wrote this book. It contains my thoughts and I will not retract them."[23] While the conversation was lighthearted—"We laughed like children"—Diderot was serious about the philosopher's duty to tell the truth, consequences be damned. "How I would suffer to retract the truth, to speak against my beliefs after having written according to my beliefs, to behave like a coward in the eyes of my judges, fellow citizens and loved ones, to deprive my statements of their authority and to refuse the sacrifices demanded by the truth."[24] But while his freethinking companions mocked him for his apparent desire "to be burned at all cost," Diderot reassured Sophie that he had no intention of starring in his own *auto-da-fé*. "The time for such foolishness has long since passed. I don't think highly enough of myself to defend my own cause."[25]

At one level this was a well-honed performance of humility. But at a deeper level it represented Diderot's growing doubts about his accomplishments. There was, of course, his deep pride in his family. His new role as patriarch and grandfather was deeply gratifying, even if he sometimes fell short of his grandchildren's expectations. "I love your children madly," he told Angélique, "even though they think I'm poorly educated ever since the day I was unable to tell them where Charlemagne died."[26] And he had even reached a modus vivendi with Nanette, who had suddenly and unexpectedly developed a love of literature. In order to replace a friend's book—Alain-René Lesage's best-selling *Gil Blas*—that Angélique had lost, Nanette bought a new copy. Idly opening the novel, Nanette began to read and, Diderot reported, could not stop. This might well be, he exclaimed, the cure for Nanette's "vapors." And so, he began a daily regimen with his wife, in which he served as her physician: "I administer three doses of *Gil Blas* every day; one in the morning, another in the afternoon, and one at night." According to Diderot's prognosis, a few hundred readings of other books over a few years would "complete the cure"—especially as Nanette had the habit of repeating to visitors what she had just read, thus "doubling the remedy's effectiveness." Joking that he had discovered a recipe for all manner of vapors, he identified yet other essential "drugs," which the doctor would vary according to need, ranging from *Don Quixote* to, yes, *Jacques the Fatalist*.[27]

But, in the end, posterity was no laughing matter for Diderot. Notwithstanding his dedication to the well-being of his children and grandchildren, he was also dedicated to the well-being of the statue he had made of himself. Would posterity judge it as favorably as it would, say, Falconet's sculpture of Peter? Had he not, in fact, told Falconet that "posterity would truly be ungrateful if it forgot me completely, given that I have been thinking about it so much"? This question led him, in the last years of his life, to undertake one last intellectual endeavor. Rather than turn to his beloved Socrates, however, Diderot appealed to another, though less-beloved thinker from antiquity. In a letter to his faithful Naigeon, Diderot proclaimed his plan to "examine without bias the life and writings of Seneca, and avenge the insults, if they are unjust, borne by this great man, or if they are founded, learn from his wise and powerful lessons."[28]

Diderot had always been partial when it came to the life and character of Lucius Annaeus Seneca—Roman statesman, philosopher, and dramatist—but not always for the same reasons. In his 1745 translation of Shaftesbury's *Inquiry Concerning Merit, or Virtue,* the young Diderot dismissed Seneca as a dissembler and double-dealer who, more interested in "adding to his wealth than seeing to his perilous duty," had made himself "complicit, through his shameful silence, in the death of a few brave men" under the reign of Nero.[29] This harsh judgment, embedded in a long and winding footnote, was based on Diderot's reading of Tacitus. "I treat this philosopher [i.e., Seneca] a little sternly," the youthful idealist admits, "but Tacitus's account makes it impossible to think better of him."[30]

That was then. Nearly four decades later—a span of time marked by repeated exposures, some terrifying, others edifying, to the exercise of absolute power—Diderot was ready to think better of Seneca. In 1782 he published his *Essay on the Reigns of Claudius and Nero, and on the Manners and Writings of Seneca.* The essay, which Diderot published under his own name, runs over 500 pages. As with so many of Diderot's writings, the essay is a revision of a text he had published three years earlier. Despite his faltering health and failing eyesight, Diderot stunned friends and family by the time he devoted to the project. Looking back on this period, when her father spent fourteen hours a day reading and writing, Angélique concluded that this extraordinary spurt of energy effort shortened his life.[31]

Shortened, perhaps, but also sweetened—or so Diderot claimed. In his letter to Naigeon—which was subsequently published as the book's introduction—Diderot insisted that the time he had spent researching and writing the book was "one of the sweetest periods of my life."[32] Yet it was a period where his attention was fastened not just on the distant past and Rome, but also on the near past and Saint Petersburg. As late as 1781 Diderot held to the tattered hope that Catherine might yet metamorphose into the legislative reformer he had long hoped she would become. That summer he recommended to Catherine the services of Pierre Charbit, a young man whose recently published book on legislative practice in France had impressed Diderot. In his letter Diderot praised Charbit's integrity and utility. His sole desire, he explained, is "to be useful." And where could his abilities be of greater use than in Russia, whose sovereign "thinks night and day about the happiness of her people"?[33] But Catherine, who never replied to Diderot's letter, made clear she had no use for Charbit's skills. Her interest in legislative reform, diminished by the resistant reality of Russian society, as well as her preoccupation by military and diplomatic matters, might explain her silence. A more prosaic and painful possibility—one that Diderot must have considered—was that Catherine had decided that her French philosophes were largely useless.

For Denis le philosophe, this possibility had nearly existential ramifications. More so than any other episode in his life, Diderot's time at the Hermitage forced him to reflect on what he had accomplished and how posterity, and not just his grandchildren, would remember him. It was less a matter of being able to tell his grandchildren where Charlemagne died than tell them why he, Diderot, had lived. The question haunted Diderot, especially as he felt his life was reaching an end. He had reached the age, he told Grimm in 1776, where "one counts the years, followed by the age where one counts the months, leading to the age when one lives a day at a time."[34] A year later, in another missive to Grimm, he returned to the theme. "My spirit and heart remain in their infancy, but the rest of my body is slouching toward the cemetery."[35]

Now that the time had come to take stock, Diderot looked to Seneca: the parallels in their lives and work were, at least in the philosophe's eyes, too great to ignore. Both had achieved fame—and a degree of infamy—as men who, because of their philosophizing, became advisors to emperors.

Seneca played a pivotal role in Rome's imperial government as Nero's tutor and advisor, whereas Catherine had Diderot—at least in his version of their relationship—"stay by her side and work on texts dealing with legislation."[36] For both men, the proximity to power became ethically problematic. There was, of course, the awkward matter of imperial munificence. With Nero's complicity, Seneca became one of the empire's richest men—a tricky position for a practicing Stoic who professed great disdain for wealth. And while Diderot could not boast of vast estates and wealth, he could breathe freely in his later years thanks to Catherine's many acts of generosity. Every time he referred to his great collection of books as her library, every time he received his salary as her librarian, every time he earned a commission for her art purchases, he wondered if he had become, not her philosopher, but her courtier. When he protested that he wanted nothing but a memento of the empress and reimbursement for his travel costs when he took his leave, he might well have asked himself if he was protesting too much. If Diderot had always been, as he told Catherine, a free man in Russia, why did he demand a public show of that freedom? Did he suspect that he had already made the sort of concessions and compromises that Rameau's nephew would have gladly flaunted? Did he have reason to recall his effort to persuade Rulhière to bury his account of Catherine's role in the "revolution" of 1762? Had his praise for the empress who combined the qualities of Brutus and Cleopatra begun to ring hollow?

These persistent questions crowded on Diderot as he looked to his past in order to better forecast his future. The pressure was so great that Diderot did both himself and Catherine a disservice by insisting too forcefully on the parallels to Seneca and Nero. Nero's palace was a theater of cruelty and murder, after all, whereas Catherine's court was often steeped in intrigue and jealously but never in blood (at least after Peter's death). Catherine sought to reform penal law and eliminate torture in Russia, of course, whereas Nero relished the power of life and death over his court and subjects. And though the empress bankrupted the treasury to fund her imperial adventures abroad and imperial spectacles at home, her private life remained modest and unpretentious—two adjectives that do not apply to Nero's public or private lives.

The bridges that Diderot tried to build between his own life and Seneca's were, in certain respects, even flimsier. Whereas Seneca was a very prolific and public writer, Diderot had relegated his philosophical writings, ever since his stay at Vincennes, to his desk drawers; the Roman was a pivotal figure in politics and served as Nero's advisor for eight years, whereas the Parisian had Catherine's ear for scarcely four months. Diderot tried (and failed) to persuade Rulhière to kill the publication of his book, but this pales in comparison to Seneca's defense of Nero's killing of his stepbrother Britannicus and mother, Agripinna. Finally, Nero was still a child when Seneca was called to Rome to shape his charge's mind; Catherine was a forty-year-old empress who knew her own mind when she called Diderot to Saint Petersburg.

And yet, despite the smudges and cracks in this particular mirror, Diderot saw a resemblance. The reader of his essay, he warned, "will not need long to see that it is my own self that I portray as much as that of the different historical actors in my essay."[37] As he veers from historical synopsis to polemical jousting, interpretations of Seneca's writings to justifications of his actions, Diderot presents a defense not just of the Roman but also of himself. He defends Seneca against the charges of corruption and hypocrisy partly by recalling his remark to Mme Necker about painted and real tigers. He chastises his contemporaries who, while enjoying a delicious meal in the comfort of a well-heated room, disparage Seneca.[38] These critics clearly had never experienced the exercise of absolute power so intimately and intensely as had Seneca—or, Diderot insinuates, he himself. The only tigers these detractors know are those framed on the walls of their well-appointed salons. Had not Nero, upon learning of a conspiracy against his life, become like a "maddened tiger"? "Put yourself in the place of the philosopher, teacher and minister," he proclaims, "and try to do better than he did."[39]

In fact, Diderot continues, Seneca did do better than his critics claim. No doubt thinking about his own efforts to help struggling writers, Diderot swats away the issue of Seneca's supposed greed. But he did not simply hoard his wealth. "Yes, Seneca's wealth was well known! Yet have his good actions and aid for the unfortunate been forgotten?"[40] Moreover, Seneca's decision to remain in his post while Nero's crimes compounded daily was less a dereliction than affirmation of duty. "Were he to have saved the honor of a single woman, shielded one son for his father or one daughter for her mother, or protected one good citizen," he would have accomplished far more than if he had openly resisted or retired. When he did retire in 62 CE, following the death of his powerful ally Burrhus, he recognized that he alone could no longer orchestrate even these modest instances of goodness.[41]

But should not have Seneca, as Stoic sage, been indifferent to these impossible conditions? Indeed, isn't death itself a "thing indifferent" for true Stoics? As Diderot's imaginary interlocutor asks: "Doesn't the teacher owe the truth to his student?" Yes, Diderot replies, but Nero was no longer Seneca's student. Instead, he had become emperor, and one could no more treat an emperor like a student than a tiger like a cub. Indeed, Diderot insisted, even religious ministers would quaver and retreat into silence in such situations. "There are still, I believe, dissolute and evil rulers. I would like to know which of their godly ministers would dare remonstrate with them, and how their sovereigns would welcome such audacity. . . . How would such wise and respectable men behave at such moments? Despite the imposing authority of their characters, they would scrape and be silent."[42]

In the end, Diderot concluded, even "great men like Seneca are not always admirable." But this was not the real issue. Instead, it had to do with the source of Seneca's greatness. His eminence was based, in part, on his brilliantly persuasive guides to Stoicism. Yet he failed to act upon those same teachings, at least until the moment of his death. What was to be said about the yawning gap between a moralist's words and actions?

Was it enough to reply, as does Diderot, that Seneca's inability to act on his teachings was irrelevant? "What does the contradiction, true or false, between Seneca's conduct and morals matter to us?" What truly mattered, ultimately, were the contents of the philosophy, and not the character of the philosopher. Let us learn from Seneca's writings, even if we cannot learn from his life. "We do not need Seneca's example to know that it is easier to give than follow good advice."[43]

Yet Diderot's unease with his own argument becomes clear when he comes to Seneca's celebrated suicide in 65 CE. Never, he declares, "did a man die with greater firmness and fearlessness."[44] Yet as the Roman historian Tacitus implies in his account of Seneca's suicide, never has a man also died with greater determination to stage-manage his death. However, as the classicist Emily Wilson notes, Seneca found himself wrestling with the same failures in his death as he did in his life. His initial efforts to kill himself—first cutting his wrists, next his knees, finally drinking hemlock—all flopped. It was only when he had his slaves lift him into a hot bath that the old man finally died of suffocation. One can mock Seneca's series of failures and compromises, concludes Wilson, or instead admire his tenacity in overcoming the former and achieving the latter.[45]

The same holds true for Seneca's flawed, yet determined, defender. When he learned that Nero had ordered his death, Seneca told his family and friends that he would bequeath them the pattern, or image, of his life to remember him by.[46] It was at the moment of his death, Seneca believed, that he could not only speak truth to power, but also most effectively speak about himself to posterity. This was the case for Diderot, as well. As his remaining years dwindled into months, which in turn trickled into days, Diderot turned to the statue of himself he wished to leave to posterity. He knew that it had been scored and scratched by life. Such was the fate of all statues, but it was even more the case for statues buffeted by the unchecked powers of emperors and empresses. Over time, Diderot lamented, the power wielded by despotic governments "narrows our minds without our knowledge. We come to shun, without thinking, certain kinds of ideas the way we avoid those obstacles that can harm us. Once accustomed to this circumspect and cowardly attitude, we regain our honesty and audacity with only great difficulty. It is only from our graves that we can think and speak openly."[47]

Upon the publication of the revised essay, Diderot's lament was given a tragicomic illustration worthy of *Jacques the Fatalist.* Diderot had persuaded the police chief of Paris, Jean-Charles-Pierre Le Noir, to allow 600 copies of the essay to be sold in Paris. When Louis XVI learned about the book, however, he burst into anger. "This philosopher, the enemy of religion," he announced, "must be punished."[48] Yet neither Le Noir nor Armand-Thomas de Miromesnil, the official tasked with this assignment, had the slightest desire to *embastiller,* or imprison, the aged and ailing philosopher. Giving a generous gloss to the king's order, Miromesnil called Diderot to his bureau and limited the punishment to a severe lecture. Once Miromesnil finished chastising Diderot, the guilty party promptly fell to his knees, declaring that he deserved "to be punished more for the mistakes of my old age than for my youthful extravagances. Please deign to accept my confession and repentance."[49] In a subsequent letter to Le Noir, Diderot echoed his regrets: "You have given me a good and kind lesson and I stand corrected for the rest of my life."[50]

Was Diderot sincere? Or, instead, did he play a role just as Miromesnil and Le Noir seemed to do? All we know with certainty, as did Diderot himself did, is that what remained of his life would be measured in months.

Epilogue

Diderot's darkly comic turn for Miromesnil resembles the comedies Rameau's nephew performed for his patron. There was only so much room for free thought and expression in a world of rigid hierarchies and despotic monarchies. But the resemblance went only so far. Whereas the nephew had his eye on his next meal, Diderot had his eye on his last meal. By early 1784 it had become painfully clear that his time had nearly run out. In February, while chatting with Angélique, Diderot suddenly fell quiet. Walking to a mirror, he pointed to his mouth, which seemed askew. Unable to move his other hand, he looked at Angélique. "A stroke," he observed. Shuffling to his bed, he kissed Nanette and Angélique, told them where they would find a stack of books he had borrowed, and bid his farewells.

But the moment for farewells had not yet arrived. After a brace of doctors had arrived, bleeding him in several places, Diderot slipped into a delirium that lasted three days. He recited and translated Greek and Latin epitaphs, quoted Horace and Virgil, and constantly asked for the time. By the fourth day the fever passed, but his family was unable to celebrate the news. As Diderot began to recover, his granddaughter, Minette, suddenly died. A devastated Angélique managed to keep the news from her father, being as incapable of telling Diderot that Minette had died as he was of telling his beloved granddaughter where Charlemagne had died.

Grimm reported Diderot's failing health to a deeply concerned Catherine. When she learned of Minette's death, the empress's shock was sincere. "I am very upset Diderot is so ill and with the terrible news concerning his granddaughter. Never have I heard of a similar case: Mother Nature's ways are inexhaustible."[1] Despite their widening political and personal differences, Grimm's attachment to Diderot remained fast. This was also the case for Catherine, as became clear in her sharp reply to Grimm's suggestion that they secure a ground-floor residence for Diderot where he would not have to climb stairs as he did at Rue Taranne. His doctors had warned that given his weak heart, it was a matter of life and death. "You should have done this without asking my permission," she chastised Grimm. "Find a suitable apartment for my library and my librarian." But Catherine's orders revealed not just her concern for Diderot, but also her concern for posterity when she ordered Grimm to make absolutely certain not to "misplace a single shred of paper" from Diderot's manuscripts.[2]

The new quarters that Grimm rented in July 1784, a spacious and stately apartment on the fashionable Rue de Richelieu, pleased Diderot greatly. Angélique reported that her father, who had "always lived in a hovel, found himself in a palace."[3] But the palace was little more than a way station. On July 30, while workers debated where to place a new bed Grimm had bought for Diderot, the dying man joked: "My friends, you are taking a great deal of trouble over a piece of furniture that will not be used for more than four days."[4] Later that day, while she listened to a discussion between Diderot and friends about the nature of philosophy, Angélique heard her father observe: "The first step towards philosophy is incredulity." That night, he slept peacefully.

They were the last words she would ever hear him say. The following day, July 31, he spent the morning chatting with his old comrade in arms, the Baron d'Holbach, then lunched with Nanette on soup and mutton.

"It's been such a long time," he exclaimed, "since I've eaten with so much pleasure." When he reached for an apricot, his wife tried to stop him. "What in the devil's name," Diderot laughed, "do you think it can do to me?" A few minutes later, Nanette, whose head was turned, heard him cough softly. Asking about the cough, but not getting a reply, she turned to look at her husband. With less display and more humanity than his hero Seneca, Diderot had died.[5]

If the first step to philosophy, for Diderot, is incredulity, Catherine's first step away from her philosopher also began in incredulity, though of a different kind. In French, incredulity shades into several meanings, denoting shock and disbelief, but also astonishment and amazement. In October 1785—little more than twelve years to the day after Diderot landed in Saint Petersburg—his library and manuscripts, packed and posted by Angélique, reached the Russian capital. On October 22 Catherine notified Grimm: "Diderot's library has arrived."[6] Shortly thereafter, having studiously ignored Diderot's earlier invitation, in 1773, to read his observations on her *Nakaz,* Catherine read the manuscript. She was, quite simply, incredulous. In a blistering letter to Grimm, she erupted: "This piece is genuine babble, bereft of experience, prudence, and foresight. If I had written the *Nakaz* to suit Diderot's taste, it would have meant turning the world upside down." Catherine concluded that Diderot had undoubtedly written this screed after he had left Russia, "as he never spoke to me about it."[7]

Two years later Catherine's anger was no longer molten, but the ashes now darkened her recollection of Diderot. In a conversation with the new French ambassador, Count Louis-Philippe de Ségur, the empress offered a remarkable revision of the past. When Ségur asked Catherine for her impressions about the philosophe—a title, Ségur primly suggested, Diderot "did not perhaps merit"—Catherine was pitiless. She confided that during her conversations with Diderot, she could hardly get a word in edgewise. She did not say a word about the excited philosopher who would grab her arm or slap her thigh as he made a point, or the sympathetic empress who insisted that such candid exchanges "between men" was to be expected. The tableau had changed dramatically: "As I listened more than I spoke, an outsider observing the scene would have taken him for a stern teacher and me for a humble student. After awhile, when he realized that my government had not adopted any of the great innovations he had proposed, he expressed his surprise with a kind of proud displeasure."

At this point, Catherine continued, she reclaimed her imperium and rapped Diderot's knuckles. "Monsieur Diderot, I have listened with great pleasure to everything that your brilliant mind has inspired. But your grand principles, which I understand quite well, make for good books and bad actions. Your plans for reform neglect the difference between our two positions. You work on paper, which accepts everything. It is smooth, supple and offers no opposition to either your imagination or pen. But I, a poor empress, work on human skin, which is rather irritable and sensitive." Having recalled—or recreated—this exchange, Catherine paused and smiled. "From this moment on, I am certain, he took pity on me, convinced that I had a vulgar and narrow mind. Politics disappeared from our conversation, and all he would speak about was literature."[8]

Of course, Catherine hardly needed Diderot—or, for that matter, Voltaire—to remind her that literature was politics by other means. If she had read Diderot's memoranda, in her possession since his departure in 1774, Catherine also knew that they reveal that politics kept popping up in their conversations till the very end. Finally, she knew from her correspondents in Paris that Diderot unfailingly praised, in private and public conversations, her intellect and character. That he despised despotism was no secret, but it was also no secret that he remained devoted to Catherine to his dying day.

But if Catherine judged Diderot too harshly on these matters, she also pointed to an uncomfortable truth concerning Diderot's own judgment. This truth is best seen in the different attitudes the two of them had toward Montesquieu. Despite his dutiful acknowledgment of Montesquieu's genius, Diderot was deeply conflicted over *The Spirit of the Laws.* He disliked what struck him as a streak of political relativism, and subsequent tolerance for despotism, that ran through the work. Yet what Diderot dismissed as relativism, Catherine embraced as realism. On more than one occasion Diderot joked that *The Spirit of the Laws* had become Catherine's breviary. But it was a decidedly odd breviary, offering not supplications to God but instead the implications of geography and climate for a people. In an enlightened but empirical approach that emphasized factors like history and geography, Montesquieu sought to portray society as it was. In his devotion to enlightened and universal ideals, Diderot instead presented society as it ought to be.[9]

Catherine and Diderot often expressed impatience, even outrage, at one another's positions. As they aged, the outrage came more easily. They had, by the 1780s, gravitated toward their respective extremes. Though Diderot died five years before the start of the French Revolution, Catherine lived until 1796. At first she had allowed the news about the Bastille, and subsequent events from France, to be reported and debated in the Russian press. But by 1792, with the overthrow of Louis XVI and the creation of the French Republic, Catherine was haunted by the revolution's increasingly bloody progress. Two years later, when France was in the throes of the Terror, the empress renounced her earlier attachment to the philosophes. Their writings, she now told Grimm, "served only to destroy," paving the way to "calamities without end and innumerable wretched people."[10]

Yet much in the lives and conversations of Diderot and Catherine reveals the common ground between the man who wrote on paper and woman who wrote on human skin. Diderot would have undoubtedly shared the revulsion Catherine (rightly) expressed over the Terror. And if they had continued to correspond, the two might have allowed that just as the empress's rule had largely been inspired by ideals espoused by the editor of the *Encyclopédie,* the editor of the *Encyclopédie* had accepted the need for incremental, not revolutionary, reform. Both were inevitably flawed and fallible, but what is less inevitable and perhaps more important is that they both remained fully attached to the party of humanity. Though these two remarkable individuals precede us by nearly three centuries, their public ideals, which are increasingly besieged in the west, and their private decency, increasingly scarce among our leaders, are more important than ever.

NOTES

ACKNOWLEDGMENTS

INDEX

Notes

PROLOGUE

1. *Denis Diderot: Correspondance,* ed. Georges Roth and Jean Varloot (Paris: Éditions de Minuit, 1966), 13:219.
2. Malcolm Bradbury, *To the Hermitage* (London: Picador, 2000), xxi.
3. Ibid.
4. Denis Diderot, *Jacques the Fatalist,* trans. Michael Henry (London: Penguin, 1986), 80.
5. Diderot, "Observations on the Nakaz," in *Diderot: Political Writings,* ed. John Hope Mason and Robert Wokler (Cambridge: Cambridge University Press, 1992), 82.
6. Maurice Tourneux, *Diderot et Catherine II* (Paris: Calmann Lévy, 1899), 519–520.

1. THE SEA AT SCHEVENINGEN

1. *Denis Diderot: Correspondance,* ed. Georges Roth and Jean Varloot (Paris: Éditions de Minuit, 1966), 13:31.
2. Simon Schama, *The Embarrassment of Riches* (New York: Vintage, 1997), 403.
3. Ibid.
4. Diderot, *Voyage de Hollande,* in *Oeuvres inédits de Denis Diderot* (Paris: Brière, 1821), 123.
5. Alain Corbin, *Le Territoire du vide* (Paris: Aubier, 1988), 45.
6. Schama, *The Embarrassment of Riches,* 263.
7. Diderot, *Oeuvres inédits,* 292.
8. Corbin, *Le Territoire du vide,* 47.

9. Ibid., 286.
10. *Denis Diderot: Correspondance,* 12:63.
11. Ibid.
12. Ibid., 12:232.
13. Diderot, Paris Art Salon of 1765. *Oeuvres,* ed. André Billy (Paris: Pléiade, 1969), 305.
14. Diderot, "Regrets on Parting with My Old Dressing Coat," in *Diderot: Rameau's Nephew and Other Works,* ed. Jacques Barzun and Ralph H. Bowen (Indianapolis: Hackett, 2001), 315.
15. Diderot, *Supplement to the Voyage of Bougainville,* in Barzun and Bowen, *Diderot: Rameau's Nephew,* 180–181.
16. Diderot, Paris Art Salon of 1765. In *Oeuvres,* ed. Billy, 307.
17. P. N. Furbank, *Diderot: A Critical Biography* (New York: Knopf, 1992), 285.
18. Ibid., 280.
19. Ibid., 285.
20. *Encyclopédie,* s.v. "Beau."
21. Furbank, *Diderot,* 372.
22. *Denis Diderot: Correspondance,* 13:51.
23. Benedetta Craveri, *The Age of Conversation,* trans. Teresa Waugh (New York: New York Review of Books, 2005), 302.
24. Arthur Wilson, *Diderot: The Testing Years, 1713–1759* (New York: Oxford University Press, 1957), 224.
25. Elisabeth de Fontenay, *Reason and Resonance* (New York: George Brazillier, 1982), 259.
26. Craveri, *The Age of Conversation,* 337.
27. Ibid., 354.
28. Ibid., 362.
29. Furbank, *Diderot,* 103.
30. Ibid., 102.
31. Roy Porter, *Flesh in the Age of Reason* (New York: W. W. Norton, 2003), 130–138.
32. Carol Blum, *Diderot: The Virtue of a Philosopher* (New York: Viking, 1974), 20–21.
33. Diderot, "Éloge de Richardson," in *Oeuvres,* ed. André Billy (Paris: Pléiade, 1951), 1062.
34. Ibid., 1066.
35. Ibid.
36. Ibid., 1067.
37. Blum, *Diderot,* 77.
38. *Denis Diderot: Correspondance,* 3:292
39. Diderot, *Entretiens sur Le Fils Naturel,* in *Oeuvres,* ed. André Billy (Paris: Pléiade, 1951), 1213.
40. Wilson, *Diderot: The Testing Years,* 245.
41. Stephen Nadler, *Spinoza: A Biography* (Cambridge: Cambridge University Press, 2001), 296.

42. Ibid.
43. Jonathan Israel, *Radical Enlightenment* (Oxford: Oxford University Press, 2002), 286.
44. Diderot, *Voyage de Hollande,* 92.
45. *Denis Diderot: Correspondance,* 13:35.
46. Ibid., 13:22, July 1773.
47. Raymond Trousson, *Diderot* (Paris: Gallimard, 2007), 254.
48. *Lettre sur l'homme,* ed. Georges May (New Haven, CT: Yale University Press, 1964), 2–3.
49. Trousson, *Diderot,* 258.
50. Lester Crocker, *Diderot's Chaotic Order* (Princeton: Princeton University Press, 1974), 77.
51. Jonathan Israel, *Democratic Enlightenment* (Oxford: Oxford University Press, 2011), 669.
52. Helvétius, *Essays on the Mind,* trans. W. Mudford (London: M. Jones, 1807), 41.
53. *Lettres de Mme de Graffigny,* ed. Eugène Asse (Paris: Charpentier, 1897), 291.
54. Wilson, *Diderot: The Testing Years,* 311.
55. Ernest Cassirer, *The Philosophy of the Enlightenment* (Princeton: Princeton University Press, 1951), 26.
56. Wilson, *Diderot: The Testing Years,* 312.
57. *Denis Diderot: Correspondance,* 2:112.
58. D. W. Smith, *Helvétius: A Study in Persecution* (London: Oxford University Press, 1965), 34.
59. Israel, *Democratic Enlightenment,* 664.
60. Ibid., 670.
61. *Denis Diderot: Correspondance,* 13:56.
62. Furbank, *Diderot,* 374.
63. Blum, *Diderot,* 147.
64. Ibid., 36–37.
65. Ibid., 142.
66. *Encyclopédie,* vol. 5, s.v. "Encyclopédie."
67. Denis Diderot, *Lettres à Falconet,* ed. J. Assézat and M. Tourneux (Paris: Garnier, 1922), 231.
68. Albert Lortholary, *Le Mirage russe en France au XVIIIème siècle* (Paris: Éditions contemporaines, 1951), 97–98.

2. READING VOLTAIRE IN ST. PETERSBURG

1. *Documents of Catherine the Great,* ed. W. F. Reddaway (New York: Russell and Russell, 1931), 188.
2. *Voltaire and Catherine the Great: Selected Correspondence,* trans. A. Lentin (Oxford: Oriental Research Partners, 1974), 34.

3. *The Memoirs of Catherine the Great,* trans. Mark Cruse and Hilde Hoogenboom (New York: Modern Library, 2005), 31–32.
4. Ibid., 10–11.
5. Ibid., 5.
6. Ibid., 148–149.
7. Ibid., 120.
8. Ernest Cassirer, *The Philosophy of the Enlightenment* (Princeton: Princeton University Press, 1951), 162.
9. *Memoirs of Catherine the Great,* 123.
10. Lucien Lévy-Bruhl, "Voltaire: His Conception of Philosophy, Theology and Universal History," *The Open Court* 13, no. 2 (February 1899): 70.
11. Isabel de Madariaga, *Politics and Culture in Eighteenth-Century Russia* (London: Longman, 1998), 238.
12. Ibid.
13. *Documents of Catherine the Great,* 2.
14. Tacitus, *The Annals of Imperial Rome,* trans. Michael Grant (New York: Penguin, 1989), 34.
15. *Memoirs of Catherine the Great,* 137.
16. Ibid., 51.
17. Simon Dixon, *Catherine the Great* (New York: HarperCollins, 2009), 102.
18. John T. Alexander, *Catherine the Great: Life and Legend* (New York: Oxford University Press, 1989), 48.
19. *Memoirs of Catherine the Great,* 185.
20. Ibid., 207.
21. Ibid., 216.
22. Ibid., 208.

3. R IS FOR RIGA

1. *Denis Diderot: Correspondance,* ed. Georges Roth and Jean Varloot (Paris: Éditions de Minuit, 1966), 13:12.
2. Denis Diderot, *Lettres à Sophie Volland* (Paris: Gallimard, 1930), 2: 63.
3. Philipp Blom, *Enlightening the World: Encyclopédie, the Book That Changed the Course of History* (New York: Palgrave, 2004), xxv.
4. Denis Diderot, *Lettre sur les aveugles* (Paris: Flammarion, 2000), 59.
5. Arthur Wilson, *Diderot: The Testing Years, 1713–1759* (New York: Oxford University Press, 1957), 106.
6. Denis Diderot, "Encyclopédie," in *Political Writings* (New York: Cambridge University Press, 1992), 21–22, 25.
7. Blom, *Enlightening the World,* 113.
8. Ibid., 120.

9. Ibid., 228.
10. Diderot, *Lettres à Sophie Volland,* 1:87.
11. *Denis Diderot: Correspondance,* 4:119–120.
12. P. N. Furbank, *Diderot: A Critical Biography* (New York: Knopf, 1992), 172–173.
13. Blom, *Enlightening the World,* 247.
14. *Voltaire and Catherine the Great: Selected Correspondence,* trans. A. Lentin (Oxford: Oriental Research Partners, 1974), 7.
15. Voltaire, *History of Russia under Peter the Great,* in *The Works of Voltaire,* trans. Tobias Smollett (Akron, OH: Werner, 1901), 35:120.
16. John Alexander, *Catherine the Great: Life and Legend* (Oxford: Oxford University Press, 1989).
17. Ronald Grimsley, *Jean d'Alembert: 1717–1783* (London: Oxford University Press, 1963), 172.
18. Isabel de Madariaga, *Russia in the Age of Catherine the Great* (London: Phoenix Press, 2002), 336.
19. *Denis Diderot: Correspondance,* 4:174–175.
20. This was the phrase the Abbé de Saint-Pierre used when he advised the young Voltaire on his proper vocation in 1740. See Geoffrey Turnovsky, "The Making of a Name: A Life of Voltaire," in *The Cambridge Companion to Voltaire,* ed. Nicholas Cronk (Cambridge: Cambridge University Press, 2009), 22.
21. Jonathan Israel, *Democratic Enlightenment* (Oxford: Oxford University Press, 2011), 621.
22. Maurice Tourneux, *Diderot et Catherine II* (Paris: Calmann-Lévy, 1899), 4–5.
23. *Denis Diderot: Correspondance,* vol. 4, April 24, 1765.
24. Ibid., November 17 / 28, 1765.
25. Ibid., November 29, 1766.
26. Wilson, *Diderot: The Testing Years,* 546.
27. Denis Diderot, *Lettres à Falconet,* ed. J. Assézat and M. Tourneux (Paris: Garnier, 1922), 256.
28. Ibid.
29. Wilson, *Diderot: The Testing Years,* 257.
30. *Denis Diderot: Correspondance,* 8:128.
31. Ibid., vol. 8, October 25, 1766.
32. Ibid., 8:231.
33. Ibid., vol. 8, September 12, 1761.
34. Diderot, *Lettres à Sophie Volland,* vol. 2, September 16, 1762.
35. *Denis Diderot: Correspondance,* 8:231.
36. Ibid., vol. 12, September 13, 1772.
37. A later generation of spies was also there, little less than a century later, when Karl Marx and Friedrich Engels first met one another in 1844 and launched their world-historical collaboration.

38. Diderot, *Rameau's Nephew,* in *Diderot: Rameau's Nephew and Other Works,* ed. Jacques Barzun and Ralph H. Bowen, trans. Jacques Barzun (Indianapolis: Hackett, 2001), 79.
39. Ibid., 35.
40. Ibid., 66.
41. Ibid., 76.
42. Ibid.
43. Ibid., 81
44. Ibid., 74.
45. Elisabeth de Fontenay, *Diderot, ou le matérialisme enchanté* (Paris: Grasset, 1981), 200.
46. Furbank, *Diderot,* 354.
47. Diderot, *Rameau's Nephew,* 83.
48. Ibid.
49. Ibid., 85.
50. Israel, *Democratic Enlightenment,* 270.
51. Peter Gay, *The Enlightenment: The Science of Freedom* (New York: Norton, 1969), 477.
52. Roger Pearson, *Voltaire Almighty* (London: Bloomsbury, 2005), 144.
53. Ibid., 222.
54. Diderot, "Lettre de M. Denis Diderot sur l'Examen de l'essai sur les préjugés," in *Oeuvres,* ed. André Billy (Paris: Pléiade, 1951), 3:168.
55. *Denis Diderot: Correspondance,* 9:64–65.
56. Ibid., 11:172.

4. GLASNOST

1. David Ransel, *The Politics of Catherinian Russia* (New Haven, CT: Yale University Press, 1975), 62–63.
2. *The Memoirs of Catherine the Great,* trans. Mark Cruse and Hilde Hoogenboom (New York: Modern Library, 2005), 198.
3. Isabel de Madariaga, *Russia in the Age of Catherine the Great* (London: Phoenix Press, 2002), 32.
4. Ibid., 32.
5. Simon Dixon, *Catherine the Great* (New York: HarperCollins, 2009), 128.
6. Ibid., 128–129.
7. Ibid., 132.
8. Dena Goodman, *The Republic of Letters: A Cultural History of the French Enlightenment* (Ithaca, NY: Cornell University Press, 1994), 74.
9. Benedetta Craveri, *The Age of Conversation,* trans. Teresa Waugh (New York: New York Review of Books, 2005), 296.
10. Antoine Lilti, *The World of the Salons: Sociability and Worldliness in Eighteenth-Century Paris,* trans. Lydia Cochrane (Oxford: Oxford University Press, 2005), 87.

11. Ibid., 219.
12. Madariaga, *Russia in the Age,* 334.
13. *Documents of Catherine the Great,* ed. W. F. Reddaway (New York: Russell and Russell, 1931), 7.
14. Ibid., 8.
15. Ibid., 7.
16. Albert Lortholary, *Le Mirage russe en France au XVIIIe siècle,* (Paris: Boivin & Cie, 1951), 74.
17. Voltaire, *Russia under Peter the Great,* trans. M. F. O. Jenkins (Rutherford, NJ: Fairleigh Dickinson University Press, 1983), 23, 251.
18. Ibid., 65.
19. Larry Woolf, *Inventing Eastern Europe: The Map of Civilization on the Mind of the Enlightenment* (Palo Alto, CA: Stanford University Press, 1994), 206.
20. Isabel de Madariaga, *Politics and Culture in Eighteenth-Century Russia* (London: Routledge, 2014), 215.
21. *Documents of Catherine the Great,* 190.
22. Jonathan Israel, *Democratic Enlightenment* (Oxford: Oxford University Press, 2011), 272.
23. Dixon, *Catherine the Great,* 224.
24. Isabel de Madariaga, *Catherine the Great* (New Haven, CT: Yale, 1990), 4.
25. See Madariaga, *Russia in the Age,* 79–104.
26. Ibid., 74.
27. Madariaga, *Politics and Culture,* 239.
28. Ibid., 238.
29. Robert Massie, *Catherine the Great: Portrait of a Woman* (New York: Random House, 2012), 305.
30. John Alexander, *Catherine the Great: Life and Legend* (Oxford: Oxford University Press, 1989), 116.
31. Dixon, *Catherine the Great,* 156.
32. *Memoirs,* 22.
33. Henri Troyat, *Catherine the Great* (New York: Meridian Books, 1994), 179.
34. *Documents of Catherine the Great,* Voltaire to Catherine, June 19, 1771.
35. Madariaga, *Russia in the Age,* 151.
36. Madariaga, *Politics and Culture,* 238.
37. Ransel, *The Politics of Catherinian Russia,* 53.
38. *Documents of Catherine the Great,* 7–8.
39. Madariaga, *Politics and Culture,* 113.
40. *Documents of Catherine the Great,* 7–8.
41. Dixon, *Catherine the Great,* 174.
42. *Documents of Catherine the Great,* 13.

43. Alexander, *Catherine the Great,* 112.
44. Denis Diderot, *Lettres à Falconet* (Paris: Garnier, 1922), 231.
45. Alexander, *Catherine the Great,* 119.
46. *Lettres à Falconet,* Diderot to Falconet, July 1767.

5. THE SHADOW LANDS

1. *Denis Diderot: Correspondance,* ed. Georges Roth and Jean Varloot (Paris: Éditions de Minuit, 1966), 13:19.
2. Ibid., 13:28.
3. Ibid.
4. Ibid., 13:49.
5. *Denis Diderot: Correspondance,* vol. 15 (Diderot to Rey, April 14, 1777).
6. Denis Diderot, *Jacques the Fatalist,* trans. Michael Henry (New York: Penguin, 1986), 63.
7. Ibid., 22.
8. Ibid., 104–105.
9. Ibid., 152.
10. Ibid., 26.
11. Ibid., 37.
12. Quoted in Wayne Booth, *The Rhetoric of Fiction* (Chicago: University of Chicago Press, 1961), 42.
13. Denis Diderot, *This Is Not a Story and Other Stories,* trans. P. N. Furbank (Oxford: Oxford University Press, 1991), 17.
14. Ian Watt, *The Rise of the Novel* (Los Angeles: UCLA Press, 2000), 11.
15. Diderot, *Jacques the Fatalist,* 32.
16. Ibid., 214.
17. Ibid., 212.
18. Ibid., 166.
19. Ibid., 158.
20. Ibid., 166.
21. Ibid., 74.
22. Ibid., 236.
23. Arthur Wilson, *Diderot* (Oxford: Oxford University Press, 1972), 629.
24. Roland Mortier, *Diderot en Allemagne* (Paris: Presses universitaires de France, 1954), 33.
25. Ibid., 39.
26. Maurice Tourneux, *Diderot et Catherine II* (Paris: Calmann Lévy, 1899), 76.
27. *Denis Diderot: Correspondance,* 13:51–52.
28. Ibid., 13:65.
29. Jeremy Black, *The Grand Tour in the Eighteenth Century* (New York: Saint Martin's Press, 1992), 110, 139.

30. Mortier, *Diderot en Allemagne,* 36.
31. Ibid., 35.
32. Ibid., 37.
33. *Denis Diderot: Correspondance,* 13:53.
34. Ibid., 13:56.
35. Ibid., 13:57–58.
36. Ibid., 13:71.
37. Albert Lortholary, *Le Mirage russe en France au XVIIIe siècle* (Paris: Boivin & Cie, 1951).
38. Larry Wolff, *Inventing Eastern Europe: The Map of Civilization on the Mind of the Enlightenment* (Palo Alto, CA: Stanford University Press, 1994), 15.
39. Ibid., 345.
40. Ibid., 293.
41. *Documents of Catherine the Great,* 177.
42. Ibid., 181.
43. Wolff, *Inventing Eastern Europe,* 21.
44. Ibid., 22.
45. P. N. Furbank, *Diderot: A Critical Biography* (New York: Knopf, 1992), 374–375.
46. *Denis Diderot: Correspondance,* 13:60.
47. Ibid., 13:65.

6. THE HERMITAGE

1. Lurana Donnels O'Malley, *The Dramatic Works of Catherine the Great* (Aldershot, UK: Ashgate, 2006), 33.
2. *Documents of Catherine the Great,* ed. W. F. Reddaway (New York: Russell and Russell, 1931), 170–171.
3. Ibid., 97.
4. Ibid., 135.
5. Simon Dixon, *Catherine the Great* (New York: HarperCollins, 2009), 208.
6. John Alexander, *Catherine the Great: Life and Legend* (Oxford: Oxford University Press, 1989), 135.
7. Ibid., 136.
8. Robert Massie, *Catherine the Great: Portrait of a Woman* (New York: Random House, 2012), 416.
9. Dixon, *Catherine the Great,* 218.
10. *Denis Diderot: Correspondance,* ed. Georges Roth and Jean Varloot (Paris: Éditions de Minuit, 1966), vol. 12, Diderot to Falconet, May 30, 1773.
11. *Denis Diderot: Correspondance,* 13:49.
12. Maurice Tourneux, *Diderot et Catherine II* (Paris: Calmann Lévy, 1899), 73.

13. *Denis Diderot: Correspondance,* 13:66.
14. Ibid.
15. Denis Diderot, *Lettres à Falconet,* ed. J. Assézat and M. Tourneux (Paris: Garnier, 1922), 237.
16. *Denis Diderot: Correspondance,* 13:124.
17. Denis Diderot, *Oeuvres,* vol. 3, ed. Laurent Versini (Paris: Laffont, 1995), 169.
18. Diderot, *Lettres à Falconet,* 236.
19. Alexander, *Catherine the Great,* 114.
20. Carol Blum, *Diderot: The Virtue of a Philosopher* (New York: Viking, 1974), 42.
21. P. N. Furbank, *Diderot: A Critical Biography* (New York: Knopf, 1992), 182.
22. *Denis Diderot: Correspondance,* 13:87.
23. Ibid., 88.
24. Denis Diderot, "Mélanges pour Catherine II," in *Oeuvres,* ed. Versini, 3:227.
25. Furbank, *Diderot,* 79.
26. Ibid., 117.
27. Inna Gorbatov, *Catherine the Great and the French Philosophers of the Enlightenment* (Bethesda, MD: Academica Press, 2006), 213.
28. Dena Goodman, *The Republic of Letters: A Cultural History of the French Enlightenment* (Ithaca, NY: Cornell University Press, 1994), 46.
29. Antoine Lilti, *The World of the Salons: Sociability and Worldliness in Eighteenth-Century Paris,* trans. Lydia Cochrane (Oxford: Oxford University Press, 2005), 112.
30. Goodman, *The Republic of Letters,* 47.
31. Ibid., 164.
32. Furbank, *Diderot,* 81.
33. Lilti, *World of the Salons,* 165.
34. *Denis Diderot: Correspondance,* 13:84.
35. Ibid., 13:102–103.
36. Dixon, *Catherine the Great,* 223.
37. *The Memoirs of Catherine the Great,* trans. Mark Cruse and Hilde Hoogenboom (New York: Modern Library, 2005), 93.
38. Ibid., 97.
39. Alexander, *Catherine the Great,* 99–100.
40. Gary Hamburg, *Russia's Path to Enlightenment* (New Haven, CT: Yale, 2016).
41. Denis Diderot, *Paradoxe sur le comédien,* in *Oeuvres*, ed. André Billy (Paris: Gallimard, 1951), 1006.
42. Furbank, *Diderot,* 268.
43. Diderot, *Paradoxe sur le comédien,* 1022.
44. Ibid., 1027.
45. Ibid., 1026.
46. *Denis Diderot: Correspondance,* 13:73.

47. *Oeuvres,* ed. André Billy, 943.
48. "Propos de Diderot sur l'Impératrice de Russie (Fragment inédit de Suard)," in Tourneux, *Diderot et Catherine II,* 580.
49. Ibid., 125.
50. Geoffrey Bremner, *Order and Chance: The Pattern of Diderot's Thought* (Cambridge: Cambridge University Press, 1983), 124.
51. Diderot, "Salon de 1761," in *Oeuvres,* ed. André Billy 10:113.
52. "Salon de 1763," *Oeuvres,* ed. André Billy, 10:208.
53. Ibid.
54. Ibid., 210.
55. Diderot, *Lettres à Falconet,* March 20, 1771.
56. Dixon, *Catherine the Great,* 193.
57. Malcolm Bradbury, *To The Hermitage* (London: Picador, 2000), 165.
58. Bremner, *Order and Chance,* 126.
59. Ibid.
60. Denis Diderot, *Lettres à Sophie Volland* (Paris: Gallimard, 1930), 3:256.
61. Alexander Schenker, *The Bronze Horseman: Falconet's Monument to Peter the Great* (New Haven, CT: Yale University Press, 2003), 79–80.
62. Diderot, *Lettres à Falconet,* February 15, 1766.
63. Ibid., December 25, 1765.
64. Ibid., September 6, 1768.
65. Ibid., Catherine to Falconet, February 18, 1767.
66. Ibid., Catherine to Falconet, May 10, 1769.
67. Ibid., Catherine to Falconet, March 28, 1767.
68. Ibid., Falconet to Diderot, July–August, 1767.
69. Schenker, *The Bronze Horseman,* 100.
70. Ibid., 125.
71. Ibid., 126–127.
72. Ibid., 131.
73. Anne Betty Weinshecker, *Falconet, His Writings and His Friend Diderot* (Geneva: Droz, 1966), 7.
74. *Lettres à Falconet,* July 1767.
75. Ibid., December 6, 1773.
76. Ibid.

7. EXTRAORDINARY MEN AND EVENTS

1. Written by Vasily Trediakovsky, the *Tilemakhida* recounts the travels of Odysseus's son Telemachus. Based on Greek hexameter, the effort was admired even though the result was unreadable.

2. Isabel de Madariaga, *Politics and Culture in Eighteenth-Century France* (London: Routledge, 2014), 268.
3. Isabel de Madariaga, *Russia in the Age of Catherine the Great* (London: Phoenix Press, 2002), 322–333.
4. John Alexander, *Autocratic Politics in a National Crisis: The Imperial Russian Government and Pugachev's Revolt* (Bloomington: Indiana University Press, 1969), 9.
5. Ibid., 36.
6. Ibid., 72–73.
7. Madariaga, *Russia in the Age,* 267.
8. Simon Dixon, *Catherine the Great* (New York: HarperCollins, 2009), 229.
9. *Denis Diderot: Correspondance,* ed. Georges Roth and Jean Varloot (Paris: Éditions de Minuit, 1966), 14:108.
10. *The Memoirs of Catherine the Great,* trans. Mark Cruse and Hilde Hoogenboom (New York: Modern Library, 2005), 34.
11. Ibid., 7.
12. Ibid.
13. Ibid., 20.
14. Geoffrey Bremner, *Order and Chance* (Cambridge: Cambridge University Press, 2009), 99–100.
15. Locke, *Second Treatise on Civil Government,* chap. 14, sec.164.
16. *Memoirs of Catherine the Great,* 126–127.
17. Ibid., 21.
18. *Denis Diderot: Correspondance,* 13:102–103.
19. Maurice Tourneux, *Diderot et Catherine II* (Paris: Calmann Lévy, 1899), 581.
20. *Documents of Catherine the Great,* ed. W. F. Reddaway (New York: Russell and Russell, 1931), 192.
21. Ibid.,196.
22. Ibid., 194.
23. *Denis Diderot: Correspondance,* 13:143.
24. Ibid., 13:111.
25. Inna Gorbatov, *Catherine the Great and the French Philosophers of the Enlightenment* (Bethesda, MD: Academica Press, 2006), 171.
26. *Denis Diderot: Correspondance,* 13:134.
27. Ibid., 13:146.
28. Arthur Wilson, *Diderot* (Oxford: Oxford University Press, 1972), 636.
29. John Alexander, *Catherine the Great: Life and Legend* (Oxford: Oxford University Press, 1989), 74.
30. *Denis Diderot: Correspondance,* 13:101.
31. Tourneux, *Diderot et Catherine II,* 78–79.
32. *Memoirs of Catherine the Great,* 285n59.

33. Wilson, *Diderot,* 636.
34. *Denis Diderot: Correspondance,* 13:123.
35. Ibid., 13:71.
36. Ibid., 13:79.
37. Ibid., 13: 81.
38. *Memoirs of Catherine the Great,* 37.
39. Ibid., 40.
40. Ibid., 43.
41. Wilson, *Diderot,* 636.
42. *Memoirs of Catherine the Great,* 44.
43. Ibid., 55.
44. Ibid., 199.
45. Madariaga, *Russia in the Age,* 503.
46. *Memoirs of Catherine the Great,* 99–100.
47. Ibid., 108.
48. Ibid., 106.
49. Ibid., 109.
50. *Supplement to the Voyage of Bougainville,* in Denis Diderot, *Rameau's Nephew and Other Works,* ed. Jacques Barzun and Ralph H. Bowen (Indianapolis: Hackett, 2001), 185.
51. Ibid., 180.
52. Ibid., 208.
53. Quoted in Wilson, *Diderot,* 225.
54. *The Major Political Writings of Jean-Jacques Rousseau,* trans. and ed. John Scott (Chicago: University of Chicago, 2012), 103.
55. "Compte-rendu du Voyage de Bougainville," in *Supplément au Voyage de Bougainville,* ed. Michel Déon (Paris: Gallimard, 2002), 183.
56. Ibid., 187.
57. Ibid., 197.
58. Ibid., 198.
59. Ibid., 198–199.
60. Ibid., 212.
61. Ibid., 218.
62. Ibid., 225.
63. Ibid., 22.
64. Lester Crocker, *Diderot's Chaotic Order* (Princeton: Princeton University Press, 1974), 81.
65. *Major Political Writings of Jean-Jacques Rousseau,* 133.
66. Diderot, *Supplement,* 227–228.

8. COLIC AND CONSTITUTIONS

1. Denis Diderot, *Supplement to Bougainville's "Voyage,"* in Rameau's Nephew and Other Works, trans. Jacques Barzun and Ralph Bowen (Indianapolis: Hackett, 2001), 228.
2. *Documents of Catherine the Great,* ed. W. F. Reddaway (New York: Russell and Russell, 1931), 192.
3. *Denis Diderot: Correspondance,* ed. Georges Roth and Jean Varloot (Paris: Éditions de Minuit, 1966), 13:144.
4. Ibid., 13:141.
5. Ibid., 13:142.
6. Ibid., 13:140.
7. Ibid.
8. Ibid., 13:142.
9. Ibid., 13:140
10. Ibid., 13:148.
11. Maurice Tourneux, *Diderot et Catherine II* (Paris: Calmann Lévy, 1899), 469.
12. David Ransel, *The Politics of Catherinian Russia* (New Haven, CT: Yale University Press, 1975), 114. See also Isabel de Madariaga, *Politics and Culture in Eighteenth-Century Russia* (London: Routledge, 2014), 227–228.
13. P. N. Furbank, *Diderot: A Critical Biography* (New York: Knopf, 1992), 80–81.
14. *Denis Diderot: Correspondance,* 13:71.
15. Ibid., 13:114.
16. Ibid., 13:143.
17. *Documents of Catherine the Great,* 192.
18. *The Memoirs of Catherine the Great,* trans. Mark Cruse and Hilde Hoogenboom (New York: Modern Library, 2005), 255.
19. Diderot, "Portrait de Diderot" in *Oeuvres choisies,* ed. François Tulou (Paris: Garnier, 1901), 408.
20. We don't know what Diderot said about the portrait, but it seems to have pleased him. In his will, he left it to his unmarried and beloved sister, Denise Diderot.
21. "When I tried to show her Highness the wrong she committed, she made fun of me." *Denis Diderot: Correspondance,* 13:103.
22. Ibid., 13:121.
23. Ibid., 13:142.
24. Solomon Volkov, *St. Petersburg: A Cultural History* (New York: Free Press, 1997), 14.
25. *Memoirs of Catherine the Great,* 178.
26. Ibid., 181.
27. Ibid., 304n286.

28. In the opening of the memorandum, he duly notes that Catherine believed that "Moscow could become the imperial seat in one hundred years" (*Memoirs of Catherine the Great,* 55).
29. Ibid., 55.
30. Ibid., 63.
31. Ibid.
32. Ibid., 55.
33. Ibid., 199.
34. Ibid., 197.
35. Ibid., 56.
36. Ibid., 2.
37. Ibid., 9.
38. Ibid., 117.
39. Diderot, "Observations on the *Nakaz,*" in *Diderot: Political Writings,* ed. John Hope Mason and Robert Wokler (Cambridge: Cambridge University Press, 1992), 89.
40. *Encyclopédie,* s.v. "Éclectisme," 5:284.
41. Montesquieu, *The Spirit of the Laws,* bk. 5, chap. 13.
42. *Memoirs of Catherine the Great,* 10.
43. Ibid., 123.
44. Ibid., 12.
45. Montesquieu, *Spirit of the Laws,* bk. 2, chap. 4.
46. Ibid., bk. 3, chap. 10.
47. *Memoirs of Catherine the Great,* 235.
48. John Alexander, *Catherine the Great: Life and Legend* (Oxford: Oxford University Press, 1989), 202.
49. Douglas Smith, *Love and Conquest: Personal Correspondence of Catherine the Great and Gregory Potemkin* (DeKalb: Northern Illinois Press, 2005), 21.
50. Robert Massie, *Catherine the Great: Portrait of a Woman* (New York: Random House, 2012), 416.
51. *Documents of Catherine the Great,* 194.
52. Simon Dixon, *Catherine the Great* (New York: HarperCollins, 2009), 230.
53. *Denis Diderot: Correspondance,* 13:146.
54. Ibid., 13:142.
55. Ibid., 13:134.
56. Arthur Wilson, *Diderot* (Oxford: Oxford University Press, 1972), 640. Wilson incorrectly identifies the date as December 5.
57. *Memoirs of Catherine the Great,* 86.
58. Ibid., 86–89.
59. Peter Gay, *The Enlightenment: The Science of Freedom* (New York: Norton, 1969), 499.

60. Isabel de Madariaga, *Russia in the Age of Catherine the Great* (London: Phoenix Press, 2002), 490.
61. Montesquieu, *Spirit of the Laws,* bk. 4, chap. 3.
62. Madariaga, *Russia in the Age,* 491.
63. Ibid., 492.
64. *Memoirs of Catherine the Great,* 129.
65. Ibid.
66. Madariaga, *Russia in the Age,* 488.
67. *Memoirs of Catherine the Great,* 127.
68. Ibid., 63.
69. Alexander Schenker, *The Bronze Horseman: Falconet's Monument to Peter the Great* (New Haven, CT: Yale University Press, 2003), 87.
70. *Memoirs of Catherine the Great,* 78.
71. Ibid.
72. Ibid., 79.
73. Ibid.
74. Ibid., 83.

9. THE ROAD NOT TAKEN

1. *The Memoirs of Catherine the Great,* trans. Mark Cruse and Hilde Hoogenboom (New York: Modern Library, 2005), 224.
2. *Denis Diderot: Correspondance,* ed. Georges Roth and Jean Varloot (Paris: Éditions de Minuit, 1966), 13:138.
3. Maurice Tourneux, *Diderot et Catherine II* (Paris: Calmann Lévy, 1899), 549, 552.
4. *Denis Diderot: Correspondance,* 13:216.
5. Arthur Wilson, *Diderot* (Oxford: Oxford University Press, 1972), 642.
6. *Denis Diderot: Correspondance,* 13:140.
7. Ibid., 149.
8. John Alexander, *Catherine the Great: Life and Legend* (Oxford: Oxford University Press, 1989), 166–167.
9. Wilson, *Diderot,* 641.
10. *Memoirs of Catherine the Great,* 265.
11. Ibid., 259.
12. A photograph of the title page is found in the Vernière edition of the *Mémoires,* xxiii.
13. *Denis Diderot: Correspondance,* 13:151.
14. Mme Necker, *Nouveaux Mélanges extraits de ses manuscrits,* vol. 1 (Paris: Pougens, 1801), 229–230.
15. Denis Diderot, *Lettres à Sophie Volland,* vol. 3, ed. André Babelon (Paris: Gallimard, 1930), 252.

16. Ibid., 3:253.
17. Ibid., 3:250.
18. *Denis Diderot: Correspondance,* 13:203.
19. Ibid., 13:199.
20. Ibid.
21. Denis Diderot, "Paradoxe sur le comédien," in *Oeuvres,* ed. A. Billy (Paris: Gallimard, 1951), 1022.
22. Ibid., 1023.
23. P. N. Furbank, *Diderot: A Critical Biography* (New York: Knopf, 1992), 389.
24. Ibid., 212.
25. Wilson, *Diderot,* 653.
26. Ibid.
27. Ibid., 654.
28. *Denis Diderot: Correspondance,* 13:231.
29. Ibid., 13:230.
30. Ibid., 14:35.
31. Ibid., 14:33.
32. Ibid., 14:63.
33. Ibid., 14:78–79.
34. Ibid., 14:80.
35. Ibid., 14:80–81.
36. Ibid., 14:85.
37. Ibid., 14:72–73.
38. Ibid., 14:84.
39. Denis Diderot, *Principes de politique des souverains,* in *Oeuvres completes,* vol. 2, ed. J. Assézat (Paris: Garnier, 1875), 467.
40. Ibid., 477.
41. Wilson, *Diderot,* 651.
42. *Denis Diderot: Correspondance,* 14:55, 68.
43. Diderot, *Observations on the Nakaz,* in *Diderot: Political Writings,* ed. John Hope Mason and Robert Wokler (Cambridge: Cambridge University Press, 1992), 81.
44. Ibid., 82.
45. Ibid., 81.
46. Ibid., 83.
47. Ibid., 84.
48. Ibid., 85.
49. Ibid., 89.
50. Ibid., 93.
51. Ibid., 101.
52. Ibid., 127.

53. Ibid., 126.
54. Ibid., 112.
55. Ibid., 150.
56. Ibid., 113.
57. Ibid., 164.
58. Ibid., 98.
59. *Denis Diderot: Correspondance,* 14:119.
60. Isabel de Madariaga, *Politics and Culture in Eighteenth-Century Russia* (London: Routledge, 2014), 200–201.
61. *Denis Diderot: Correspondance,* 14:102.
62. Ibid., 14:65–66.

10. SEND FOR SENECA

1. *Denis Diderot: Correspondance,* ed. Georges Roth and Jean Varloot (Paris: Éditions de Minuit, 1966), 14:104.
2. Ibid., 14:75.
3. Ibid., 14:117.
4. Arthur Wilson, *Diderot* (Oxford: Oxford University Press, 1972), 657.
5. *Denis Diderot: Correspondance,* 14:123.
6. Ibid., 14:102.
7. Ibid., 15:48.
8. Ibid., 15:226.
9. Wilson, *Diderot,* 684.
10. Robert Darnton, *The Forbidden Best-Sellers of Pre-Revolutionary France* (New York: Norton, 1995), 73.
11. P. N. Furbank, *Diderot: A Critical Biography* (New York: Knopf, 1992), 418.
12. *Denis Diderot: Correspondance,* 15:149–150.
13. Denis Diderot, *Histoire des deux Indes,* in *Diderot: Political Writings,* ed. John Hope Mason and Robert Wokler (Cambridge: Cambridge University Press, 1992), 177.
14. Ibid., 175–176.
15. Ibid., 171.
16. Ibid., 173.
17. Ibid., 207–208.
18. Ibid., 204.
19. *Denis Diderot: Correspondance,* 15:211.
20. Ibid., 15:213.
21. Ibid., 15:227.
22. Ibid.
23. Ibid., 9:112.

24. Ibid.
25. Ibid., 9:115.
26. Ibid., 15:148
27. Ibid., 15:255.
28. Ibid., 15:112.
29. Denis Diderot, *Essai sur les règnes de Claude et de Néron,* in *Ouevres de Denis Diderot,* ed. Jacques-André Naigeon (Paris: Desray, 1798), 210.
30. Ibid., 211.
31. Furbank, *Diderot,* 406.
32. *Denis Diderot: Correspondance,* 15:111.
33. Ibid., 15:266–267.
34. Ibid., 14:218.
35. Ibid., 15:59.
36. Ibid., 15:266.
37. Diderot, *Essai sur les règnes,* 11.
38. Ibid., 51.
39. Ibid., 65–66.
40. Ibid., 154.
41. Ibid., 111.
42. Ibid., 112.
43. Ibid., 168.
44. Ibid., 167.
45. Emily Wilson, *The Greatest Empire: A Life of Seneca* (Oxford: Oxford University Press, 2014), 211–212.
46. Tacitus, *The Annals and the Histories,* trans. Alfred Church and William Brodribb (New York: Random House, 2003), 336–337.
47. Diderot, *Essai sur les règnes,* in *Oeuvres*, ed. Laurent Versini (Paris: Laffont), 1234.
48. *Denis Diderot: Correspondance,* 15:300–301.
49. Ibid., 15:301.
50. Ibid., 15:303.

EPILOGUE

1. *Denis Diderot: Correspondance,* ed. Georges Roth and Jean Varloot (Paris: Éditions de Minuit, 1966), 15:334.
2. Ibid., 15:328.
3. Ibid., 15:338.
4. Ibid.
5. Ibid., 15:339.
6. Maurice Tourneux, *Diderot et Catherine II* (Paris: Calmann Lévy, 1899), 519.

7. Ibid., 520.
8. Louis-Philippe de Ségur, *Mémoires, souvenirs, et anecdotes,* vol. 1, ed. M. Barrière (Paris: Librairie de Firmin Didot Frères, 1859), 444–445.
9. Citing the work of Sergio Cotta, Isabel de Madariaga proposes this contrast. See Madariaga, *Politics and Culture in Eighteenth-Century Russia* (London: Routledge, 2014), 231.
10. Simon Dixon, *Catherine the Great* (New York: HarperCollins, 2009), 310.

Acknowledgments

First, I have a confession to make. While I have studied Montesquieu's *Spirit of the Laws,* I have not devoured, as Catherine the Great did, the entire book cover to cover a half dozen times. And while I have read my share of Voltaire, I suspect I will never read nearly as much of his oeuvre as did the Empress of All Russias. Chances are that I have not read as widely in the works of yet other thinkers of the age, whether it is Pierre Bayle or Cesare Beccaria, as did Catherine. Though I began this book several years ago, I remain as astonished by Catherine's sure grasp of the philosophy of the Enlightenment as I am by her stubborn attachment to its spirit.

This same attachment brought to Saint Petersburg the individual who, to my mind, was the Enlightenment's most compelling—and most subversive—thinker, Denis Diderot. I can safely state—if only because so much of his work was published posthumously—that I have read much more of Diderot than Catherine ever did. Yet Catherine had the great fortune that I will never have: to spend dozens of afternoons, over the course of several months, in private conversation with this man, reputed to be his age's greatest conversationalist. It was Diderot's voyage to and stay in Saint Petersburg as Catherine's honored guest that gave me the means to acquaint myself, if only at a distance, with both of these remarkable individuals.

Equally important, it was the means to measure the impact of philosophical and political ideas on the practice and policies of a ruler. For many of the age's great thinkers, after all, the realization of their enlightened ideals could be achieved only with the complicity and collaboration of enlightened rulers. By the end of Diderot's stay, his expectations of Catherine had changed dramatically, as had Catherine's impressions of Diderot. Similarly, my own sense of these two individuals has changed since I first began this book. Yet as I came to discover the flaws and failings of both Catherine and Diderot, my admiration for both of them in fact deepened. Though both of them were inevitably human, there was nothing at all inevitable in the ways they sought, in very different ways, to translate enlightened convictions into reality.

During the writing of this book, my admiration, and gratitude, also deepened for those who helped along the way. I need to thank, first of all, the scholars who have written on Catherine, Diderot, and their times. As a newcomer to Russian history, I am indebted to the work of biographers like Robert Massie, Simon Dixon, and John Alexander, and to the authoritative historical accounts of the late Isabel de Madariaga. Though I am much less of a newcomer to eighteenth-century French thought, Arthur Wilson's massive biography of Diderot was an invaluable resource, as were the works of P. N. Furbank, Carol Blum, Raymond Trousson, and Lester Crocker. My thanks to friends and colleagues John Scott, Paul Slavin, Lois Zamora, and Karen Valihora for reading portions of the book, and to Robert Cremins, who introduced me to his former teacher Malcolm Bradbury's extraordinary novel *To the Hermitage.* I must thank, as well, Robert Massie for his invaluable encouragement when I was still wondering if this story merited a book.

My deepest thanks go to the manuscript's three anonymous readers; I was humbled by their many corrections and suggestions, just as I was by their unwavering encouragement. Had it not been for the backing of my first editor at Harvard University Press, John Kulka, the book would never have gotten off the ground; were it not for the generous support and wise advice of my second editor, Sharmila Sen, the book would never have safely landed. I am grateful to both of them, as I am to their assistant, Heather Hughes, who once again proved far more understanding and patient than this anxious academic deserved. My copyeditor, Wendy Nelson, was a sharp-eyed and smart reader. The unwavering support provided at the University of Houston by William Monroe, dean of the Honors College, and Hildegard Glass, chair of the Department of Modern and Classical Languages, was crucial: my sincere thanks to both of them. I also wish to thank Jennifer Johnston for her work on proofreading and indexing the book.

Finally, I need to thank my children, Ruben and Louisa, for their enlightened ways. And I am dedicating this book to my wife, Julie, to whom I owe this book and so much more.

Index